Public Private Partnership for WTO Dispute Settlement

Dedicated to

My dearest parents, Gurdip and Anita
&
The love of my life, Ankit
…

Public Private Partnership for WTO Dispute Settlement

Enabling Developing Countries

Amrita Bahri

Assistant Professor of Law, Instituto Tecnológico Autónomo de México (ITAM University), Mexico City, Mexico

EE Edward Elgar PUBLISHING

Cheltenham, UK • Northampton, MA, USA

Published by
Edward Elgar Publishing Limited
The Lypiatts
15 Lansdown Road
Cheltenham
Glos GL50 2JA
UK

Edward Elgar Publishing, Inc.
William Pratt House
9 Dewey Court
Northampton
Massachusetts 01060
USA

A catalogue record for this book
is available from the British Library

Library of Congress Control Number: 2017953159

This book is available electronically in the **Elgar**online
Law subject collection
DOI 10.4337/9781786437495

FSC www.fsc.org MIX Paper from responsible sources FSC® C013056

ISBN 978 1 78643 748 8 (cased)
ISBN 978 1 78643 749 5 (eBook)

Typeset by Servis Filmsetting Ltd, Stockport, Cheshire
Printed and bound in Great Britain by TJ International Ltd, Padstow

Contents

Foreword

This book, *Public Private Partnership for WTO Dispute Settlement: Enabling Developing Countries* by Professor Amrita Bahri, represents a critical area of international trade law research. If law is to be legitimate, it must be broadly available to all. Formalised law is not sufficient. As legal realists and law and society scholars have long explained, formalized law does not mean right prevails over might. Power rather manifests itself in new forms. Those able to wield the law deploy it to advance their interests. Once more, the haves can come out ahead.

We thus must look behind formal rules to see how law operates in practice. The book *Defending Interests: Public-Private Partnerships in WTO Litigation* showed how trade officials in the United States and Europe work with the private sector and lawyers hired by it to advance their reciprocal interests and attempt to shape legal interpretation and dispute settlement in the WTO. I concluded it by asking, 'If the United States and EC depend on assistance from private firms and trade associations, what does this bode for developing country participation in the system?' Professor Bahri takes up that challenge.

Her book is important because it gives voice to the experiences of those outside of the United States and Europe through a study of three emerging economies—Brazil, India and China—who invested significant resources in building trade-related legal capacity in government and the private sector. Professor Bahri studied this process through a research method that is too infrequently used in legal academia. She left the comfort of her office and traveled to meet with trade officials from these countries to understand their challenges and experiences with the WTO's legal system. She draws from this original fieldwork, combined with existing and parallel work of other scholars, to explain how WTO dispute settlement works. Going further, she assesses what important lessons can be drawn from these countries' experiences for themselves as well as for developing countries more generally.

Scholarship is a collective endeavour. It is a cumulative, never-ending process. It tests and verifies and renews what has come before. This work by Professor Bahri is an important contribution to a corpus of scholarship assessing the importance of building legal capacity if countries are to be full stakeholders in the international trading system. When countries broadly are able to participate effectively to use the WTO legal system, then one can envision a rule of law for international trade. Yet history is never-ending and that hope is now under threat. Professor Bahri's work shows what can be done if countries invest in law and legal institutions. They now have a stake in the system. Let us hope that vision prevails during these difficult times.

Gregory Shaffer
Chancellor's Professor, University of California, Irvine School of Law

Acknowledgements

I am indebted to Professor Gregory Shaffer, who has encouraged and guided me throughout this academic journey. His research works on WTO dispute settlement and developing countries are a source of inspiration for this work. I consider him and often refer to him as the 'father' of this area of law. I would also like to express my special appreciation and thanks to Dr Luca Rubini who has been a wonderful mentor and guide. Also, thanks to Dr Rilka Dragneva-Lewers, Mr N Jansen Calamita and Dr Celine Tan for their comments and feedback.

My words cannot express how grateful I am to the distinguished participants and interviewees who have made this work possible. I am particularly thankful to Niall Meagher, Ricardo Melendez-Ortiz, Harsha Vardhana Singh, Rajan Sudesh Ratna, Abhijit Das, Anant Swarup, Petros Mavroidis, Henry Gao, Lothar Ehring, Marco Bronckers, Erwan Berthelot, William Davey, Celso de Tarso Pereira, Eduardo Chikusa, Lu Xiankun and Toufiq Ali, all of whom have enriched this work with their invaluable insights.

I am also indebted to ITAM University and my colleagues for giving me the best possible environment to accomplish this work within strict timelines and ongoing work constraints. Thanks to Andres Hernandez, an ITAM student, for his feedback and help with proofreading. I also thank my alma maters, University of Birmingham and London School of Economics, as they have played a vital role in shaping my thoughts, understanding and ambitions.

I want to express how grateful I am to Michael Flay (Mike), whom I met on a train to Birmingham, who then became a very special friend, and taught me some wonderful lessons about work and life, and then left the carriage of life to live in my heart and mind forever. Mike, this book will always remind me of our discussions in that next-door cafeteria, during train journeys and over drinks with our better-halves. I cherish the role you have played in my life.

I fall short of words to thank my mother, who has spent many sleepless nights and monotonous days to keep me going. I cannot wait to see the smile this book will bring to her face. Thanks to my role model, my father, who has always been a constant source of inspiration and encouragement.

Finally, thanks to my dearest husband, Ankit, who has given me a life full of love and comfort. My love, this book would not have been possible without your faith in me.

Abbreviations

AB	Appellate Body
ACWL	Advisory Centre on WTO Law
ADR	Alternative Dispute Resolution
BIC	Brazil, India and China
BOFT	Bureau of Fair Trade for Imports and Exports
BTC	Bangladesh Tariff Commission
CAMEX	Interministerial Chamber of Foreign Trade (Câmara de Comércio Exterior – CAMEX)
CEB	Brazilian Business Coalition
CGC	Unit for General Coordination of Disputes
CNI	National Confederation of Industry
CONEX	Private Sector Consultative Council
DSM	Dispute Settlement Mechanism
DSU	Dispute Settlement Understanding
FTA	Free Trade Agreement
GATT	General Agreement on Tariffs and Trade
GDP	Gross Domestic Product
GNI	Gross National Income
ICTSD	International Centre for Trade and Sustainable Development
IIFT	Indian Institute of Foreign Trade
IMF	International Monetary Fund
ITAC	Industry Trade Advisory Center
ITEC	Interagency Trade Enforcement Center
LDC	Least Developed Countries
MIC	Middle Income Country
MOFCOM	Ministry of Commerce
MPEDA	Marine Products Export Development Authority
MSMEs	Micro, Small and Medium Enterprises
NGO	Non-governmental Organisation
OECD	Organisation for Economic Co-operation and Development
PIL	Public Interest Litigation
PMI	Permanent Mission of India

PPP	Public Private Partnership
PTA	Preferential Trade Agreement
RTI	Right to Information
SCM	Subsidies and Countervailing Measures
SEAI	Seafood Exporters Association of India
SPS	Sanitary and Phytosanitary Measures
TBI	Trade Barrier Investigation
TBIM	Trade Barrier Investigation Mechanism
TBR	Trade Barrier Regulation
TBT	Technical Barriers to Trade
TEXPROCIL	Cotton Textiles Export Promotion Council of India
TFA	Trade Facilitation Agreement
TPD	Trade Policy Division
TPRM	Trade Policy Review Mechanism
UBABEF	Brazilian Poultry Association and the Brazilian Chicken Producers and Exporters Association
UN	United Nations
USTR	United States Trade Representative
WTO	World Trade Organization

Table of cases

WTO CASES

Short Title	Full Case Title and Citation
Brazil – Aircraft	Appellate Body Report, *Brazil – Export Financing Programme for Aircraft*, WT/DS46/AB/R, adopted 20 August 1999 32, 36, 60, 131–133
Canada – Aircraft	Appellate Body Report, *Canada – Measures Affecting the Export of Civilian Aircraft*, WT/DS70/AB/R, adopted 20 August 1999 32, 36, 60, 131–133
Canada – Renewable Energy / Canada – Feed-in Tariff	Appellate Body Reports, *Canada – Certain Measures Affecting the Renewable Energy Generation Sector / Canada – Measures Relating to the Feed-in Tariff Program*, WT/DS412/AB/R / WT/DS426/AB/R, adopted 24 May 2013 15
China – Electronic Payment Services	Panel Report, *China – Certain Measures Affecting Electronic Payment Services*, WT/DS413/R, adopted 31 August 2012 172
China – Auto Parts	Appellate Body Reports, *China – Measures Affecting Imports of Automobile Parts*, WT/DS339/AB/R / WT/DS340/AB/R / WT/DS342/AB/R, adopted 12 January 2009 108, 119
China – Raw Materials	Appellate Body Reports, *China – Measures Related to the Exportation of Various Raw Materials*, WT/DS394/AB/R, WT/DS395/AB/R, WT/DS398/AB/R, adopted 22 February 2012 15
EU and Member State – Seizure of Generic Drugs in Transit	*European Union and a Member State – Seizure of Generic Drugs in Transit*, WT/DS409, in consultations on 12 May 2010 16, 61, 158
EU and Member State – Seizure of Generic Drugs in Transit	*European Union and a Member State – Seizure of Generic Drugs in Transit*, WT/DS408, in consultations on 11 May 2010 16, 158
EC – Bed Linen	Appellate Body Report, *European Communities – Anti-Dumping Duties on Imports of Cotton Type Bed Linen from India*, WT/DS141/AB/R, adopted 12 March 2001 164–167, 169, 210

COURT OF FIRST INSTANCE OF THE EUROPEAN UNION CASE

Table of legislation

EU REGULATIONS

EU DECISIONS, NOTICES AND TREATIES

WTO AGREEMENTS AND PROTOCOLS

FOREIGN LEGISLATIONS AND CONSTITUTIONS

Introduction

1.1 INTRODUCTORY REMARKS

Trade across borders affects our lives in many disciplines. The selection of international foods and beverages that we enjoy, the variety of competitively priced clothing, footwear, accessories and cosmetics available at shops next door, the education and training we receive, the services we provide and avail, and the technology that impacts the way we work, travel and live – are all conditioned upon international trade. The World Trade Organization (WTO), an instrument of international trade governance, facilitates as well as regulates the international trade. It promotes free trade and open markets through multilaterally negotiated trade agreements. With its near-universal membership, impressive reduction of tariff and nontariff barriers to trade, and enforceability of rules through a dispute settlement forum, the WTO has emerged as the biggest achievement of the multilateral trading system.

Over the past two decades of its operation, the WTO Dispute Settlement Understanding (DSU)[1] has played a vital role in the protection and enforcement of rights under the multilateral trading system. By providing a consultative as well as litigatory forum to resolve foreign trade conflicts amongst its Member States, it has established itself as one of the most successful dispute resolution mechanisms at the international level. Yet, it has been a subject of criticism since its very inception. The system has been criticised for various reasons, including the poor enforcement mechanisms provided under the WTO DSU, its ambiguous special and differential treatment provisions seen as paying lip service to the concerns of developing country members, and the asymmetrical use of WTO DSU provisions by developed and developing Member States.[2] This book is concerned

[1] Understanding on Rules and Procedures Governing the Settlement of Disputes ('Dispute Settlement Understanding') (15 April 1995) LT/UR/A-2/DS/U/1.

[2] For details, see Robert R Baldwin, *Doha and Beyond: The Future of the Multilateral Trading System* (Cambridge University Press 2004) 46; Andrew D Mitchell, 'A Legal Principle of Special and Differential Treatment for WTO Disputes' (2006) 5(3) *World Trade Review* 445; Christina L Davis and Sarah

with the last-mentioned point of criticism; that is, the utilisation of the WTO Dispute Settlement Mechanism (DSM) by the developing Member States of the WTO.

In particular, four characteristics of WTO DSU introduce and define the focus of this book. *First*, the WTO DSM is a costly avenue for dispute resolution and it is therefore not equally affordable to all WTO Member States. In contrast to developed country members, developing countries have faced considerable problems while invoking WTO DSU provisions because they do not possess sufficient resources to monitor and enforce their international trade rights. Due to resource constraints, they have faced problems in monitoring foreign trade practices and identifying or investigating trade barriers. They have also struggled in negotiating a settlement, challenging trade barriers, defending trade interests or ensuring compliance even after a favourable ruling is given by the Panel or Appellate Body (AB). The book, in the following chapters, discusses these challenges as it is broadly concerned with how developing countries can overcome the participation challenges they currently face at WTO DSU.

The *second* characteristic is that, in practice, WTO DSM is a two-tier mechanism. The *first* tier is domestic handling of trade disputes and the *second* tier is international adjudication. Both tiers are interdependent and interconnected. A case that is poorly handled (perhaps because the impugned trade barrier is insufficiently investigated or the arguments are not examined by experienced litigators or the claims are poorly substantiated) at the domestic level will stand a relatively lower chance of success at the international level.[3] Hence, in practice, the outcome of WTO litigation is partially predetermined by the way it is handled at the domestic level. With this ethos in mind, the book focuses on the first tier; that is, how the disputes can be effectively handled at the domestic level in order to improve the performance and participation of developing countries at the second tier; that is, at WTO DSU.

The *third* feature of the dispute settlement system is that every trade disagreement which grows into a formal legal action at WTO

Blodgett Bermeo, 'Who Files? Developing Country Participation in GATT/WTO Adjudication' (2009) 71(3) *The Journal of Politics* 1033.

[3] Marie Wilke, 'Practical Considerations in Managing Trade Disputes' (December 2012) ICTSD Information Note 11, at 1, accessed 27 March 2017 at http://ictsd.org/downloads/2013/02/practical-considerations-in-managing-trade-disputes.pdf. (The author notes that '. . .countries can take advantage of the rule of law only if they can effectively pursue their rights in this complex legal regime, which largely depends on having an adequate number of experienced legal, economic, and diplomatic staff and a well informed and active private sector.').

DSU (if not resolved or diffused by way of negotiations or consultations) generally emanates from cross-border commercial relationships between exporters and importers or business entities and public-sector authorities. Violation of WTO rules, in essence, directly affects business interests of exporters, importers, manufacturers and producers. Moreover, business entities are suitably placed to identify trade barriers and provide the required information to investigate a foreign trade measure or prepare a legal case. Exporters and importers can gather information, evidence and documents concerning foreign trade measures and their impact during the course of conducting their everyday business activities. In light of these observations, read together with the *first* and *second* characteristics mentioned above, one can infer that the engagement of affected industries is an enabling element for any government action that is undertaken to safeguard or expand business interests.

The *fourth* characteristic is that WTO dispute settlement is an intergovernmental process and the exclusive authority to file or respond to WTO litigations is conferred on the governments of Member States. This positions the government as the key participant of WTO DSM. This characteristic of DSU, when read together with the *third* characteristic, logically indicates that the governments should handle WTO disputes in close coordination with the affected industries. The book accordingly focuses on how governments can manage disputes by engaging the affected private stakeholders and what problems, if any, the governments can face in doing the same. In doing so, it analyses the approach of public private partnership (PPP), which in the context of this book, refers to the synergy of resources between a government and an industry during the conduct of WTO dispute settlement proceedings.

The underlying argument of this book is two-fold: *First*, the participation problems that developing countries face at WTO DSU should be addressed at domestic level, and *second*, an effective PPP arrangement can enable developing countries to mobilise resources at domestic level and thereby better enable them to utilise the provisions of WTO DSU. Effective utilisation of the provisions of WTO DSU can further lead to better protection and enforcement of WTO rights, improved market access conditions for the developing world, and enhanced integration of developing countries into the world trading system. Better integration of developing countries into the world trading system will positively affect the legitimacy of WTO as an institution of global trade governance and a forum for the settlement of foreign trade disputes. These arguments, read together with the above-mentioned characteristics of WTO DSU, introduce and define the focus of this book.

The book seeks to bring out the challenges, experiences and best practices of certain successful users of DSM, and thus enlighten the deliberation and debate over what can be done by developing countries for improved access to WTO DSM. To achieve this purpose, the author reflects on the dispute settlement partnership experiences of the European Union (EU), the United States of America (US), Brazil, China and India as they are the top DSU users from the developed and the developing world. With this experience-driven analysis, the book enables developing countries to consider and critically evaluate a diverse range of PPP strategies, and determine individual approaches towards the future handling of foreign trade disputes.

2.1 SELECTED WTO MEMBERS: THE EU, THE US, BRAZIL, CHINA AND INDIA

Mavroidis, Horn and Johannesson have categorised WTO members into five groups, depending upon their level of WTO DSU experience, level of development and foreign trade interests.[4] These groups are as follows:

1. G2 (the European Union and the United States): The group includes the US and the Member States of the EU.[5]
2. IND (other industrialised countries): It includes OECD members and non-OECD members that have a very high per capita income.[6] Countries under this group are classified as high-income countries by the World Bank.

---

[4] Henrik Horn, Louise Johannesson & Petros C Mavroidis, 'The WTO Dispute Settlement System 1995–2010: Some Descriptive Statistics' (2011) 45(6) *Journal of World Trade* 1107, 1138.

[5] In the paper, '[t]he EU is taken to be EU-15, since the enlargements came relatively late. . .' (Horn et al, 'The WTO Dispute Settlement System' (n 4) 1138). However, this book treats G2 as comprising the US and the 28 Member States of the EU as on 14 January 2017.

[6] 'Economic Cooperation and Development (OECD) members, the non-OECD members among the twelve countries that most recently became members of the EU, those that are currently at an advanced stage of their accession negotiations, as well as countries that are not OECD members but have a very high per capita income, such as Singapore.' (Horn et al, 'The WTO Dispute Settlement System' (n 4) 1138). This book follows the same composition for IND, except for the fact that it excludes the 12 countries that are now EU Member States and hence included in the G2.

3. BIC (Brazil, India, and China): The group comprises Brazil, India and China, who are developing yet emerging market economies with a distinctly high rate of participation at WTO DSU. China and Brazil are upper middle income countries, and India is a lower middle income country.
4. DEV (developing countries other than least developed countries): 'The DEV group consists of all countries that do not fit into either of the above mentioned categories and are not BIC countries either.'[7] These countries are classified as upper middle, middle or lower middle income countries by the World Bank.
5. LDC (least developed countries): This group comprises the list of LDCs prepared by the United Nations. These countries are classified as low income countries by the World Bank.

The book actively focuses on the experiences of two groups: G2 and BIC. The chapter on G2, which is presented after the chapter on conceptual analysis, will provide an extension of the theoretical review as it will further clarify the conceptual underpinnings of the PPP approach in the context of WTO DSU. Moreover, it will introduce and examine an arrangement of government-industry coordination which is based on a system of 'rights and obligations' often referred to as a formal PPP system. With formal systems of PPP in place almost since the creation of WTO, their governments and industries have gained a wealth of dispute settlement partnership experience to share with the developing world.

The chapters on BIC will provide detailed case studies, and these case studies will build upon the previous chapters with the help of empirical fact-finding and analysis. BIC countries have certain things in common. All three countries are among the most active developing country users of WTO DSM. They have made use of effective dispute settlement strategies and are therefore better enabled to litigate and defend their trade interests at WTO. They are important international trade players with certain common economic and strategic interests.[8] They are members of BRICS, which is a trading alliance of major emerging market economies.[9] They have collaborated to form BASIC, which is a geopolitical alliance of newly

[7] Horn et al, 'The WTO Dispute Settlement System' (n 4) 1138.

[8] In China, from 5% of GDP in 1970, exports and imports have expanded to 55% of GDP 2011. In India, from 8% in 1970, exports and imports have increased to 46% of GDP in 2011. In Brazil, from 14% in 1970, it has expanded to 25% of GDP in 2011 (The World Bank DataBank 2015).

[9] Namely Brazil, Russia, India, China and South Africa. For more information, see The BRICS Post, accessed 10 March 2017 at <http://thebricspost.com>.

industrialised and developing country superpowers.[10] They are members of Group of 77 (G-77), which is a coalition of developing nations at the United Nations.[11] They have also come together under Group of 20, which is an international alliance of economies that collectively accounts for almost 80 per cent of world trade.[12] Hence, they are emerging powers with certain common interests but hugely different domestic circumstances and global ambitions.

At the same time, Brazil, China and India continue to be (self-) designated as 'developing countries' under the WTO agreements, as they face many problems that the developing world shares.[13] For example, India has low standards of living, poor health and sanitation conditions and an acute problem of high population growth. Brazil faces the problem of governmental ineffectiveness and weak regulation. China faces high population growth and dependency burden, rapid urbanisation and challenges to environmental sustainability. They all, in common with other developing countries, face high levels of corruption, low GDP per capita, wide inequality of income, and lack of transparency and free flow of information.[14]

Similar to other developing countries, BIC countries have also faced multiple challenges while litigating or defending actions at WTO DSU. These participation challenges can directly be linked to their common domestic conditions, which include, but are not limited to, resource-constrained governance, lack of transparency and information flow, unorganised, under-represented and disengaged industries, poor observance of the rule

---

[10] Karl Hallding, Marie Olsson, Aaron Atteridge, Marcus Carson, Antto Vihma & Mikael Roman, 'Together Alone: Brazil, South Africa, India, China (BASIC) and the Climate Change Conundrum' (August 2011) Stockholm Environment Institute (SEI), accessed 15 June 2016 at <http://www.sei-international.org/mediamanager/documents/Publications/Climate/sei-basic-preview-jun2011.pdf>.

[11] For information on the G-77, see the Group of 77 of the United Nations, accessed 15 March 2017 at <http://www.g77.org/>.

[12] For information on G-20, see John J Kirton, *G20 Governance for a Globalised World* (Ashgate 2013) 1.

[13] A development economist, Michael P Todora, has devised a list outlining the common characteristics of developing countries. The characteristics are as follows: (i) Low standards of living, characterised by low incomes, inequality, poor health and inadequate education; (ii) Low levels of productivity; (iii) High rates of population growth and dependency burdens; (iv) High and rising levels of unemployment and underemployment; (v) Substantial dependence on agricultural production and primary product exports; (vi) Prevalence of imperfect markets and limited information; (vii) Dominance, dependence and vulnerability in international relations. (Jocelyn Blink & Ian Dorton, *Economics* (Oxford University Press 2007) 314–320).

[14] The World Bank DataBank 2015.

of law, limited knowledge and expertise of WTO law on the part of government officials, lack of legal expertise, and language barriers.[15] Hence, to see how their peers have overcome, at least to some extent, similar capacity problems which they are confronting today at WTO DSU can be an effective way of learning for other developing countries. As developing country superpowers and the most active DSU users among developing countries, BIC countries can provide some practical insights and motivation on capacity-building measures to their peers; that is, DEV countries.

3.1 RESEARCH METHODOLOGY

This book is based on five years of investigation which was carried out with the help of pragmatic empirical methods, extensive review of literature, reports and surveys. Moreover, a case study approach was used to conceptualise and propose generalisations about the PPP mechanism, its best practices and effective elements. These methods were used to gain an in-depth and comprehensive understanding of the issues, to investigate and develop the presumptions, and to check and cross-check the validity of the findings gathered from different sources.

For the original empirical investigation, the author conducted semi-structured interviews and discussions with the help of selectively designed and individuated sets of questions. The interviewees were identified using a purposive snowball sampling approach as it enabled the author to make an 'initial contact with a small group of people' that were related to the area under investigation and then utilise these to establish further related contacts.[16] With this approach, it became possible to identify those officials who, in various capacities, have been engaged in the process of WTO dispute settlement, and could therefore share their first-hand experiences and provide practical insights into this work.

Different perspectives from government officials, private sector representatives, lawyers, academics and diplomatic officials were taken into account. The claims made by government officials were verified and cross-checked against the observations provided by private sector representatives, and vice versa. Their claims and perceptions were further corroborated, endorsed or refuted in the statements received from lawyers, academics and officials from international and intergovernmental organisations.

---

[15] Gregory C Shaffer, Marc Busch & Eric Reinhardt, 'Does Legal Capacity Matter? A Survey of WTO Members' (2009) 8 *World Trade Review* 559, 561.

[16] Alan Bryman, *Social Research Methods* (Oxford University Press 2012) 202.

For the case study of India, additional empirical research methods were employed as the information was also sought through written applications filed by the author and responses received from the Government of India under India's Right to Information Act 2005. Moreover, additional facts were gathered from accessing and surveying the official documents (relating to WTO disputes) available at the offices of the Ministry of Commerce and the Permanent Mission of India to WTO.[17] These additional methods were employed only for the case study of India because the author (as an Indian national) has the right to inspect documents and seek information on issues concerning public welfare.

4.1 BENEFITS TO READERS

The book is an interdisciplinary work that draws on relevant literature and empirical findings, with an argumentative and analytical framework that extends to the pragmatically informed study of varied dispute settlement experiences. The author hopes that the topical area of this book and its unique insiders' driven approach will benefit its readers in multiple ways. It will interest readers who are keen to learn about the DSU experiences of developing countries and the impact of private sector engagement in the intergovernmental process of WTO DSU. It will also invoke interest in the academics, policymakers, government officials, business officials and lawyers who contribute to the management of foreign trade disputes in developed as well as developing countries. In particular, the benefits that different categories of readers can expect to achieve from this book are the following:

4.1.1 Policy Audience

This book aims to influence the policy review and reform in developed as well as developing country users of WTO DSM. The book will be of importance to the policymakers in the US and the EU. With expanding volumes and complexity of trade and investment, disputes in these areas will continue to rise, generating major conflicts that will require a joint management approach. Hence, with a critical evaluation of the dispute

---

[17] For example, the author browsed through the internal files with India's Ministry of Commerce including the written memorandum of request that was filed by the private steel companies in India before the *US-Carbon Steel* case was launched by India at WTO.

settlement partnership approach, this text can influence the review of dispute management practices and policies currently employed by the United States Trade Representative and the European Commission in the US and the EU respectively.

The text will particularly be appealing amongst the policy audience in developing countries. The policy experts in China, Brazil and India can use this text to review the performance and effectiveness of their dispute settlement practices and identify some key challenges and even suggestions for improving their trade defence performance. It will also be useful for the policymakers and advisers in other similarly developed countries (such as Mexico, Argentina, Chile, Turkey and Thailand which also are active DSU users among developing countries) to assess the relevant experiences of their peers and hence gain practical insights.

The book will enable the policy audience from developing countries to consider and critically evaluate a diverse range of capacity-building strategies for the management of trade disputes. It will also allow them to observe the benefits of engaging the private sector in the intergovernmental process of WTO dispute settlement, and to identify the reforms that will be needed for devising a workable domestic framework for handling trade disputes. Additionally, the book highlights for them the important issues, concerns and possible challenges that need consideration by developing countries in general before any legal, institutional, regulatory and procedural reforms related to dispute settlement and capacity building are carried out.

4.1.2 Government Officials

The book will also benefit readers from various government departments that deal directly with the management of foreign trade disputes. The book will answer some difficult questions for these government officials, such as the following:

i) What role can industries play in building the WTO dispute settlement capacity of developing countries?
ii) When and how will an affected industry be willing to invest its resources for the settlement of disputes?
iii) How can industries be approached when a dispute that needs industry's intervention arises?
iv) What actions can government officials take to help industries better organise themselves and hence coordinate with governments?
v) How have governments and industries coordinated their efforts and resources towards the successful resolution of certain landmark WTO disputes in various developed and developing countries?

vi) What are the downsides of partnering with industries during settlement of international disputes, and how are other DSU users coping with such problems?

By answering these difficult questions that government officials dealing with trade disputes commonly face, the text will act as a practical guidebook for national trade gateways such as the United States Trade Representative in the US, Director General for Trade at European Commission in the EU, Ministry of Commerce in China, Trade Policy Division in India and Dispute Settlement Unit in Brazil.

4.1.3 Industry Officials

Industry representatives from private companies, export promotion councils, trade association and confederation of industries will also find this book useful as various chapters will guide them on several systemic issues. Such issues, amongst others, include the following:

i) Which informal strategies and formal avenues can industries use to approach the relevant public officials to discuss foreign market access issues?
ii) What kind of issues are at stake when a government is considering initiating a dispute with an offending government, and in light of that, how can the affected industries convince their government to initiate a dispute at the earliest opportunity?
iii) How can industries weigh the anticipated cost and benefits of approaching the government with a trade concern and the subsequent possibility of multilateral consultations or a fully-blown WTO litigation triggered by this communication?
iv) How and in what ways can industries assist the government during pre-litigation, litigation and post-litigation stages of dispute settlement?
v) What type of problems can industries, especially in developing countries, confront while coordinating with the government during the settlement of trade disputes, and how can such problems be overcome?

4.1.4 Private Lawyers

The book will also interest private law firms and practitioners. The discussions on legal services and legal expertise in the chapters on BIC experiences are of commercial relevance to private law firms as these chapters draw on the lawyers, government officers and industry officials' experiences on the following issues:

i) How can the government and industry officials hire trade lawyers for matters relating to trade disputes and disagreements?
ii) What kind of services can they be hired for?
iii) What kind of expertise and skills are required for working on such international cases?
iv) How can law firms ambulance-chase the governments and industries to expand their practice and attract more business?
v) How can lawyers and law firms expand their experience and expertise in the field of international trade law without significant cost repercussions?
vi) How can lawyers communicate the market access concerns of their industry clients to the relevant government officials?

4.1.5 Academics, Students and Researchers

The book will be of great interest to academics, researchers and students in many disciplines including international trade law, development studies, political science, economics, international relations, and international dispute settlement. Researchers from these fields can work together, and in light of the proposed guidelines, prepare an adaptation plan of the proposed dispute settlement partnership model for a specific developing country. Moreover, the book identifies other promising areas of investigation that the readers will discover throughout in the subsequent chapters. The book can also be a useful teaching aid for the many specialist courses that are currently blossoming around the world in the areas of WTO dispute settlement and developing countries participation in the WTO legal regime.

5.1 OUTLINE OF THE BOOK

The book contains eight chapters. Chapter 1 provides a conceptual background on the WTO DSU participation benefits, participation challenges that developing countries face at WTO DSU, and how these challenges can be overcome. In doing so, it outlines various capacity-building solutions that can be employed at the international as well as domestic levels, with a special focus on strategies that can be employed at the domestic level. Chapter 2 provides a conceptual framework for this book. By identifying, describing and analysing the important concepts and issues, the chapter seeks to prepare a benchmark against which the theoretical and empirical findings presented in the following chapters should be assessed and analysed by the reader. Most importantly, it conceptualises PPP in the context of WTO DSM.

Chapter 3 deals with the dispute settlement partnership experiences of the two most active users of WTO DSU: the US and the EU. They have established a substantial set-up for public-private interaction during dispute settlement, which is built on a system of 'rights and obligations'. The US and the EU are therefore important examples useful for understanding and examining the benefits and weaknesses of a formalised PPP arrangement. Chapter 4 focuses on China's dispute settlement experience. It throws light on certain capacity-building strategies that have strengthened the dispute settlement capacity of this relatively new and developing Member State of the WTO. The combination of China's expanding foreign trade, its developing nature, the creation of a formal system of 'rights and obligations' closely following the one in the US, and the overall evolution of its dispute management approach makes this chapter a very interesting read.

Chapter 5 presents a distinct PPP arrangement, as it introduces and examines a PPP framework built and operated on the basis of specialised and dedicated institutions, intergovernmental institutional coordination and pre-defined procedures. This chapter examines the capacity-building strategies that Brazil has employed to manage foreign trade disputes with a coordinated approach. Chapter 6 focuses on the dispute settlement partnership experience of India. This chapter reviews and analyses the characteristics, weaknesses and capacity-building potential of a purely informal, ad hoc PPP approach. A review of India's dispute settlement partnership experience in this chapter therefore introduces a fresh dimension to this investigative work as it examines a different form of dispute settlement partnership arrangement.

Deriving lessons from the dispute settlement experiences of the selected developed and developing countries, Chapter 7 puts forward certain practical suggestions on how developing countries can enhance their dispute settlement capability and thereby defend their trade interests by harnessing the resources and expertise possessed by affected industries. Chapter 8 concludes the book.

1. Developing countries at WTO Dispute Settlement Understanding: strengthening participation

The World Trade Organization (WTO) dispute settlement system is a remarkable example of international 'rule of law' and multilateral adjudication. The WTO grants several rights to its members, and the WTO Dispute Settlement Understanding (DSU) provides a rule-oriented consultative and judicial mechanism to protect and enforce these rights in cases of WTO-incompatible trade infringements. The quasi-universal (and unceasingly increasing) WTO membership, significant use of dispute settlement mechanism, enthusiastic multilateral negotiations, and notable media coverage of WTO developments and disputes – all goes to show that the WTO system is here to stay as it renders trade benefits to its Member States. However, there is no denying the fact that these trade benefits have come at heavy costs; these costs are even more onerous when it comes to the protection of WTO rights because WTO DSU is a formidably resource-demanding system. This has, to a large extent, swung the pendulum of WTO DSU in favour of developed countries, as resource-constrained developing countries have often stumbled over the costs and complexities of WTO DSU.

The book examines how developing countries can deal with the capacity constraints they have faced at WTO DSU. To begin with, this chapter gives a brief account of the participation benefits, participation challenges and options to overcome those challenges that developing countries can possibly avail. In doing so, Section 1.1 provides a brief overview of how individual countries and business entities can benefit from the system, and which factors influence the nature and extent of possible DSU benefits. Section 2.1 clarifies and narrows down the typology of 'developing countries' as it will be used in this book. In doing so, it usefully identifies a specific group of developing countries that could benefit directly from the analysis and suggestions provided in this work. Section 3.1 talks about various capacity-related challenges that developing country participants have had to cope with at WTO DSU.

Readers at this stage should envisage WTO DSU as a two-level mechanism. The *first* level is domestic, where trade barriers are identified and investigated at the domestic level. The *second* level is international, where consultations are conducted or disputes are launched and fought in the form of international adjudications. Following this logic, in Section 4.1, we will look at the possible options at international and domestic levels that can strengthen the dispute settlement capacity of developing countries. Readers are reminded that the subject matter of this book is the capacity-building measures that can be taken at the domestic level. Therefore, the focus of this chapter lies in providing a conceptual background on how the disputes can be effectively handled at the domestic level in order to improve the performance and participation of developing countries at the second level; that is, at WTO DSU.

1.1 PARTICIPATION AT WTO DSU: BENEFITS FOR MEMBER STATES AND BUSINESS ENTITIES

The WTO empowers its Member State to protect and expand its foreign market access by challenging foreign trade practices and defending its measures through a time-defined procedure of consultation, litigation and implementation. One of the key objectives of WTO DSU is to enhance a country's overall economic growth and development, by reducing trade barriers and expanding foreign trade through multilateral regulation.

In essence, the market access benefits from participation at WTO DSU are mainly realised by business entities that conduct foreign trade. Non-state entities do not enjoy any direct rights and remedies under WTO DSU provisions as only governments are authorised to bring disputes to WTO.[1] However, it is mainly the trade interests of business communities that are defined, clarified and protected through dispute settlement procedures. Exporters and importers are the direct beneficiaries and victims of international trade regulation, and it is, in practice, the regulation of their business conduct and conflicts that gives rise to the burgeoning jurisprudence on international trade law.

Open markets and an increase in foreign trade activities can create more employment and investment opportunities, and thereby contribute to a country's better living standards and overall development.[2] More

---

[1] As an exception to this inter-state rule, the Agreement on Preshipment Inspection (art 2.21) confers a direct right to an individual to petition the WTO's Independent Entity if its rights guaranteed under the said Agreement are violated by an importing country. (Agreement on Preshipment Inspection (15/04/1994) LT/UR/A-1A/6, arts 2–4).

[2] On the contrary, certain scholars have vehemently argued that free trade can have a damaging impact on the living standard, human welfare, sustainable

particularly, WTO dispute settlement experience can enhance the Member States' understanding of, and expertise in, international trade law, which the governments can utilise in identifying WTO-incompatible foreign trade practices and invoking WTO DSU provisions. With the experience, expertise and confidence to invoke the WTO rules, the governments can develop bargaining strategies, which they can employ to amicably resolve (and diffuse) trade conflicts and thereby protect their industries' trade interests in the 'shadow of a potential WTO litigation'.[3] Galanter refers to this process as 'litigotiation', as he observes that 'the career of most cases does not lead to full-blown trial and adjudication but consists of negotiation and manoeuvre in the strategic pursuit of settlement through mobilization of the court process.'[4] In this manner, developing countries can strengthen their negotiating abilities once they have strengthened their litigation abilities.

With better bargaining and litigation strategies, and with the consequentially enhanced capacity to raise credible litigation threats, Member States can improve the terms on which they can trade with other member countries. This can generate further wide economic, social and environmental benefits for their economic sectors and society at large. The overarching ambit of WTO dispute settlement now encompasses areas other than commerce, as the Panels and Appellate Body have interpreted and clarified issues that go well beyond law and economics, such as those relating to strategic raw material,[5] green technology,[6] consumer welfare,[7]

---

economic growth and employment aspects. See, for example, Sarah Joseph, 'The WTO, Poverty, and Development', in Sarah Joseph, *Blame it on the WTO: A Human Rights Critique* (Oxford Scholarship Online, September 2011).

[3] Benefits from WTO DSU participation are discussed at length in Gregory Shaffer, 'Developing Countries Use of the WTO Dispute Settlement System: Why it Matters, the Barriers Posed', in James Hartigan (ed), *Trade Disputes and the Dispute Settlement Understanding of the WTO: An Interdisciplinary Assessment* Vol 6 (Emerald Group Publishing 2009) 172.

[4] M Galanter, 'Contract in Court; Or Almost Everything You May or May Not Want to Know about Contract Litigation' (2001) 3 *Wisconsin Law Review* 577, 579.

[5] Appellate Body Report, *China – Measures Related to the Exportation of Various Raw Materials*, WT/DS394/AB/R, WT/DS395/AB/R, WT/DS398/AB/R, adopted 22 February 2012.

[6] Appellate Body Report, *Canada – Certain Measures Affecting the Renewable Energy Generation Sector / Canada – Measures Relating to the Feed-in Tariff Program*, WT/DS412/AB/R / WT/DS426/AB/R, adopted 24 May 2013.

[7] Appellate Body Report, *United States – Measures Concerning the Importation, Marketing and Sale of Tuna and Tuna Products*, WT/DS381/AB/R, adopted 13 June 2012.

public health[8] and purely social concerns.[9] Hence, one can understand how, against a limited legal representation by Member States, WTO DSM can generate far-reaching economic and non-economic benefits for governments as well as business entities. However, these benefits differ from country to country and case to case.

The nature of a dispute, chances of winning and implementation of award, a country's negotiating clout and its retaliation capacity can impact its ability to realise the full benefits of WTO DSU participation. For instance, a Member State with poor retaliation capacity and bargaining power may prefer not to invoke DSU provisions even if a WTO-inconsistent measure injures its trade interests. This is especially so in cases where the challenged measure is maintained by an important trading partner or a country with a relatively stronger bargaining, litigation and retaliation capacity. Moreover, a country may decide against launching a formal action after unsuccessful rounds of bilateral negotiations with an offending Member State if the anticipated cost and time involved in dispute settlement procedures exceed the expected benefits of settlement, or if the nature of a dispute makes a formal action socially, diplomatically or politically undesirable due to reasons beyond economics.

Furthermore, a country with small market size[10] and small absolute trading stakes[11] will generally face poor economies of scale and high cost of mobilising resources for DSU participation.[12] This is because their low volumes of trade and profit margins may not justify covering any non-economic (that is, litigation) costs required for the removal of WTO-incompatible trade barriers. This is mainly due to the fact that the WTO litigation costs are insensitive to the economic stakes or market size of a country involved in a dispute. Hence, a country with small market size and stakes is less likely to participate repeatedly at WTO DSU. Due to this low participation rate, such countries would have little incentive to enhance their in-house dispute settlement capacity to fully realise the

---

8 *European Union and a Member State – Seizure of Generic Drugs in Transit*, WT/DS408, in consultations on 11 May 2010.

9 Appellate Body Report, *United States – Measures Affecting the Cross-Border Supply of Gambling and Betting Services*, WT/DS285/AB/R, adopted 20 April 2005.

10 Market size is a measurement of total volume of a given market; or put differently, the total number of buyers and sellers in a particular market.

11 Absolute trading stakes are the aggregate of a country's overall exports and imports (including the value, volume and variety of exports and imports).

12 Shaffer, 'Developing Country Use of the WTO Dispute Settlement System' (n 3) 182.

benefits of WTO DSU. For that reason, low economies of scale would generally be accompanied by high start-up costs as additional resources may be required for hiring overseas lawyers and economic consultants, or for purchasing information and evidential documents from external agencies in the absence of standing monitoring institutions, information repositories and in-house expertise. In this manner, the high cost of WTO litigation can significantly reduce the anticipated economic benefit that a country's economic sector could expect to make from the removal of a trade barrier.

Bohanes and Garza observe that 'larger WTO members trade greater volumes of more diversified trade to a greater number of trading partners, which in turn leads to a greater number of potential trade frictions and greater propensity to bring disputes'.[13] Shaffer and Sutton have also observed a positive correlation between the size of market and the capacity to participate and power to retaliate or negotiate. They observe that '[power] in the international trading system roughly corresponds to the size of a country's market – measured in terms of the ability of a country to exercise leverage by offering market access, or threatening to withdraw access, for foreign goods and services'.[14]

Let us consider the examples of India and China to further illustrate this correlation. Both are developing country members of WTO with low per capita income, but they have made an active use of WTO DSU provisions. Figures 1.1 and 1.2 are indicative of a somewhat positive and symmetrical correlation between the value of the export of goods and services in China and India and their respective rate of participation at WTO DSU (as complainant, respondent and third party).[15]

---

13 Jan Bohanes & Fernanda Garza, 'Going Beyond Stereotypes: Participation of Developing Countries in WTO Dispute Settlement' (2012) 4(1) *Trade Law and Development* 45, 57.

14 Gregory Shaffer & Charles Sutton, 'The Rise of Middle Income Countries in the International Trading System', in Randall Peerenboom, Tom Ginsburg (eds), *Law and Development of Middle-Income Countries: Avoiding the Middle-Income Trap* (Cambridge University Press 2014) 59, 64.

15 The overall period covered in the figures is 2005–2013, and they reflect a cumulative sum of data from 2013–2011, 2010–2008 and 2007–2005. Exports of goods and services (BOP, US Dollars) 'comprise all transactions between residents of a country and the rest of the world involving a change of ownership from residents to nonresidents of general merchandise, net exports of goods under merchanting, nonmonetary gold, and services'. This data is shown on the right axis. Data is compiled from The World Bank Database < https://data.worldbank.org/ > (accessed 8 June 2016). Data on WTO disputes is compiled from World Trade Organization, Database < http://stat.wto.org/Home/WSDBHome.aspx?Language= > (accessed 9 June 2016). The year of dispute indicates the year

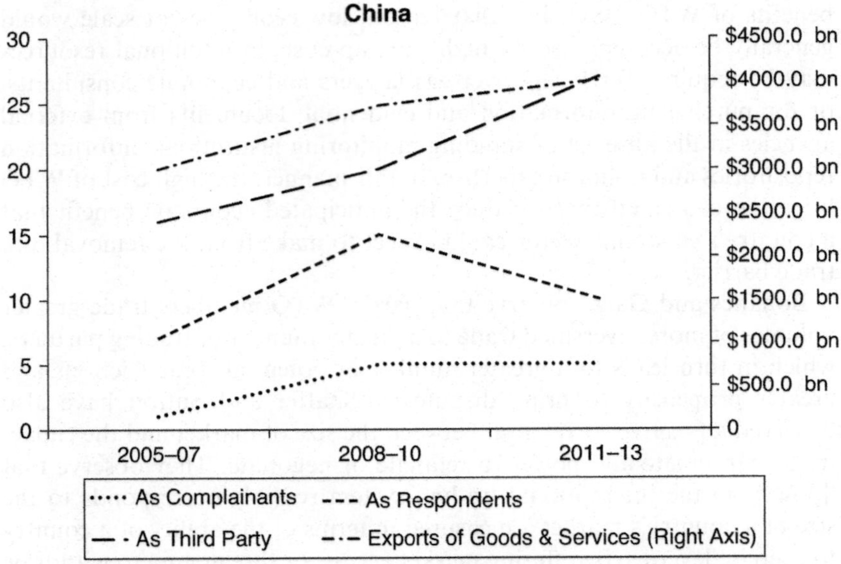

Figure 1.1 WTO DSU participation versus exports of goods and services in China

Figure 1.1 illustrates that China had minimal litigation experience (other than third party participation) until the year 2005. However, by the years 2010 and 2013, the increasing value of exports in China was accompanied by its higher relative participation as a complainant and respondent at WTO DSU. Now, let us have a look at how this correlation has played out in the case of India.

Figure 1.2 also shows a positive correlation between the increased value of exports and number of WTO complaints filed by the government in India, although this correlation is not as strong as we have seen in the case of China. Together, both figures show that with increase in exports, China and India have significantly increased the number of times they have joined disputes as third parties. This can partly be attributed to their increase in trading stakes, and to some extent to their growing willingness to enhance their understanding of, and expertise in, WTO law. High aggregate trading stakes, export-oriented economic structure and a wealth of DSU experience, which have further resulted in high economies of scale

in which consultations were requested by the complainant(s). This data is shown on the left axis.

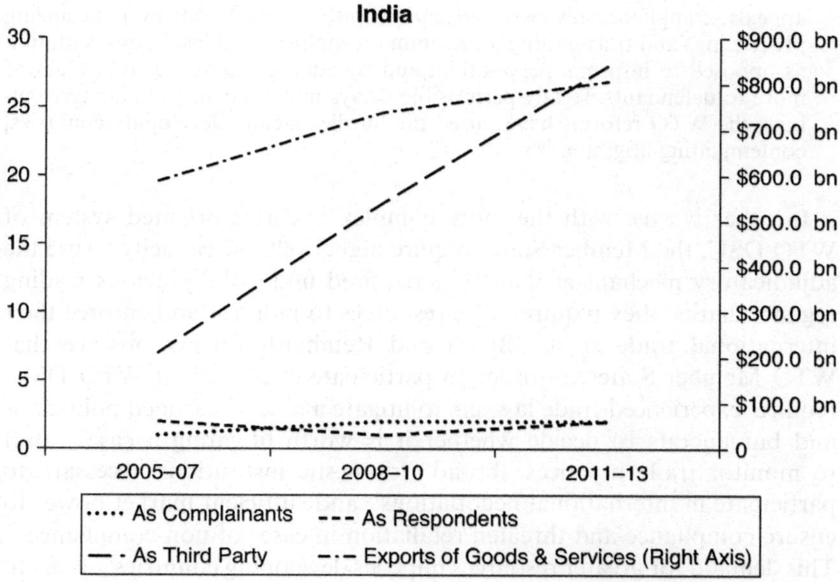

Figure 1.2 WTO DSU participation versus exports of goods and services in India

and low start-up costs in building in-house dispute settlement capacity, have better enabled these countries to self-enforce their WTO rights.

Moreover, it may be fair to argue that their rapidly growing market size and position in the global economy have strengthened their capacity to negotiate a settlement, threaten retaliation or face a retaliation threat, although it is very difficult (and beyond the scope of this book) to assess or measure the same. As a result, these countries can generally benefit more from a successful WTO litigation because their in-house capacity enables their governments to litigate and defend the market access interests of their industries in a cost-effective manner. Hence, high trading stakes and market size have, to some extent, contributed to making these countries less susceptible to high participation costs at WTO DSU.

The above observations reinforce the claim that DSU participation benefits come at a cost and these costs may not be equally affordable by all WTO members. Busch and Reinhardt explain the problem of increased cost and the complexity of WTO DSM as follows:

> By adding 26,000 pages of new treaty text, not to mention a rapidly burgeoning case law; by imposing several new stages of legal activity per dispute, such as

> appeals, compliance reviews, and compensation arbitration; by judicializing proceedings and thus putting a premium on sophisticated legal argumentation as opposed to informal negotiation; and by adding a potential two years or more to defendants' legally permissible delays in complying with adverse rulings, the WTO reforms have raised the hurdles facing [developing countries] contemplating litigation.[16]

In other words, with the more complex and rule-oriented system of WTO DSU, the Member States require higher relative capacity to use the adjudicatory mechanism than they required under the previous trading regime; that is, they require more resources to monitor and enforce their international trade rights. Busch and Reinhardt further observe that WTO Member States, in order to participate effectively at WTO DSU, require 'experienced trade lawyers to litigate a case', 'seasoned politicians and bureaucrats to decide whether it is worth litigating a case', 'staff to monitor trade practices abroad', 'domestic institutions necessary to participate in international negotiations', and sufficient market power to ensure compliance and threaten retaliation in cases of non-compliance.[17] This demand for greater resources impedes developing countries' access to WTO DSM, which in turn negatively impacts the legitimacy of WTO as a global forum for negotiations and dispute settlement.

Before we look at developing countries' participation challenges and ways to overcome them, let us try to understand the term 'developing countries', which is commonly used in a very broad and ambiguous manner as it often groups high income, middle income and low income countries under the same category. This terminology lacks a universally accepted definition. The use of purely economic indicators by the World Bank and International Monetary Fund (IMF), social and economic indicators by the United Nations (UN), and of self-identification process employed by WTO to categorise countries and define development has, to some extent, diluted the meaningfulness of this term. Hence, before we proceed, it is vital to define and categorise 'developing countries' as will be used in the context of this book, and hence, to neatly identify the group of countries that remain the focus of attention of this work.

---

16 Marc Busch & Eric Reinhardt, 'Testing International Trade Law: Empirical Studies of GATT/WTO Dispute Settlement', in Daniel LM Kennedy (ed) & James D Southwick (ed), *The Political Economy of International Trade Law: Essays in Honor of Robert E. Hudec* (Cambridge University Press 2002) 457, 467.

17 Marc Busch & Eric Reinhardt, 'The WTO Dispute Settlement Mechanism and Developing Countries' (April 2004) Trade Brief, Swedish International Development and Cooperation Agency, 3-4, accessed 15 November 2016 at <http://www9.georgetown.edu/faculty/mlb66/SIDA.pdf>.

2.1 DEVELOPING COUNTRIES: MEANING AND CLASSIFICATION

Under the General Agreement on Tariffs and Trade (GATT) 1947, the term 'developing' was used for those countries where the economies '. . . [could] only support low standards of living and [were] in the early stage of development'.[18] The WTO agreements have not provided any definition or classification of the term, as they have incorporated a system of self-classification. The WTO allows Member States to self-designate themselves as developed or developing countries, and it adheres to the UN's definition and classification of least developed countries (LDCs), which is based on GNP per capita, human assets and economic vulnerability indicators.[19]

The WTO's self-classification system has given rise to a broad and heterogeneous group of 'developing countries', as it ranges from small economies that are predominantly based on subsistence agriculture, to large and emerging economies such as China, Brazil, Mexico and India.[20] At one end of this category, you have high income countries such as Argentina and Korea. At the other end, the same group comprises least developed countries with very low per capita income and GDP. These diversely developed countries have very different levels of development, market size and foreign trade interests. Moreover, they have hugely diverse experience of participation at WTO DSU as some of them have participated actively, while others have had a minimal or no DSU participation experience. For instance, from January 1995 to January 2017, Brazil has filed 30 complaints and responded to 16 complaints, while Cuba has filed a single complaint and responded to none at WTO DSU. It is therefore neither practicable nor meaningful to identify and analyse the usefulness and weaknesses of common strategies that can be employed, broadly speaking, by any 'developing' country member that is endeavouring to enforce its WTO rights.

In light of this, the book seeks to analyse specific capacity-building strategies that a specific group of developing country members can practically employ in the future. To achieve this purpose, it centres its attention

---

[18] General Agreement on Tariffs and Trade 1947 (55 UNTS 194) 61 STAT pt 5; TIAS 1700, art XVIII: 1

[19] UNCTAD website: United Nations Recognition of the Least Developed Countries, accessed 2 May 2016 at <http://archive.unctad.org/Templates/Page.asp?intItemID=3618&lang=1>.

[20] Out of the 164 WTO members (as on 26 January 2017), only 37 are developed countries. More than 80% of WTO members have self-designated themselves under the wide category of 'developing countries'.

Table 1.1 *Participation of middle income countries at WTO DSU (1995–2017)*

Country	Complainants	Respondents	Third Party	Total Participation
China	15	39	135	**189**
India	23	24	123	**170**
Brazil	30	16	106	**152**
Mexico	23	14	80	**117**
Thailand	13	4	72	**89**
Turkey	3	9	71	**83**
Guatemala	9	2	36	**47**
Ecuador	3	3	33	**39**
Indonesia	10	14	17	**41**
Honduras	8	0	26	**34**
Peru	3	5	19	**27**
Philippines	5	6	14	**25**
Vietnam	3	0	25	**28**

on the experience and interests of those developing country members of WTO that are classified as middle income countries (MICs) (including upper middle, middle and lower middle income countries as on 15 April 2017) by the World Bank. The economies and markets of MICs have risen faster than the rest of the world, and they have shown increasing enthusiasm for creating new market opportunities and defending domestic policies through the use of WTO DSU.[21] More particularly, large MICs such as Brazil, China, India, Mexico and Thailand have become more advanced in using WTO DSU to restore and protect their foreign market access. This can be seen in Table 1.1, as it illustrates the total number of times some of the most active DSU users among MICs have participated as a complainant, respondent and third party.[22]

Table 1.1 clearly ranks the leading developing countries, Brazil, India and China (BIC), as the top three users of DSU among MIC countries, with Mexico and Thailand following the trail of participation. The table

[21] In the past two decades, the contribution of foreign trade to GDPs in middle income countries has increased substantially. From 20% of GDP in 1970, it has grown to an astonishing 56% in 2011 (The World Bank Database 2016, accessed 21 January 2017).

[22] The data is compiled from World Bank Database and WTO website (accessed 21 January 2017). It includes the number of times these middle income countries have acted as complainant, respondent and third party at WTO DSU from 1 January 1995 to 19 January 2017.

also indicates that MICs, including the larger ones, have been relatively more comfortable in joining the disputes as third parties, as compared to participating as complainants or respondents. This reflects, to some extent, that the top three users of DSU too have their reasons to avoid the costly system of litigation; however, their continuing interest in DSM is evident from their striking rate of participation as third parties.

Third parties to WTO disputes enjoy substantial rights of participation: (i) they can be physically present in substantive meetings at consultative, Panel and Appellate stage; (ii) they can deliver written and oral submissions during the first round of litigation; (iii) they can receive the first submissions filed by the complainant(s) and respondent(s); and (iv) they can also be granted additional rights on a case-by-case basis.[23] The provision allows Member States to comprehensively observe dispute settlement proceedings, and they can utilise this experience of observation to expand their understanding of WTO laws and dispute settlement system in a cost-effective manner. Along with many other MICs, BIC countries have clearly realised these benefits, as they have participated frequently as third party participants to improve their understanding of the system by 'learning through observation'. Given this enthusiasm, it is an opportune time to evaluate the strategies MICs, particularly large MICs, have employed to develop in a cost-effective way their WTO dispute settlement capacity.

3.1 PARTICIPATION CHALLENGES AT WTO DSU: DEVELOPING COUNTRIES

Academics, lawyers, economists and political scientists have written extensively about the participation challenges faced by various developing countries at WTO DSM.[24] The developing countries have faced problems in monitoring foreign trade practices and identifying or investigating foreign trade barriers. They have struggled in negotiating a settlement or conducting successful bilateral or multilateral consultations. They have also faced obstacles in litigating trade barriers at WTO DSU. Moreover, on several notable occasions, developing countries have found it difficult

---

[23] For information on the rights of third parties, see DSU Agreement, arts 4, 10 and 17.

[24] For details, see Busch & Reinhardt, 'The WTO Dispute Settlement Mechanism and Developing Countries' (n 17); Michael Ewing-Chow, 'Are Asian WTO Members Using the WTO DSU "Effectively"?' (2013) 16(3) *Journal of International Economic Law* 669; Shaffer, 'Developing Country Use of the WTO Dispute Settlement System' (n 3) 182–185.

to ensure compliance even after a favourable ruling has been given by the Panel or Appellate Body (AB). The key reasons behind these obstacles that have impeded developing countries' access to WTO DSU are as follows:

i) First and foremost, developing countries lack the monitoring capacity that is required to monitor foreign trade practices, identify trade barriers and ensure compliance by offending Member States.
ii) Paucity of in-house legal and economic expertise and experience in WTO law further impedes their effective access to WTO DSU, as these resources are essential to investigate a trade barrier, conduct consultations and adjudicate a WTO case.
iii) Insufficient financial resources also constrain their capacity as such resources may be required for the hiring of overseas trade lawyers and economic consultants to assist during the consultation, litigation and implementation stages (especially in the absence of domestic expertise and experience).
iv) Another striking constraint is the paucity of political, diplomatic and subject-matter expertise within the government, as that may be required to gather information and coordinate tasks with the affected industry, overseas governments and various WTO divisions. Political expertise and efficient bureaucracy is also required to make appropriate determinations in respect of bilateral/multilateral actions that are required to be undertaken in cases of infringements.
v) Poor information channels and ineffective governance structures lead to problems in gathering evidentiary documents relating to trade barriers, their impact, nature and magnitude of injury and their WTO-inconsistency.
vi) Inadequate powers of retaliation and bargaining lead to difficulties during negotiations or in ensuring compliance after a favourable ruling is adopted by the Dispute Settlement Body (DSB).
vii) Fears of adverse diplomatic and economic retaliation from stronger market powers and powerful trade partners further persuade the governments to stay away from any confrontation in the shape of formal consultation or litigation.
viii) Insufficient knowledge and awareness about the benefits of WTO DSU provisions among government officials and business entities further constrain developing countries' ability to manoeuvre and utilise the DSU provisions for their legitimate trade interests.

Bohanes and Garza confirm that the main challenges which various developing countries have faced in the process of enforcing international trade rights are the lack of legal capacity, weak domestic governance, insufficient retaliatory powers and fears of political consequences and pressures.[25] Shaffer succinctly describes these challenges as '. . .constraints of legal knowledge, financial endowment, and political power, or, more simply, of law, money, and politics.'[26]

Multiple participation challenges, as listed above, are central to the most common problem that most developing countries have faced: the problem of capacity constraint. The term 'capacity' in this book has a broad connotation as it includes a country's political, legal and financial power, and it generally refers to a country's overall ability to utilise the WTO dispute settlement provisions. Capacity, in the context of WTO DSU, should not be measured on purely economic indicators (such as a country's per capita income) as a country can have low per capita income but large export markets and, therefore, advanced expertise and experience of participation at WTO DSU.

India, for example, has low indexed per capita income, but it is a major emerging economy which has participated actively at WTO DSU and has demonstrated the capacity to mobilise the required resources to monitor and enforce its WTO rights. Hence, the dispute settlement capacity should be measured by taking systemic account of a country's ability to mobilise resources, as and when required, for monitoring and enforcing its WTO rights. The problem of 'capacity constraint' refers to a situation where a country is unable to effectively and fully utilise the WTO DSU provisions due to lack of required resources and expertise. Insufficient capacity therefore impedes a country's ability to utilise the remedies available under WTO DSM, be it in litigating or defending a dispute, conducting formal or bilateral consultations with foreign governments, or ensuring proper implementation and compliance.

The problem of insufficient capacity becomes even more severe if a developing country challenges a measure or if its measure is challenged by a developed country. Busch and Reinhardt observe that 'the WTO has exaggerated the gap between developed and developing complainants with respect to their ability to get defendants to liberalize disputed policies. In short, wealthy complainants have become significantly more likely to secure their desired outcomes under the WTO, but poorer complainants have not.'[27] This situation can be more appropriately described as the

---

[25] Bohanes & Garza (n 13) 69.

[26] Gregory C Shaffer, Marc Busch & Eric Reinhardt, 'Does Legal Capacity Matter? A Survey of WTO Members' (2009) 8 *World Trade Review* 559, 572.

[27] Marc Busch & Eric Reinhardt, 'Developing Countries and General Agreement on Tariffs and Trade/World Trade Organization Dispute Settlement' (2003) 37(4) *Journal of World Trade* 729.

problem of 'capacity gap' between the developing and the developed world.

'Capacity gap' here refers to a situation where developing countries lack the capacity to identify a potential trade barrier, arrive at a negotiated settlement, conduct WTO litigation, defend their practices or ensure compliance due to paucity of resources required for each task, as against a sufficiently resourced and developed country in opposition. 'Equal access to justice is a measure of the legitimacy of any legal order'[28] and the WTO's international adjudicatory mechanism therefore 'must ensure that inequalities between its members do not grow too large'.[29] An obvious response to this situation would be to raise the following questions: Can this resource gap between developed and developing country members be bridged? How can developing countries enhance their capacity to resolve trade disputes through WTO DSM? These issues are addressed in the following section.

4.1 OVERCOMING THE PARTICIPATION CHALLENGES

Broadly, there are two options that can be explored for addressing the capacity-related challenges. The *first* option is to introduce changes at the international level (which can include changing WTO rules), and the *second* option is to find solutions at the domestic level. The first option can be explored through proposals presented by developing countries, and by academics and organisations committed to the notion of WTO reform The second option can be explored by making use of the first-hand experiences of certain upper middle, middle and lower middle income countries that have employed varied strategies to mobilise resources for the utilisation of DSU provisions.

4.1.1 Options for Overcoming Participation Challenges

4.1.1.1 First option: what can be done at international level?

The WTO has introduced certain favourable provisions for enabling its developing country members to participate effectively at WTO DSU. These provisions include, but are not limited to, the requirement of non-reciprocity in trade negotiations between developed and developing

[28] Bohanes & Garza (n 13) 48.
[29] Ibid.

countries, grant of extra time to fulfil commitments, legal assistance extended by the Secretariat and the Advisory Centre on World Trade Organization Law (ACWL), improved and greater market access opportunities, requirement to safeguard developing countries' interests by WTO membership, and additional technical assistance. However, in practice, these provisions are far too limited and inadequate to provide developing countries with an effective DSU access. The reasons behind this claim are discussed at length in various scholarly works.[30] Hence, we should now turn our attention to those changes that are currently proposed at the multilateral level.

Developing countries have submitted multiple proposals aimed at levelling the playing field at WTO DSU. These proposals, amongst others, include introduction of retrospective and mandatory financial compensation in place of suspension of concession[31] and/or collective suspension of concession as powerful remedies for developing countries.[32] Developing Member States have also requested the creation of a fast track, simplified procedure for the adjudication of cases with established precedents.[33] Another suggestion which has occupied some prominence in WTO Ministerial Conferences is the strengthening of special and differential treatment provisions in order to make them precise, effective and operational.[34]

Academics have also proposed several changes to WTO DSU rules. These proposals, amongst others, include the appointment of a special WTO prosecutor for developing countries, introduction of an additional provision for technical and administrative assistance, and training of adjudicators on special and differential treatment provisions contained in the WTO agreements. Scholars have also argued in favour of allowing

---

[30] For information on the limitations of special and differential treatment provisions, see F Roessler, 'Special and Differential Treatment of Developing Countries under the WTO Dispute Settlement System', in F Ortino & EU Petersman (eds), *The WTO Dispute Settlement System 1995–2003* (Kluwer Law International 2004) 88.

[31] World Trade Organization, Dispute Settlement Body, Special Session, 'Contribution of Ecuador to the Improvement of the Dispute Settlement Understanding of the WTO' submitted by Ecuador [TN/DS/W/9] 8 July 2002.

[32] World Trade Organization, Dispute Settlement Body, Special Session, 'Text for the African Group Proposals on Dispute Settlement Understanding Negotiations' submitted by Kenya in the name of African Group [TN/DS/W/42] 24 January 2003.

[33] World Trade Organization, Dispute Settlement Body, Special Session, 'Responses to Questions on the Specific Input from China' submitted by China [TN/DS/W/57] 19 May 2003.

[34] World Trade Organization, General Council, 'Preparation for the Fourth Session of the Ministerial Conference' [WT/GC/W/442] 19 September 2001.

direct applicability of WTO law in national courts for enabling developing countries to self-enforce favourable awards.[35] They have also proposed the establishment of additional provisions for differential and more favorable time frames and evidential requirements during dispute settlement proceedings for developing country participants.[36]

Petersmann, with a 'bottom-up approach' towards WTO law, proposes that private parties should be granted direct litigation rights so that 'corporations and other private actors may enforce WTO law through national courts'.[37] Nordstrom and Shaffer, on the other hand, maintain a 'top-down approach' as they put forward a different proposal for granting easier WTO access to developing countries. They propose that developing countries with small trading stakes and market size (amidst high litigation cost) can benefit significantly from a small claims procedure established at WTO.[38] They argue that a small claims procedure, which can be made available for a specific monetary value of non-complicated claims (with established precedents) and limited to a well-defined group of developing country governments, can result in prompt and cost-effective settlement of trade disputes.

Other academics, as well as policymakers, have criticised these proposals. One of the criticisms posed by academics is that not all developing country members require financial or legal aid; all developing members do not have similar financial needs. For instance, the financial needs and conditions of Brazil and China with respect to the utilisation of WTO DSM will be very different from those of Bangladesh. In order to implement proposals which seem to indiscriminately favour all (self-classified) developing country members, the WTO members would need to better define and categorise the term 'developing countries'.[39] Other critiques come from

---

[35] See, for instance, Alberto Alemanno, 'Private Parties and WTO Dispute Settlement System' (2004) 1 Cornell Law School Inter-University Graduate Student Conference Papers, accessed 8 August 2016 at <http://scholarship.law.cornell.edu/lps_clacp/1>.

[36] Ibid.

[37] Ernst-Ulrich Petersmann, *Constitutional Functions and Constitutional Problems of International Economic Law: International and Domestic Foreign Trade Law and Foreign Trade Policy in the United States, the European Community and Switzerland* (University Press 1991) 243, 463.

[38] Hakan Nordstrom & Gregory Shaffer, 'Access to Justice in the World Trade Organization: The Case for a Small Claims Procedure?' (2008) 7(4) *World Trade Review* 587, 589.

[39] Sheila Page & Peter Kleen, 'Special and Differential Treatment of Developing Countries in the World Trade Organization' (2005) 2 *Global Development Studies* 45, 79.

the fact that adopting these (and other similar) proposals would require multilateral re-negotiations and complex trade-offs between more than 164 WTO Member States (as of 20 January 2017), all of which have 'varying interests, values, levels of development, and priorities'.[40]

The WTO's long-standing ineffectiveness in striking multilateral agreements makes the *first* option less feasible and somewhat unachievable in the present circumstances. Moreover, changing WTO rules to favour developing countries is an option that has been resisted and challenged by developed countries throughout the GATT and WTO era. A trade policy advisor confirms that any endeavour to achieve a consensus among WTO members for changing WTO rules would be similar to 'finding a needle in a haystack'.[41] However, developing countries can possibly influence the WTO jurisprudence through active participation in WTO Ministerial Meetings, its Committee System and Dispute Settlement Proceedings. As Michalopoulos observes: 'The capacity of the developing countries to promote changes to the system of rules governing international trade that will benefit their development depends very much on the effectiveness of their participation in the WTO.'[42] This observation brings the discussion back to its original concern; that is, the need to explore an attainable solution to help developing countries enhance their WTO DSU participation capacity.

There are other proposals which may not require changes to WTO rules, but would nevertheless call for action at international level. For example, Bown has proposed that an international institution should be established to monitor compliance on behalf of developing countries and generate requisite information for the government and private sector.[43] It is also proposed that dispute settlement funds should be created at international level, and developed countries and international financial institutions should contribute to the building up of these funds. The proposed funds could be utilised to strengthen the legal aid mechanism for developing countries. Shaffer suggests that the ambit of the ACWL should be expanded and, in coordination with international non-governmental

---

40 Gregory C Shaffer, *Defending Interests: Public-Private Partnerships in WTO Litigation* (Brookings Institution Press 2003) 156.

41 Aurelie Walker, 'The WTO has failed developing nations' *The Guardian* (14 November 2011), accessed 8 June 2016 at <http://www.theguardian.com/global-development/poverty-matters/2011/nov/14/wto-fails-developing-countries>.

42 Constantine Michalopoulos, *Developing Countries in the WTO* (Palgrave 2001) 152.

43 Chad P Bown, *Self-Enforcing Trade: Developing Countries and WTO Dispute Settlement* (Brookings Institution Press 2009) 208.

organisations (NGOs) and intergovernmental organisations, it should extend enhanced legal, informational, monitoring and technical support to developing countries.[44]

Certain scholars have extended support to changes proposed at international and multilateral levels with the argument that increased participation of developing countries at WTO will result in better integration of developing countries into the world trading system, thereby creating new trade opportunities for the entire world.[45] Some have also argued that the institution of WTO can only be more acceptable and credible if all WTO members participate effectively.[46] On the other hand, these proposals are opposed on multiple grounds by the developed world. Developed countries have argued that it is not fair to extend favourable treatment to all developing Member States without making any distinction or establishing parameters based on their level of development and size of economy. It is also argued that implementing these proposals at international level, especially if they also favour emerging market economies such as China and Brazil, would generate external benefits that would go beyond (and sometimes against) the interests of developed countries.[47] These divergent views can cause undue delay in the consideration and implementation of these proposals. Moreover, all proposals discussed under this *first* option have a common limitation; that is, they require developing countries to seek intervention from external agents that are beyond their control and influence. On the other hand, the *second* option discussed in the following section does not attract such points of criticism.

4.1.1.2 Second option: what is being done at domestic level?

The *second* option for developing countries is to explore possible ways to build their in-house WTO participation capacity by introducing changes at the domestic level. This book embraces the domestic approach because most of the capacity-related challenges faced by developing countries are deeply rooted in the domestic context of these countries and therefore solutions can best be found at the domestic level. For example, paucity of lawyers and government officials trained and experienced in WTO law can, to some extent, be blamed for high litigation costs as the lack of

---

44 Gregory C Shaffer, 'The Challenges of WTO Law: Strategies for Developing Country Adaptation' (2006) 5(2) *World Trade Review* 177, 189.

45 Bohanes & Garza (n 13) 50.

46 Tuula Honkonen, *The Common But Differentiated Responsibility Principle in Multilateral Environmental Agreements* (Wolters Kluwer 2009) 54.

47 Page & Kleen (n 39) 45, 79.

domestic legal expertise necessitates hiring expensive overseas lawyers. In accord with this, an Indian trade lawyer observes the following:

> With more number of cases being litigated by and against India mainly from the year 2001, the government has decided to expand its legal expertise. It is not feasible and economically viable to hire expensive Geneva based lawyers, especially in the cases where India is challenged. The government therefore has started to rely more on domestic expertise for cutting down the high litigation cost.[48]

Likewise, paucity of information and evidential documents with a complaining or responding government is mainly due to lack of inter-ministerial coordination and disengaged private stakeholders, and it sometimes results in increasing the litigation cost as data is purchased from overseas agencies. In *EC – Export Subsidies on Sugar (Thailand)*, for example, the sugar industries in Brazil, Australia and Thailand had to get together and jointly purchase the evidential data from LMC International for substantiating and updating their litigation briefs and responses. This led to a massive increase in the litigation costs for the complainants.[49] It is therefore important that these constraints are directly dealt with at the domestic level.

This option can be explored practically with the help of first-hand dispute settlement experiences of certain developing Member States. Certain MICs have made significant progress in overcoming the participation challenges, as they have learnt to utilise WTO DSM more effectively than other WTO members from the developing world. Most notably, Brazil, China and India, all emerging yet developing economies, have rigorously explored the *second* option as they have employed different domestic strategies for overcoming the challenges they have faced during identification of barriers, settlement of disputes and enforcement of awards. These Member States are the top three developing country users of WTO DSU, and hence, their experience of managing trade disputes can motivate and guide other developing countries to meaningfully consider the in-house remedies.

After the US, the EU and Canada, Brazil is the fourth most active complainant at WTO DSU, and its successful performance at WTO DSU, especially in strategically important cases won against the EU and the

---

48 Interview with a trade lawyer, Luthra & Luthra, Delhi, India, 21 June 2013.

49 Appellate Body Report, *European Communities – Export Subsidies on Sugar*, Complaint by Thailand, WT/DS265/AB/R, WT/DS266/AB/R, WT/DS283/AB/R, adopted 19 May 2005.

US (such as *EC – Export Subsidies on Sugar (Brazil)*[50] and *US – Upland Cotton*[51]), is recognised nationally and internationally. China, the world's fastest growing economy, after its accession to WTO in December 2001, has promptly established itself as a prominent DSU user by successfully litigating and defending cases against powerful trading partners such as the US and the EU. India, again an ambitious emerging economy, has joined the club of active and successful DSU users by presenting strong litigation and defence in significant WTO cases against developed as well as developing Member States. The nature and extent of their participation exhibits their continuing commitment towards expanding their in-house ability to further utilise DSU provisions.

At the same time, it is important to note that these ambitious economies too have faced various capacity-related problems in accessing WTO DSM. For example, the *Canada – Aircraft*[52] and *Brazil – Aircraft*[53] cases exhibited the emergent need to expand the dispute settlement capacity in Brazil. During these disputes, the government realised that an institutional reorganisation, additional financial and information resources and legal expertise were required for successful litigation and compliance proceedings.[54] Similarly, China, during the initial WTO litigations, faced high litigation costs due to insufficient domestic trade law expertise and lack of litigation experience.[55] India has also faced multiple difficulties in identifying trade barriers, locating in-house expertise, gathering information and ensuring compliance.[56] However, Brazil, China and India have learnt from their past dispute settlement experience and, to some extent, from the enormous experience of the US and the EU. As will be seen in the following chapters, they have evolved distinct capacity-building strategies at the domestic level.

---

[50] Appellate Body Report, *European Communities – Export Subsidies on Sugar*, Complaint by Brazil, WT/DS265/AB/R, WT/DS266/AB/R, WT/DS283/AB/R, adopted 19 May 2005.

[51] Appellate Body Report, *United States – Subsidies on Upland Cotton*, WT/DS267/AB/R, adopted 21 March 2005.

[52] Appellate Body Report, *Canada – Measures Affecting the Export of Civilian Aircraft*, WT/DS70/AB/R, adopted 20 August 1999.

[53] Appellate Body Report, *Brazil – Export Financing Programme for Aircraft*, WT/DS46/AB/R, adopted 20 August 1999.

[54] Interview with an official, Permanent Mission of Brazil to the WTO, Geneva, Switzerland, 16 September 2013.

[55] Henry Gao, 'Taking Justice into Your Own Hand: The TBI Mechanism in China' (2010) 44 *Journal of World Trade* 633.

[56] Interview with an official, Permanent Mission of India to the WTO, Geneva, Switzerland, 13 April 2013; verified in the interview with an official, Centre for WTO Studies, Indian Institute of Foreign Trade, New Delhi, Delhi, India, 5 June 2013.

Broadly, Brazil, China and India have strengthened their DSU participation with the help of multiple strategies. These strategies include the following: (i) expansion of DSU understanding and experience with the help of 'third party participation'; (ii) enhancement of domestic legal expertise in WTO law with the help of increased WTO-focused education and training; (iii) creation of dedicated laws, institutions and procedures to manage WTO disputes at the levels of ministries and WTO Mission; (iv) creation of in-house monitoring capacity to better identify and monitor foreign trade barriers with the help of voluntary sector and local law firms; and (v) engagement of business entities for the settlement of trade disagreements and disputes (government-industry coordination). Although the potential of all these strategies cannot be ignored, this book focuses particularly on the last-mentioned strategy; that is, government-industry coordination.

The government departments of certain developed and developing countries have actively coordinated and exchanged resources with industries during the handling of WTO disputes. The available literature presents the EU and the US, the two most active DSU users, as the leaders of this coordination approach. Moreover, Shaffer and Ortiz-Melendez have put forward India, China and Brazil as the most distinct examples of developing countries that have engaged their private sector for the effective conduct of dispute settlement proceedings.[57] By analysing the wealth of their DSU experience, the readers can usefully review and analyse the best practices, weaknesses and capacity-building potential of government-industry coordination.

Government-industry coordination is grounded in the notion of public private partnership (PPP). Grossman observes that 'special interest groups', which include private companies, trade associations, chambers of commerce, and unions and confederations, influence and impact almost all areas of government's policy-making and decision-making endeavours.[58] However, in the area of international trade, they are the frontrunners as cross border transactions of goods and services are mainly carried out by profit-motivated business groups. Hence, some form of coordination between government and industry, in most cases, is embedded in the nature of WTO dispute settlement proceedings as the violation of WTO rules directly affects business interests of exporters, importers,

---

[57] Gregory C Shaffer & Ricardo Melendez-Ortiz (eds), *Dispute Settlement at the WTO: The Developing Country Experience* (Cambridge University Press 2010) 21, 137, 174.

[58] Gene M Grossman & Elhanan Helpman, *Special Interest Politics* (The MIT Press 2001) 3 (the authors define 'special interest groups' (SIG) as any identifiable group with similar preferences on a subset of policy issues).

manufacturers and producers, which in most cases are private companies. Moreover, industries are a vital source of information and evidential documents.

Business entities are best placed to gather information relating to trade barriers for two primary reasons. *First*, exporters and importers can gather knowledge during the course of conducting their everyday business activities. *Second*, a member of an industry should have 'collective action interest' in gathering and building upon such information. In other words, an exporter should invest in gathering information on market access violations as removal of a trade barrier would not only benefit the special economic interests of that exporter but, more broadly, of its entire industry. Grossman and Helpman also confirm that '. . .individuals who have similar policy preferences have much to gain from pooling their resources to pursue common political aims. On the other hand, there is always the temptation to "free-ride". This is so because those who share a group's objectives can benefit from its political efforts even if they refuse to help pay the bills.'[59] In other words, business entities may not always capture this "positive externality" argument and may prefer to 'free-ride' by enjoying trade benefits generated from the investment of resources by other companies, government, industry associations and NGOs. However, an organised and combined effort by exporters with overlapping trade interests and share of the workload between government and an organised industry can result in better protection of trade interests through effective dispute settlement proceedings.

These arguments, considered together, give rise to the following questions: How should readers conceive the notion of PPP in the context of WTO DSU? What should be the readers' benchmark for judging the effectiveness of a PPP arrangement? How can PPPs enhance a country's dispute settlement capacity, and how can resources be exchanged in an effective manner? Chapter 2 responds to these questions, as it conceptualises the PPP mechanism in the context of WTO DSU.

59 Ibid 103.

2. WTO dispute settlement partnerships: a conceptual framework

Three key concepts run through this book: developing countries' participation at WTO DSU, the public private partnership approach, and domestic management of WTO disputes. Chapter 1 examined the developing countries' participation at WTO DSU. This chapter builds upon this examination further, as it prepares the conceptual benchmark against which the readers should assess the theoretical and empirical findings provided throughout this book. In other words, it provides a conceptual foundation to this book as it helps readers understand and evaluate the analysis provided in the rest of the chapters.

The chapter puts forward the PPP approach as one of the key in-house strategies that can produce positive capacity-building results in developing countries. Section 1.1 discusses the nature and forms of PPP arrangements that, broadly speaking, developed and developing country members have commonly employed. It provides the conceptual framework to this work as it demonstrates the ways in which industries can be engaged to enable countries to mobilise resources during each stage of dispute resolution. This is done with the help of a nine-stage model, wherein each stage of dispute settlement is expounded with the help of several practical examples.

Readers should consider the PPP approach with a word of caution: dispute settlement partnerships do not operate in a vacuum; you will observe throughout this work that their effectiveness depends hugely upon the domestic conditions within which they operate. In line with this, Section 2.1 outlines for readers various weaknesses, challenges and domestic conditions that can affect the nature and performance of PPP arrangements. Readers should keep these factors in mind while analysing the suitability of PPP arrangements for individual countries. In this manner, Chapter 2 provides a comprehensive analytical framework to understand and determine the effectiveness of PPP arrangements that will be examined in the subsequent chapters.

1.1 CONCEPTUALISING PUBLIC PRIVATE PARTNERSHIP

1.1.1 Public Private Partnership at WTO DSU: Meaning

While formally considered as a form of public international law, WTO DSU directly affects business interests. In the *India – Batteries* case, for instance, the anti-dumping duties imposed by India on the Bangladeshi battery imports infringed the financial interests of the battery exporters in Bangladesh.[1] In the famous *Aircraft* litigations, the complaining and responding governments contested WTO litigations primarily for restoring the market access interests of their respective aircraft manufacturers and exporters.[2] A similar correlation between a trade barrier and business interests can be seen in almost all WTO litigations. Therefore, a commercial entity that wants to protect or expand its market access interests has reasons to provide its government with the relevant resources (such as information, evidence, finances and legal expertise) required for the removal of a trade barrier. The privately owned resources can be utilised by the government to investigate a barrier, launch bilateral negotiations and WTO consultations, and litigate a dispute. In this manner, the constitutional authority of a government can be indirectly invoked by an industry (as they do not have any direct rights under WTO DSU) with the help of a privately funded government action at WTO DSU. The arrangement therefore provides industries with an indirect route to access international trade adjudication.

In general terms, a public private partnership refers to a contractual arrangement or understanding between the public and private sectors, where both sectors invest their unique resources to achieve a mutually beneficial goal and both sides share the risks and rewards emanating from the partnership. In the context of WTO DSU, PPP refers to the synergy of resources between a government and an industry during the conduct of WTO dispute settlement proceedings. At stake, during this arrangement, are the respective national and exporting interests of a government and an industry, and both sectors are mutually dependent on each other's resources for the protection of their respective interests. Their distinct yet

---

[1] *India – Anti Dumping Measure on Batteries from Bangladesh,* WT/DS306, in consultations on 28 January 2004.

[2] *Canada – Aircraft* (Appellate Body Report, *Canada – Measures Affecting the Export of Civilian Aircraft*, WT/DS70/AB/R, adopted 20 August 1999); *Brazil – Aircraft* (Appellate Body Report, *Brazil – Export Financing Programme for Aircraft*, WT/DS46/AB/R, adopted 20 August 1999).

overlapping interests can be protected with the reciprocal exchange of resources through an effective partnership arrangement.

Jan Kooiman observes that '[n]o single actor, public or private, has all the knowledge and information required to solve complex, dynamic and diversified problems.'[3] It is therefore important that the governments and industries function in a complementary manner even during the management of WTO disputes. A trade representative from the Office of the United States Trade Representative (USTR) states that: 'We at USTR rely on industry.'[4] A trade representative from the European Commission observes the following:

> None of our disputes is brought without there being an industry that is adamantly behind it and pushing for the case to be taken to the WTO. The Commission does not have the resources to monitor observance of the rules and litigate all trade concerns. So it prioritises to take those cases where there is a demand and resource support by the private sector.[5]

The resource crunch experienced by the European Commission and the USTR, which are official trade representatives of the EU Member States and the US, reinforces the argument that exchange of resources is even more vital for the resource-constrained governments of developing and least developed countries. Walter Powell explains the rationale behind the envisaged relationship in the following statement: 'A basic assumption of network relationships is that one party is dependent on resources controlled by another, and that there are gains to be had by the pooling of resources.'[6] On the basis of this rationale, the primary objective of the proposed PPP mechanism is to enable developing country governments to mobilise resources in a cost-effective manner, and thereby strengthen their capacities to protect, defend and negotiate the international trade rights. Put differently, an effective PPP mechanism should seek to facilitate the formation of 'public-private coordination', which can enable the governments to utilise the WTO dispute settlement procedures.

---

3 Jan Kooiman, 'Findings, Speculations and Recommendations' in Jan Kooiman (ed), *Modern Governance: New Government – Society Interactions* (Sage Publications 1993) 252.

4 Gregory C Shaffer, *Defending Interests: Public-Private Partnerships in WTO Litigation* (Brookings Institution Press 2003) 47.

5 Interview with an official, DG Trade, European Commission (audio conferencing), 3 June 2013.

6 Walter Powell, 'Neither Market nor Hierarchy: Network Forms of Organization' in J Frances, R Levacic, J Mitchell & G Thompson (eds), *Markets, Hierarchies & Networks: The Coordination of Social Life* (Sage Publications 1991).

The effectiveness or success of government-industry coordination, in the context of this work, will not be measured in terms of the nature and extent of resources exchanged between the partners, or the extent to which an industry has financed a dispute. A PPP strategy will be effective and advantageous if it can strengthen developing countries' WTO dispute settlement capacity. In other words, the success of a PPP mechanism will be measured in terms of its ability to achieve its objective; that is, its potential to perform a capacity-building function, by incentivising and facilitating optimal resource exchange and a regulated share of the workload between government and industry in a developing country. However, there is no standard form of PPP arrangements; PPP, as mentioned above, is a dynamic approach that acts as a foundation for different types of coordination arrangements.

As will be shown in Chapters 3, 5 and 6, dispute settlement coordination can initially and most commonly be carried out through informal means between a government and an industry as both can enter into informal dialogues and exchange resources on a reciprocal basis wherever and whenever their interests overlap. There are also instances where a more regular pattern of ad hoc coordination can be identified. A recurring formation of coordination between a particular industry and a government can eventually lead to a 'pattern of coordination' between the two. Such partnerships usually operate on a voluntary basis and are mainly prompted by cost-benefit analysis conducted by the affected industry and the government. This form of coordination is mainly discussed in Chapter 6, especially in the examples involving the textiles industry as a repeat private partner to the Government of India.

Chapters 3 and 4, which address the dispute settlement experience of the US, the EU and China, show that a dialogue between the public and private partners can also be established through legal provisions, regulations and institutions. For instance, the US has a mechanism that provides a right to its private stakeholders to petition the USTR if their trade interests are infringed. Likewise, the EU and China have similar formal provisions for the formation of partnerships during the settlement of trade disputes. Therefore, the formation of public-private coordination with the help of legal provisions, specialised institutions and regulatory procedures will be considered as a formal system of PPP.

The key distinguishing aspect of a *formal* system of PPP will be the existence of a right with private entities to petition their government if and when their trade interests are infringed by a foreign practice. Correspondingly, the government will have an obligation to administer and preliminarily examine such petitions. The government may also have an obligation to coordinate with the concerned private individuals if the government decides to pursue the matter. On the other hand, a coordination (or a pattern of coordination) formed between a government and an industry without the framework of established regulations or national legal provisions will be considered as an *informal* system of PPP.

The line of distinction between a formal and an informal partnership arrangement is not easy to draw and it can seem obscure on certain occasions. This is because the governments and industries can form and functionalise these partnership arrangements using a combination of formal and informal procedures. Alternatively, they can invoke formal provisions to form such partnerships but in practice exchange resources through informal methods. For example, as will be seen in Chapter 4, in the discussion of the *Japan – Quotas on Laver* case, partnership between the laver industry and the Ministry of Commerce was initially formed with the help of national legal provisions. However, the elements of informal exchanges were clearly visible as the industry was engaged in persuasive lobbying and bargaining practices. Therefore, the partnership in this case was a formal partnership but with certain elements of informal coordination.

It is not the focus of this book to define or distinguish the formal PPP processes from the informal ones. It *is* the book's focus to identify the elements of an effective PPP mechanism (not necessarily a formal one) for developing countries. The existence of a more formal or an informal system of coordination will only be relevant in so far as it makes the partnership more effective in building the dispute settlement capacity of developing countries. However, the key question that remains unanswered is the following: How can PPP arrangements achieve their stated objective; that is, the building of dispute settlement capacity in developing countries through resource-optimal procedures of exchange and interaction? The next section deals with this question, as it provides a conceptual framework to illustrate the significance of the PPP approach; that is, its capacity-building potential.

1.1.2 Dispute Settlement Partnerships and Capacity Building: The Key Significance

The key *significance* of a PPP arrangement lies in its ability to build the WTO dispute settlement capacity of a government through mutually beneficial exchange and coordination. The procedure and extent of coordination between a government and an industry differs from country to country and from case to case, but it is nevertheless useful to understand the underlying rationale behind the stated objective of PPP mechanism; that is, how exchange of resources at a particular stage of dispute settlement can enable a government to mobilise the required resources for conducting that stage with fewer internal costs and constraints. The importance of this section lies in the fact that it provides a conceptual framework to understand how a domestic partnership mechanism can significantly impact and influence the international trade adjudication at WTO.

Public private coordination can take place at every stage of WTO dispute settlement proceedings, and a pattern of its nature and possible extent can be explained with the help of the following illustration. The model illustrated in Figure 2.1 below has drawn inspiration from Bown's model of 'The Extended Litigation Process'.[7] Readers should treat this model as the theoretical lens of this book as it illustrates the manner in which PPP arrangements, through exchange of resources at each phase of a WTO dispute, can enhance the dispute settlement capacity of developing countries.

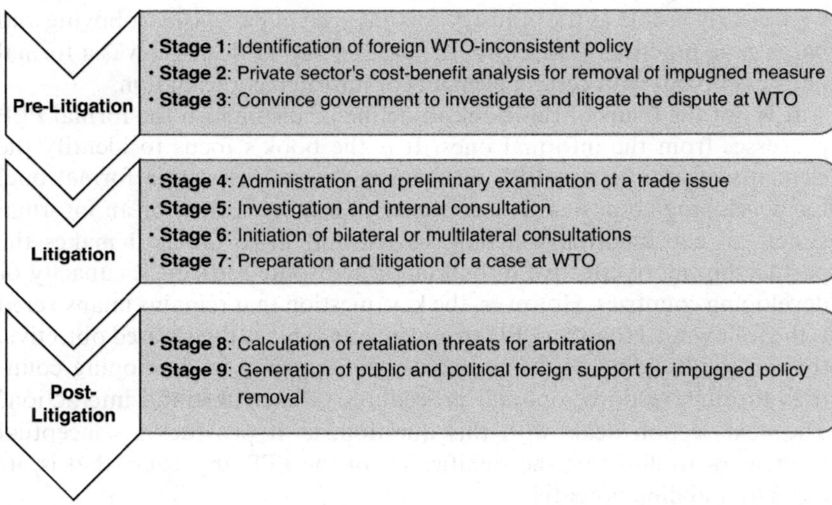

Figure 2.1 Public Private Partnership: potential stages of WTO dispute settlement

Figure 2.1 illustrates nine potential stages through which a WTO dispute (conducted by means of a public private partnership) may proceed. The operational nature and significance of dispute settlement partnerships,

---

[7] Chad P Bown, *Self-Enforcing Trade: Developing Countries and WTO Dispute Settlement* (Brookings Institution Press 2009) 112. The 'Extended Litigation Process' proposed by Bown illustrates the key procedural stages through which a foreign trade dispute can be handled. In this section, Bown's six-stage model is adapted into a nine-stage model for dispute settlement.

and the possibilities for exchange and resource mobilisation during such partnerships will be explained in the sequence of each stage (mentioned in Figure 2.1). The following discussion is therefore divided into three parts, covering three phases of WTO dispute settlement proceedings: Pre-litigation, litigation and post-litigation.

1.1.2.1 Pre-litigation phase

The key stages at the pre-litigation phase are: identification of a foreign WTO-inconsistent measure(s); cost-benefit analysis conducted by private sector for the removal of an alleged trade barrier; industries to convince the government to investigate a barrier and litigate for its removal.

To begin with, a precondition for the efficient enforcement of WTO rights is the existence of a strong monitoring mechanism. However, due to shortage of resources and poor economies of scale, developing country members are likely to find it difficult to develop and functionalise dedicated monitoring processes and institutions. The key *issue* therefore is whether the private sector can help the developing country governments to identify foreign trade barriers. Certain countries have established dedicated processes to monitor and list foreign trade barriers. For example, the International Trade Administration at the US Department of Commerce has a dedicated Market Access and Compliance (MAC) team in the Trade and Compliance Center. Similar government processes in the EU are provided within the system of 'Trade Barrier Regulation' and 'Market Access Database'.[8]

In the case of developing and particularly least developed countries, where governments may not be able to spend their scarce resources on similar monitoring provisions, division of the monitoring task between the government and industry becomes relatively more crucial. One could argue that the gap could possibly be filled by the WTO Trade Policy Review Mechanism (TPRM), but the frequency of TPRM assessments is not adequate enough, as it varies in accordance with a country's share of world trade in a given period of time. For example, TPRM assessments in the US and the EU are conducted once in every two years. This frequency

---

[8] For information on MAC initiatives, see Trade and Compliance Center, Report a Foreign Trade Barrier, accessed 9 October 2016 at <http://tcc.export.gov/Report_a_Barrier/index.asp>. For information on Trade Barrier Regulation, see Trade Defence section of the EU's official website, Europa (main website address: https://ec.europa.eu/), accessed 9 October 2016 at <http://ec.europa.eu/trade/tackling-unfair-trade/trade-barriers/>. For Market Access Database, see Trade Barriers section of Europa, accessed 9 October 2016 at <http://madb.europa.eu/madb_barriers/barriers_select.htm>.

is as low as once in six years in Bangladesh. Moreover, certain LDCs do not even enjoy that; for example, Zimbabwe (until January 2017) has been reviewed only once, in 2011. This resource deficit can effectively be filled with the help of public private coordination.

As the key beneficiaries, victims and operators of foreign trade, the affected business players are arguably best placed to identify the foreign trade barriers affecting their economic interests. In the past, the exporting firms and trade associations have identified and reported infringements to the governments. Moreover, they have outsourced the monitoring and identification of barriers to corporate law firms[9] and economic consultancies.[10] Multinational companies and powerful trade associations have also created their dedicated in-house team of lawyers and consultants to perform this function. The public-sector authorities, on the other hand, can also identify foreign trade barriers on a *suo moto* basis and reach out to the private sector (for information, evidence or other form of resources) during initial investigation or consultations.

At the *second* stage, the private sector estimates the potential economic benefits to be had from the removal of a trade barrier. At this stage, an affected firm or trade association will investigate several issues, including the expected economic benefits from the removal of an impugned barrier, the amount of resources required to be spent on investigation and overall conduct of a case, and the chances of winning the case and getting the award enforced. The extent of the private sector's participation and resource contribution will depend upon this cost-benefit analysis. The *cost* generally includes the 'cost of monitoring and information collection', 'cost of industry organisation and engaging government policymakers and legal service providers', 'cost of actual WTO enforcement litigation', and 'cost to obtain compliance'. *Benefits* would mainly include the financial benefits, chances of winning and enforcement, and other benefits, which could be social, diplomatic, political or ethical in nature.[11]

The *third* stage is where the affected private sector convinces the government to investigate and pursue a case at WTO. The industry can approach the government either through established laws and regulations, or through informal procedures of coordination. The cost incurred by the private sector at this stage can be substantial, as the government may require it to find answers to various complex questions such as: Does the

---

[9] Major law firms that pursue this practice are Sidley Austin, Van Bael & Bellis, and Winston & Strawn.

[10] Examples of such economic consultancies are Giz, Datagro, Deloitte, and KPMG.

[11] For further details on anticipated costs and benefits, see Bown (n 7) 118–132.

given trade barrier vitiate the national interest and the overall economic wellbeing of the nation? What is the extent of its impact on the economic wellbeing of the nation or an industry? What are the chances of winning the case at WTO and thereafter securing compliance? Is it politically favourable to pursue the case at WTO? How complicated is the case and how many resources are available within the government to prepare and litigate the case at WTO? Would the affected private sector supplement these governmental resources? If yes, to what extent? Combined efforts of the affected private sector and the government to find answers to these questions can be seen as another instance of resource mobilisation and joint efforts to improve performance at WTO DSU.

To assist the government in the initial examination of these issues (and for the conduct of cost-benefit analysis), the private sector entities can hire legal, economic and technical experts.[12] Moreover, they are suitably placed to provide required information to the government for examining the alleged barrier and its impact on the industry. Grossman provides the rationale behind this argument in the following words:

> Interest groups are an obvious source of information for policymakers, both because the groups are already familiar with many of the technical issues from their every-day involvement in the areas where policies are to be determined and because they are prepared to undertake research to produce information that they do not initially have.[13]

On the other hand, an analysis of the political state of affairs, the political outcome and possible repercussions of pursuing a dispute can predominantly be carried out by government departments.[14] It is the public sector which mostly delves into prioritising and listing the trade

---

[12] An example is the case of *India – Anti-Dumping Measure on Batteries from Bangladesh*, WT/DS306, in consultations on 28 January 2004. In this case, Rahimafrooz's undertaking to finance the dispute was seen as the main reason that convinced the reluctant Bangladesh Ministry of Commerce to invoke WTO DSM against India. (Interview with Former Ambassador to WTO Mission of Bangladesh (audio conferencing), 21 August 2013).

[13] Gene M Grossman & Elhanan Helpman, *Special Interest Politics* (The MIT Press 2001) 5.

[14] For example, in *India – Anti-Dumping Measure on Batteries from Bangladesh*, the Bangladesh Tariff Commission (BTC) investigated the legitimacy and significance of pursuing the dispute, and it acted as the political strategist to the Bangladesh Ministry of Commerce. (MA Taslim, 'How the DSU Worked for Bangladesh: The First Least Developed Country to Bring a WTO Claim', in G Shaffer & R Melendez-Ortiz, *Dispute Settlement at the WTO: The Developing Country Experience* (Cambridge University Press 2010) 230).

barriers, scrutinising the significant ones, and analysing the extra-WTO counter-retaliation capacity of the offending Member State. Evaluating the chances of success and enforcement, based on its retaliation capacity and the chances of extra-WTO counter-retaliation from offending states, becomes a serious issue for developing and least developed countries, especially when a dispute is against a developed and a powerful nation. In this manner, a joint identification and examination of foreign trade barriers at the pre-litigation phase of a dispute can help the governments to first identify trade barriers, and then to investigate and examine the overall viability of taking further steps for its removal.

1.1.2.2 Litigation phase

At the litigation phase, the key potential stages are: the administration and preliminary examination of a trade concern; investigation and internal consultations; initiation of bilateral or multilateral consultations; preparation and litigation of a case at the WTO DSM, including the stage of appeal if required.

To begin with, the private sector can file a complaint or informally communicate a problem to its government. The government can register a complaint and initiate the process of investigating the overall viability of pursuing a dispute. In order to estimate and assess the political, legal and economic viability of launching a dispute at WTO, the government requires commercial inputs and expert assistance of trade lawyers, economists, foreign policy experts and political strategists. The private stakeholders can provide requisite information and documents to the government. The private entities can also hire or finance the hiring of experts, and they can conduct market research, and hold joint consortiums and consultation meetings with the government and industry representatives. In *EC – Export Subsidies on Sugar (Thailand)*, for instance, Thailand's sugar association sent its experts to Geneva to hold consultations with the Permanent Mission of Thailand to the UN on the questions of initiating a dispute at WTO, its benefits, costs and the threats involved. The Thai sugar association also coordinated with the Brazilian and Australian sugar industries to gather and supply better informational and evidentiary inputs to the Thai government.[15]

Once the government has investigated a complaint and has found a measure which violates the WTO rules or which impedes its foreign trade, it would generally have several options. The government, depending upon

[15] *EC–Export Subsidies on Sugar* Appellate Body Report, *European Communities–Export Subsidies on Sugar, Complaint by Thailand*, WT/DS265/AB/R, WT/DS266/AB/R, WT/DS283/AB/R, adopted 19 May 2005.

its economic and political climate and the nature of the dispute, would either raise the matter at the relevant WTO Committee or launch bilateral and/or multilateral consultations with the offending Member State(s).[16] If the government's initiative at this stage (such as bilateral consultations or WTO Committee discussions or multilateral consultations) fails, a subsequent stage could be the development and litigation of a case at the WTO DSU. The costs incurred by the private sector and the government at this stage vary to a large extent, as the sums involved mainly depend upon the nature of the case, willingness of the partners to support each other, the stakes involved, chances of winning and enforcement, the clarity of law on the issue in question, and the complexity of gathering supporting evidence.

The main participants at this stage can be: lawyers, economists, consultants, foreign policy experts, concerned subject-specific experts (such as scientists, engineers and environmentalists), government representatives and industry representatives (and at times, NGOs). The participants can work in close coordination while they jointly prepare legal briefs, develop arguments, engage in research and fact-finding, and gather supporting evidence. A private sector representative asserts the importance of government-industry coordination at this stage in the following words:

> The Government's team of lawyers and trade policy experts can interpret the legal texts from a legal aspect, but it is only the concerned industry which can interpret these legal texts from a commercial perspective and marshal the required commercial facts, evidence and arguments. Without commercial inputs from industry, the legal analysis would remain in a vacuum.[17]

This stage provides a clear example of a burden-sharing approach between the two partners. The presentation of a case at WTO is mostly carried out by the country's Mission officials at Geneva, and the officials are often closely supported by other government representatives, private sector representatives, and the team of public and private lawyers.[18] Similar coordination and involvement of these public and private sector

---

[16] Launching a bilateral consultation is voluntary, but it is strongly encouraged as DSU Agreement gives clear preference to a mutually acceptable positive solution to a dispute (art 3.7, DSU Agreement). Launching multilateral consultations with the offending member is obligatory before the launch of a formal litigious action at WTO (art 4, DSU Agreement).

[17] Interview with an official, TEXPROCIL, Mumbai, India, 27 June 2013.

[18] The Appellate Body in the *EC – Bananas III* case clarified that private legal counsels and private law firms can participate in the WTO dispute settlement proceedings and be engaged in other related legal work. For details, see *EC – Bananas III* Appellate Body Report, *European Communities – Regime for*

agencies are again required if a Member State appeals a Panel decision. This would be the case irrespective of whether a country is acting as an appellant or an appellee.

The *EC – Export Subsidies on Sugar (Thailand)*[19] case, for example, provides an interesting instance of public private interaction in Thailand as it illustrates the potential role that can be played by private entities during the litigation of WTO disputes. The Thai sugar industry in this case coordinated with the government at every stage of the dispute settlement. Informal consultations, joint meetings and field trips were frequently organised by the industry and the Thai government during investigation, preparation and litigation of the case. The trade association and the concerned private companies offered financial contributions to the government for hiring the expert services of ACWL, LMC International and Datagro.[20] The sugar association also established dedicated legal and managerial teams to assist the government in litigating the dispute. Furthermore, the sugar industries in Brazil, Australia and Thailand jointly purchased the relevant evidential data from LMC International. They purchased this data to ensure, in a cost-effective manner, that their respective case files remained updated and well-substantiated. The case therefore is a sound example of how industries from different countries can form cross-border alliances and reduce the burden of cost imposed on each of them for the protection of their common and overlapping interests.

1.1.2.3 Post-litigation phase

There are two key stages at the post-litigation phase. These stages can also be referred to as the stages of implementation. They are: calculation of the WTO-sanctioned economic retaliation threats for arbitration; generation of public and political foreign support for the removal of WTO-inconsistent policy.

Winning WTO litigation is not always the final stage, as it may at times

---

the Importation, Sale and Distribution of Bananas, WT/DS27/AB/R, adopted 25 September 1997.

[19] *EC – Export Subsidies on Sugar* Appellate Body Report, *European Communities – Export Subsidies on Sugar, Complaint by Thailand*, WT/DS265/AB/R, WT/DS266/AB/R, WT/DS283/AB/R, adopted 19 May 2005.

[20] Interview with an official, Government of Thailand (audio conferencing) 3 February 2014; Michael Ewing-Chow, 'Are Asian WTO Members Using the WTO DSU "Effectively"?' (2013) 16(3) *Journal of International Economic Law* 669, 687. The two driving factors during the *EC – Export Subsidies on Sugar (Thailand)* case are identified by the author when he notes that 'Thailand sought the ACWL's help *and simultaneously* used financial contributions from the Thai private sector to hire a private law firm' (emphasis added).

be followed by enforcement proceedings pursued at the request of the winning Member State. A government can request the establishment of the arbitral tribunal or compliance Panel in the cases of non-compliance. There are two possible temporary remedies (pending full compliance) that can be invoked by the winning member if the offending member refuses to comply or unduly delays complying with the award: financial compensation and suspension of concessions or obligations.[21] The most commonly chosen temporary remedy is the suspension of concessions or obligations wherein the winning member may receive the DSB's authorisation to suspend tariff concessions it is granting to the offending member under market access or other WTO obligations. If a member opts for this remedy, the quantitative limits to which a member can retaliate are determined and authorised by the arbitral tribunal appointed by the DSB.[22]

During this stage, the private sector can play an important role by studying the markets and identifying the right products in order to intelligently craft the retaliatory measures. The private sector can identify products which are politically, socially or economically strategic for the offending governments and which, at the same time, would produce minimal damage to its own economy. In the past, private firms and industries have hired law firms and economic consultancies to calculate effective retaliation levels and to identify suitable products for retaliation.[23] On the other hand, governments at this stage can also be assisted by their lawyers, think tanks, policy analysts and foreign policymakers. Occasionally, the governments can also receive informational inputs from non-profit-based organisations.

The final possible task in the lifecycle of a WTO dispute could be the generation of public and political foreign support and pressure for the removal of a WTO-inconsistent policy. In cases where retaliation is not politically or economically favourable, or if it proves to be ineffective or insufficient for enforcing compliance, the potentially final stage of the enforcement phase steps in. In the words of Bown, this stage 'involves engaging other political forces to generate a public outcry within the offending country to create the momentum for policy reform

[21] Art 22.1, DSU Agreement.

[22] Art 22.3, DSU Agreement.

[23] Evidence of this is visible in the WTO services section of the Sidley Austin LLP website, which states that the firm offers advisory and legal services to business units, trade associations and the government clients on issues relating to WTO law, dispute settlement and enforcement measures. See Sidley Austin LLP: WTO Disputes, accessed 12 October 2016 at <http://www.sidley.com/wto/>.

to achieve WTO compliance.'[24] This stage may involve media campaigns and organised public relation activities, which can take place at national and international levels. This function can be carried out jointly by the government and the affected industry representatives through the use of joint workshops, exchange programmes and publications. Non-profit and intergovernmental organisations can also play an instrumental role in the organisation of public relation activities and campaigns.

A striking example of private sector initiative during the post-litigation phase can be seen in *EC – Export Subsidies on Sugar (Thailand)*, where the Thai Sugar Association, along with the sugar associations of Australia and Brazil, developed close contacts with other sugar associations under the Global Sugar Alliance.[25] The alliance undertook the responsibility of monitoring the EC's implementation of the award. The Chairman of the Global Sugar Alliance, Mr Keith De Lacy, issued a statement that the 'Global Sugar Alliance will be closely monitoring the reforms to make sure it happens'.[26] In addition to this, the 'Global Sugar Alliance members called on the world's leaders to make their commitment to the elimination of export subsidies unequivocal, not dependent on the outcome of the Round'.[27] The alliance was engaged in international campaigning to ensure effective and smooth implementation of the award and improvement in worldwide sugar trading conditions. This goes to show that the engagement of the private sector during the stage of implementation and its potential to enhance its government's enforcement (including retaliation) capacity can be seen as the notable benefits of dispute settlement partnership.

During all three phases of dispute settlement, resource exchange will be *effective* if it leads to improved dispute settlement capacity of the government and thereby achieve the stated objective of a PPP mechanism. It will be *optimal* if the deployment of public and private sector resources to dispute settlement endeavours gives rise to a condition which is conducive to a favourable outcome for both the government and industry and for the nation as a whole.

At the same time, it is important to note that a PPP mechanism may not

---

[24] Bown (n 7) 117.

[25] This is an alliance of the world's leading sugar trade associations and is officially known as Global Alliance for Sugar Trade Reform & Liberalisation.

[26] Global Alliance for Sugar Trade Reform and Liberalization, 'Global Sugar Alliance to Monitor EU Implementation of WTO Sugar Decision' 6 July 2006, accessed 17 August 2016 at <http://www.globalsugaralliance.org/resources.php?action=viewResource&id=51>.

[27] Ibid.

be able to perform a similarly positive role in building a country's capacity in cases where that country is acting as a respondent. In such cases, PPP may be constrained in facilitating an effective resource exchange and interaction as the private sector may not be as forthcoming as in the instances discussed above from a complainant's point of view. From a respondent's point of view, a private sector may not be forthcoming in assisting its government, unless the challenge has a direct and substantial implication for a specific industry's or exporter's interest.[28] It is conceivably difficult to convince a non-incentivised industry to bear the cost of litigation when an existing practice (which is challenged at WTO) does not directly and significantly affect an industry's interest. An official at the Indian Institute of Foreign Trade states that 'the extent to which an industry can participate here is rather limited and restricted. It is because the challenge has been raised against their government, and it may or may not concern an industry.'[29]

Unaware individuals may often perceive that a WTO challenge is made against a government and not an industry. With this mindset, they may fail to understand and calculate the benefits they can gain if the dispute is won or losses which they might incur if their government is made to withdraw a trade practice. Moreover, it may happen that the industry which is affected from a WTO challenge is not sufficiently equipped (with the required information, evidence and finances) to provide resource assistance to its government when a challenge arises. Therefore, substantial coordination between government and industry cannot often be observed in cases where a country is acting as a respondent. In such cases, it is more likely that a government will be required to reach out and convince an industry if the government requires its assistance to examine and investigate a measure, or it will be left on its own to manage and finance the entire dispute if the affected industries cannot be convinced. This is a limitation of the dispute settlement partnership approach, though it can partially be overcome by educating private stakeholders about the benefits of participation and devising ways for incentivising them to participate during defence litigations. In addition, there are other challenges which can impede the formation and operation of PPP arrangements.

---

[28] Interview with a trade lawyer, White & Case LLP (Geneva), London, United Kingdom, 16 May 2013; interview with a trade lawyer, Luthra & Luthra, Delhi, India, 21 June 2013.

[29] Interview with an official, Centre for WTO Studies (audio conferencing), 11 April 2012.

2.1 PPP STRATEGIES: POTENTIAL WEAKNESSES AND HINDRANCES

Public private partnership strategy is not free from weaknesses. Multiple factors operating at a domestic level in developing countries can impede the exchange of resources between the government and industry, or they can restrict the capacity-building potential of government-industry coordination. Moreover, undue and unregulated reliance on PPPs can leave a country's national interests susceptible to special private interests. It is therefore important to understand certain challenges and weaknesses of this approach, as these challenges should be examined carefully when different dispute settlement and partnership arrangements are considered or employed in developing countries. The first two challenges are (i) threat of regulatory capture, and (ii) discriminatory protection of trade interests, which are the major potential weaknesses of the PPP approach. These are considered immediately below. All other challenges, while also significant, should rather be considered as impediments or hindrances to the formation and effective functioning of PPP systems. These are discussed under Section 2.1.2 ('Potential Hindrances').

2.1.1 Potential Weaknesses

2.1.1.1 Threat of regulatory capture

Dispute settlement partnerships should lead to maximum protection of trade interests, but they should not lead to a situation where protection of trade interests injures national interests. However, there may be situations where an industry can have an economic interest the protection of which may not be in line with those of other industries or may not be in line with that of the nation as a whole. In such cases, the government might find it difficult to reconcile the conflicting interests, especially where an industry is funding the action.[30] Shaffer describes it as a situation where 'even when the private sector provides financial support for the hiring of an outside law firm, the private sector's interests may not coincide with the government's perception of the public interest'.[31]

When privately hired lawyers are preparing and presenting a case at WTO and if they are not sufficiently supervised by government officials,

---

[30] Interview with an official, Ministry of Economy (Mexico), Dubai, UAE, 1 November 2016.

[31] Gregory C Shaffer, Michelle Raton Sanchez Badin & Barbara Rosenberg, 'The Trials of Winning at the WTO: What Lies Behind Brazil's Success' (2008) 41(2) *Cornell International Law Journal* 383, 474.

they may be inclined to protect special economic interests of their financers at the cost of national interests. Public private partnerships provide business entities with an opportunity to engage in rent-seeking activities to protect their special private interests. For example, a business entity might propose making a substantial financial contribution to government provided that, in return, the government supports its attempts to protect its own financial interests. If the government attaches significant weight to the financial contributions made or proposed by private sector parties, the government may be induced to act as the business entity wishes, even if the action taken undermines wider economic, social or environmental interests. In this manner, a privately funded action may lead to a situation of private capture or corporate regulatory capture where government officials can be inclined (for various reasons) to uphold private interests at the cost of national interest.

Grossman defines 'corporate regulatory capture' as an interplay between special interest groups and government organisations that can influence and shape a nation's foreign trade policy to the detriment of other wider economic and social concerns.[32] Regulatory threats could also potentially arise through various other rent-seeking activities including bribery and lobbying. These regulatory challenges could pose a serious threat to the functioning of PPPs especially in developing countries that have high levels of corruption and poor observance of the rule of law. Poor observance of the rule of law in a country can lead to an unsupervised system of governance permeated with various forms of corruption. These impediments could jeopardise the balance between national interests and private interests, and might consequentially hamper a country's development of international trade in a sustainable manner. This is a potential weakness of the PPP approach, since capture of national interests, including wide economic, social, environmental, ethical and welfare interests, by a handful of profit-motivated organisations or individuals is never a desirable situation, and effective PPP arrangements should always try to balance such competing interests in the best interests of the nation and industry.

2.1.1.2 Discriminatory protection of trade interests

Wealth inequality among different economic sectors, which is a common condition in developing countries, can result in an unevenly organised private sector. The wealthy industries, on one hand, can potentially

---

[32] Problems of bribery, regulatory capture and lobbying emerging from private participation discussed in Gene Grossman & Elhanan Helpman, 'Protection for Sale' (1994) 84(4) *The American Economic Review* 833.

approach the concerned government officials without any assistance from industry representatives. Moreover, if they have high trading stakes in a WTO litigation, they will generally have the incentive to play an active role and invest resources that they possess. The partnership procedures can therefore enable resourceful business actors to protect their exporting interests through a privately funded government action at WTO. But the same result may not be achieved in cases where the exporting interests of resource-constrained, developing and small-scale industries are at stake. Providing resource assistance to the government can be an unaffordable option for business entities that cannot afford to collect information or 'buy in' the external expertise required for preparation and filing of DSU complaints.[33] The approach may therefore result in discriminatory protection of special economic interests, arguably on the basis of resources possessed by affected business entities.

2.1.2 Potential Hindrances

2.1.2.1 An unorganised and unaware private sector

Unorganised private sector An 'organised private sector' is a vital requirement for the establishment and smooth functioning of the proposed public private partnership in developing countries. From an economic perspective, there are multiple factors (such as productivity, workforce, economic output, profits, industry size, wage rate and literacy) that determine whether an industry is organised or unorganised. However, the term 'organised private sector' or 'organised industry' in this book is used to refer to an industry that has the following characteristics: (i) industries that are strongly represented by trade associations, confederations, export promotion councils or chambers of commerce; (ii) industries with established channels of communication and exchange between producers, manufacturers, exporters, importers and their representative organisations; (iii) industries in which the exporters, importers and their representatives are aware of international trade developments, foreign and national trade policies affecting their business interests and the possibility of approaching their governments to address trade grievances; (iv) industries that have the capacity and know-how to gather information and other required resources that may be required for presenting trade grievances in a well-substantiated and investigated manner to their governments.

---

33 Shaffer et al, 'The Trials of Winning at the WTO' (n 31) 474. The authors note the following: 'There may also be divisions within the private sector so that only that portion of the private sector with the means to fund the outside lawyers will be represented.'

The significance of an organised private sector is twofold. *First*, it facilitates an industry to represent a wide economic interest in order to influence and convince the government to initiate an investigation or consultation. *Second*, it enables industry representatives to gather and consolidate the required resources possessed by affected business entities. The industry representatives may require these resources to monitor and investigate foreign measures, and to assist the government with the investigation and overall management of foreign trade disputes.[34]

An unorganised industry can face impediments due to lack of coordination between various private stakeholders. A trade representative neatly explains this limitation in the following words:

> We lost one year in convincing the Government of India to initiate consultations with Turkey in the dispute of Turkey-Cotton Yarn. It was due to the fact that we were the only players, without constant support from the companies and confederations, who were going to the Government again and again with various trade issues. In a developing country and fragmented industry like ours, it is crucial that business entities should provide support to its trade associations for better protection of individual interests.[35]

The statement above shows that, in the absence of a resourceful and well-connected industry representative, the private sector may struggle to form an effective dispute settlement partnership with the government. As a result, the government might not be able to acquire the capacity required to identify barriers or conduct trade disputes. The situation may ultimately frustrate the aim of the proposed PPP mechanism; that is, domestic capacity building.

The case of *US – Shrimp*[36] is a classic example of 'structural asymmetry' between the insufficiently organised fisheries industry in India and the wealthy, influential and well-organised fisheries industry in the US. Although the Seafood Exporters Association of India (SEAI) in the case provided some commercial facts to the government during the proceedings at WTO, a government official contends that those facts were not comprehensive as they were detached from the realities that the fishermen in India

[34] Grossman & Helpman, *Special Interest Politics* (n 13) 103. ('An organised group can take advantage of the economies of scale by researching issues centrally and educating its rank-and-file members. The groups also may use the information they gather to win over policymakers. . .'.)

[35] Interview with an official, TEXPROCIL, Mumbai, India, 27 June 2013.

[36] *US – Shrimp* Appellate Body Report, *United States – Import Prohibition of Certain Shrimp and Shrimp Products*, WT/DS58/AB/R, adopted 6 November 1998.

faced.[37] An International Centre for Trade and Sustainable Development (ICTSD) official explains the situation in the following words:

> In the dispute, you have two actors which are structurally very different. In the US, you have an organised shrimp industry which was pushing their government with sound environmental arguments for the protection of their commercial interests. On the other hand, you have a poor, almost illiterate, and not so organised fishery industry in India which had difficulties in approaching its government during the dispute.[38]

The case exhibits that an effective interaction between an industry and a government is possible only when the private sector is well-organised, aware, interconnected and strongly institutionalised. This may not be the case with many industries, especially in developing and least developed countries.

Unaware private sector The lack of awareness among private sector entities about WTO laws and possible avenues for seeking international trade opportunities is a problem that may impede the formation of effective partnerships between government and industry. Unawareness about the possibility of approaching the government for the protection of trade interests and benefits which WTO Agreements can potentially extend to business communities can be a common characteristic of an unorganised or institutionally underdeveloped industry. Certain private stakeholders in developing countries may even opine that international trade laws and foreign trade policies are there to protect the interests of the government, and hence, the government should be solely responsible for the handling of WTO-related matters. '[T]he private industry players "may simply not know how useful the WTO DSM is", and they may "prefer adapting their businesses to the laws and practices of their trading partners, regardless of whether they are WTO consistent or not".'[39]

With such perceptions, industries tend to distance their special economic interests from the common national interests. Hence, uninformed and unaware attitudes within the private sector may act as a major hindrance to the smooth formation and functioning of PPPs. Lack of communication channels between government and industry, disconnected and inadequately organised industry, and paucity of outreach and training

[37] Interview with an official, Government of India, Mumbai, India, 17 June 2013.

[38] Interview with an official, ICTSD, Geneva, Switzerland, 11 April 2013.

[39] Ewing-Chow (n 20) 693.

opportunities for business communities can further aggravate this hindrance to the formation of PPP arrangements.

2.1.2.2 Weak governance framework

Lack of dedicated government units and interdepartmental coordination Lack of dedicated government units responsible for the management of disputes and coordination with industries can further impede such partnerships. Plasai suggests that 'it is practical to have a single mechanism at home that serves as the focal point for coordination among the various actors at the domestic level'.[40] These 'various actors' can include other government departments, industries, civil society organisations, lawyers and permanent mission at WTO. In the absence of a dedicated unit, the government may face difficulties in effectively managing WTO disputes, reaching out to industries for resource assistance, and educating them about the possibility and benefits of coordinated management of WTO disputes.

In addition, it is important to have an interdepartmental component in the domestic handling of trade disputes. Amidst the increasingly multidisciplinary and complex nature of WTO disputes, and in the absence of an interministerial component, a resource-constrained government can impose an undue resource-burden on the affected private stakeholders. The EU's Interim Evaluation Report on the Trade Barrier Regulation confirms that public private partnership provisions can impose a high burden of evidential requirements on the affected industries, and this can seriously discourage them from approaching their government.[41] It is therefore important that the concerned government department should be able to mobilise as much information as possible from the subject-specific departments without imposing an excessively deterring evidential burden on the affected industries.

Insufficient channels of communication, leading to lack of transparency and confidence Lack of confidence between government and industry is another factor that can impede the formation of effective networks

---

[40] Virachai Plasai, 'Coordinating Trade Litigation' (April 2013) ICTSD Issue Paper No 14, 4, accessed 24 September 2016 at <http://www.ictsd.org/sites/default/files/research/2013/04/coordinating-trade-litigation1.pdf>.

[41] European Commission DG-Trade, 'Final Report: Interim Evaluation of the European Union's Trade Barrier Regulation (TBR)' (June 2005) 51, accessed 25 September 2016 at <http://trade.ec.europa.eu/doclib/docs/2005/october/tradoc_125451.pdf>.

between the two. If the government authorities are not proactive in disclosing information about ongoing disputes, the system will suffer from lack of transparency and paucity of information exchange. A secrecy-favouring approach of a government and consequential lack of transparency can act as serious deterrents to the formation of PPPs as industries might be unwilling to share their trade knowledge and information with government entities that might act covertly in relation to such matters. Consequential paucity of information may constrain the government's ability to analyse, consider and incorporate overall business, national and international perspectives during investigation and decision-making. Smooth conduct of dispute settlement procedures requires a relationship of confidence and trust between government and industry, and this can be made possible if there are open channels of communication and smooth exchange of information between the two.

2.1.2.3 Cultural and psychological barriers

Certain cultural barriers can also pose a challenge to the desired engagement of the private sector. For example, a government official observes that the remnants of China's non-litigious culture are still very much ingrained in the mind-set of business entities and government officials.[42] Such psychological constraints have, in the past, deterred the affected industries from approaching the government and the government from litigating issues at WTO DSU. However, China to a large extent has overcome this barrier as it has increasingly filed complaints at WTO DSU and engaged its private sector in the overall process of dispute settlement.

Moreover, governments may have a strict inter-governmental approach of dealing with WTO disputes and, therefore, may not be inclined to seek explicit (or rather any) resource assistance from industries. A government may opine that PPPs can result in the overriding of national interests as certain government officials involved in the conduct of disputes may succumb to industry pressures and financial inducements. As discussed above under regulatory challenges (see Section 2.1.1.1), this fear is not unfounded and is based on well-reasoned possibilities of regulatory threats. Moreover, a policymaker may doubt the credibility and reliability of arguments, information and evidential documents provided by an affected industry. Grossman and Helpman explain this issue in the following words: 'We take it that policy-makers accept at face value only those assertions that a lobbyist has reason to make truthfully; otherwise,

---

42 Ewing-Chow (n 20) 677.

they discount the claims appropriately in recognition of the group's bias.'[43] Hence, government officials' cautiousness may deter a smooth flow of information between the public and private sectors. However, this obstacle may no longer act as a serious threat to PPP in this era of open market economies, more so because governments have established certain watchdog provisions to verify the reliability, validity and comprehensiveness of information.

Finally, private stakeholders may fear that partnering the government during active litigation or enforcement may lead to undesirable trading complications for their industries as it may further jeopardise their trade relations with overseas trading partners or their governments. If a government has an aggressive or confrontational mechanism for investigating a barrier or launching litigation, or if the procedures of PPP do not grant a right to the participating traders to remain anonymous, fears of unfavourable retaliation may further lower the industry's confidence and commercial motivation to seek governmental intervention.

2.1.2.4 Conflict of interests

Conflict of interests between government and industry may impede their interaction during the handling of foreign trade disputes. Government is in theory the guardian of national interests and an industry represents special economic interests. In all disputes, the national interests and special economic interests may not converge and overlap. Protection of one may, at times, lead to the violation of the other. It is therefore argued that the partnership between the two would only be formed where their interests overlap and, therefore, it may not be possible for them to coordinate and exchange resources if the national interest clashes with the special economic interest of an industry, and vice versa. Grossman and Helpman confirm that the exchange of information between government and special interest groups (including business entities) will be hampered in situations where an interest group and policymaker do not share similar objectives.[44] It is therefore important that best practices are pursued at the domestic level to ensure that government actions lead to a balance of interests.

---

43 Grossman & Helpman, *Special Interest Politics* (n 13) 23.

44 Grossman & Helpman, *Special Interest Politics* (n 13) 23. For further details on regulatory capture and lobbying emerging from private participation, see Tony Makkai & John Braithwaite, 'In and Out of the Revolving Door: Making Sense of Regulatory Capture' (1992) 12(1) *Journal of Public Policy* 61–78.

3.1 DOMESTIC CONTEXT: FACTORS AFFECTING PPP MECHANISM

Public private partnership arrangements do not operate in a vacuum. They are deeply embedded in the legal, institutional, political, economic and social environment of a country. Multiple factors working together or in isolation in a given country can shape and impact the dispute settlement partnerships. For example, the private sector's contribution in a dispute may largely depend upon the nature of the dispute, the cost-benefit analysis of launching a formal action, and the chances of winning and enforcement. If it is a complicated dispute with higher expected litigation cost, or if the anticipated time frame for the settlement of the dispute is long because the relevant law is unclear or there are no clear precedents, or if a case is being contested against an important or powerful trading partner, the affected industry might prefer to negotiate a settlement or endure the adverse impact of a trade barrier. An industry may also be reluctant to approach the government if the chances of winning the case are low, or if it is likely that the offending country will not mend its ways even after a favourable report is adopted by DSB because of the small market size and consequentially low retaliation capacity of its government (as compared to the market size and perhaps extra-WTO cross-retaliation capacity of the offending country).[45] In addition to these factors, other domestic conditions may also have a positive or an adverse impact on the effectiveness of a PPP arrangement in a given country. These factors are discussed in the following subsections.

3.1.1 Political, Social and Diplomatic Context

The nature of the political set-up in a country can influence the extent to which a government will be likely to protect individual business interests with or without engaging the affected private sector. In democratic countries with multi-party systems, for instance, governments generally are more accountable and responsive to the needs of industries, civil society organisations, media and society at large. In addition to the political

---

[45] Bernard Hoekman, Henrick Horn & Petros C Mavroidis, 'Winners and Losers in the Panel Stage of the WTO Dispute Settlement System' in Chantal Thomas and Joel P Trachtman (eds), *Developing Countries in the WTO Legal System* (Oxford University Press 2009) 151. (The authors argue that 'limited scope for credibly threatening retaliation' arising from small market size and economy can act as a key disincentive for the government and industry to bring a matter to DSU.)

motivation to remain in power through the support of the electorate, government's responsiveness in democracies may also stem from the fact that special interest groups in certain electoral campaigns provide resources to candidates and parties. They make financial contributions, or provide information and personnel for electoral campaigns, through direct and indirect circumventing procedures if direct giving is outlawed in a country. However, these contributions do not come for free. The elected governments, in turn, may tend to sympathise with the special interests of their financers. In the US, for example, business groups and corporations are the largest contributors of money in electoral campaigns. They can possibly access the Office of the United States Trade Representative (USTR) and influence its decisions relating to foreign trade matters with the help of congressmen they have supported during elections.[46]

On the other hand, policymakers in a democratic environment, being in theory accountable to their voters (consumers and society at large), also have reasons to refrain from accepting direct financial contributions for litigating cases at WTO. Grossman confirms that many voters in a democracy might hold their elected representatives in 'disdain' if they 'were to pander to special interests so blatantly'.[47] Shaffer further strengthens the observation by arguing that, in democracies, 'government leaders will be subject to demands of favoritism from particular economic sectors, whether for demanding protection from imports or government support for exports'.[48] Therefore, governments might be introvert and cautious while forging public private alliances for the protection of business interests, and government officials in that case might be wary of accepting direct or explicit contributions from business entities. This can be illustrated with the help of an example. The Government of India states in an explicit manner that all WTO disputes are financed entirely by the government, and that 'no financial assistance is taken from the industry'.[49] However, as it will be seen in Chapter 6, the private sector in India has paid the legal fees of trade lawyers, hired subject-matter experts, and

---

46 Grossman & Helpman, *Special Interest Politics* (n 13) 8, 10.

47 Ibid 242.

48 Gregory Shaffer & Charles Sutton, 'The Rise of Middle-Income Countries in the International Trading System', in Randall Peerenboom & Tom Ginsburg (eds), *Law and Development of Middle-Income Countries: Avoiding the Middle-Income Trap* (Cambridge University Press 2014) 59.

49 The information was requested by the author via Right to Information (RTI) application dated 17 September 2013. The RTI reply was received on 5 December 2013 vide Document No. 1/27/2013-TPD. (Right to Information Act 2005, India).

purchased evidential data from external agencies to assist the government during multiple WTO litigations.

An aware and free media in a democracy can possibly create domestic political pressure upon a government by educating a nation about the adverse impact of the government's failure to initiate a dispute at WTO, or the positive impact of its victory at WTO. For example, during the conduct of the *Aircraft* litigations,[50] it became important for the Brazilian government to win these disputes as the national and international media was extensively covering their developments. The issue had become a popular subject of discussion for the general public as well as academics. These cases were discussed in Brazilian newspapers just as a 'soccer match' is covered and discussed in Brazil, and they therefore became symbolically very important.[51] Mass awareness and resulting expectations of victory at WTO DSU placed domestic political pressure on the government, which at the time was engaged in a re-election campaign. Hence, strongly contesting the disputes at WTO with the full engagement of the aircraft industry became a strategic part of the government's political campaign for re-election. For such reasons, democratic governments usually tend to be relatively more particular about balancing successes against failures on the international front.

The shape and effectiveness of a PPP strategy will also depend upon the nature of political institutions in a country. For example, the intergovernmental set-up at the Commission and the Council in the EU and the political pressure from the EU governments and industries have resulted in a decentralised and fragmented form of dispute settlement coordination. On the other hand, China, with its national, state and provincial system of governance and effectively a single political party at the national level, has devised a centralised form of procedures and institutions for coordinated management of WTO disputes. Amidst increasing political decentralisation in China, the management of WTO disputes remains centralised to ensure that state and local authorities' intervention in economic affairs is kept to a minimum.

The engagement of the private sector may also depend upon the extent to which a government, as a matter of policy, would accept its assistance. Governments may want to retain entire control over the dispute settlement process and therefore may prefer to hire their own lawyers and experts. Other governments may be more liberal in this regard and less

---

[50] *Canada – Aircraft* and *Brazil – Aircraft* cases.

[51] Interview with an official, Permanent Mission of Brazil to the WTO, Geneva, Switzerland, 16 September 2013.

conservative in their policy outlook. Some governments may accept draft submissions from law firms hired by an industry. Others might be inclined to have more control and draft the submissions themselves, with or without conducting consultations with the affected individuals and their law firms.

The European Commission may accept assistance from private sector lawyers in drafting, but it will generally prepare its final submissions and present its case by itself.[52] On the other hand, Japan has accepted submissions prepared by privately hired law firms but has not invited the private sector representatives into the hearing room.[53] In simple cases, several governments may prefer to manage a case without the assistance of (and intervention from) the private sector. But the same governments may, in complicated cases, seek resources from the private sector as and when the budgetary and informational requirements become unaffordable. Hence, governments may have different approaches and political policies with respect to private sector participation, and the extent of coordination in different cases may accordingly vary in relation to the individual policy approach.

Governments may be reluctant to involve industries where a trade conflict has the potential to affect sensitive aspects of national welfare, such as those relating to public policy, health, social or moral considerations, environmental protection and consumer interests. There are several instances where governments have financed an entire dispute because it was strategically important for the country or had sensitive implications. For example, in the case of *EU and Member State – Seizure of Generic Drugs in Transit*,[54] the industry did not participate actively in spite of the fact that the dispute had significant trade ramifications for the pharmaceutical industry in Brazil. Because the dispute had the potential to adversely affect the 'right to health' of the citizens of Brazil, it was considered strategically important and was therefore entirely led and financed by the government.

Furthermore, a government might be under political or diplomatic pressure from the offending country or it may fear adverse diplomatic or extra-WTO retaliation, especially in cases where the alleged measure is maintained by an important trading partner or a powerful developed country. In the case of *Turkey – Safeguard Measures on Imports of Cotton*

---

52 Interview with an official, DG Trade, European Commission, Brussels, Belgium, 3 June 2013.

53 Interview with a WTO official (details withheld).

54 *EU and Member State – Seizure of Generic Drugs in Transit*, WT/DS409, in consultations on 12 May 2010.

Yarn,[55] TEXPROCIL initially faced difficulties in convincing the Indian government about the favourable conditions and possibilities of launching a dispute against Turkey and the dispute was therefore initiated by the unwilling government after a delay of one year. The government was unwilling because of its reluctance to challenge an important diplomatic and powerful trading partner with which it shared strong bilateral relations, and the consequent possibility of facing untoward trade and diplomatic retaliation. More so, middle income countries, and particularly larger ones, are highly dependent on the markets of high income countries for their exporting interests, and therefore they need to be cautious when considering an action against them. Hence, diplomatic state of affairs and bilateral trade relations can also have a significant bearing on the approach employed by governments towards the management of trade conflicts.

3.1.2 Economic Context

The cost of litigating a dispute at WTO is substantial, and due to poor economies of scale, it becomes even more substantial for the industries that have not been repeat participants in the process. A full-blown dispute may take around two years to reach the stage of compliance, and there might also be further delays in that time frame.[56] If an award is not implemented by the offending Member State, the process of compliance may need to be initiated, which may bring in further uncertainty, time delays, and a call for additional resource investment. Additionally, the remedies available under the WTO laws are prospective (not retrospective) and, in practice, non-compensatory in nature. Also, there is no provision that imposes financial penalty for non-compliance. Hence, invoking DSU provisions is often not an economically viable option for businesses that require immediate and predictable gains. For these reasons, the businesses may prefer to divert their exports to a different market than to resort to DSU provisions for regaining the lost market access.

Formation of partnerships for the invocation of WTO DSM may also be an unaffordable option for traders with small commercial stakes because the 'litigation costs are more or less independent of the commercial stakes

---

55 *Turkey – Safeguard Measures on Imports of Cotton Yarn (other than sewing thread)*, WT/DS428, in consultations on 13 February 2012.

56 For time frames, see WTO Dispute Settlement System Training Module: Chapter 6, accessed 24 September 2016 at <http://www.wto.org/english/tratop_e/dispu_e/disp_settlement_cbt_e/c6s1p1_e.htm>.

involved in a dispute'.[57] The small trading stakes 'are not sufficiently offset by smaller litigation costs or a reduced need for domestic WTO legal expertise'.[58] Moreover, there would be some trade frictions between industries or traders that are non-litigable and non-continuing in nature and WTO DSU may not be a viable route to address such concerns. A private entity faced with such non-litigable concerns will prefer to resolve them through informal procedures such as negotiations or bargaining, or by approaching the government to raise an issue at the WTO Committee Meetings, or with the help of Alternative Dispute Resolution (ADR) procedures. The DSU Agreement, under Article 5, provides for ADR procedures in the form of good offices, conciliation and mediation. Arbitration, provided under Article 25 of DSU Agreement, can also be opted for by Member States as an alternative to litigation. However, the nature and extent of coordination needed during committee meetings, mediation, conciliation, or negotiation will be different from those required during active litigation.

Different approaches are required for the deployment of partnership strategies in countries that have privately owned industries from the ones that have state-owned industries. Owing to the democratic set-up, privatised industries and open market economies in the US and the EU, firms and associations 'across both sides of the Atlantic find it quite natural to turn to the governments for help when they encounter trade barriers in overseas markets'.[59] The US and the EU, to further encourage and empower their enthusiastic industries, support and strengthen the dispute settlement partnerships with user-friendly provisions and institutions. However, it is important to note that their procedures of PPP are different from each other, as they have been devised as per their respective political economies. The legal provisions and procedures of interaction in the US employ a 'bottom-up' approach as their industries play a more 'aggressive' and 'proactive' role in dispute settlement. The EU, by contrast, in accordance with its interstate, institutional, legal and administrative set-up, employs a 'top-down' approach as the Commission plays a leading entrepreneurial and managerial role in PPP arrangements and only allows the industries to play a supplementary role.[60]

---

[57] Hakan Nordstrom & Gregory Shaffer, 'Access to Justice in the World Trade Organization: The Case for Small Claims Procedure?' (2008) 7(4) *World Trade Review* 587.

[58] Ibid 593.

[59] Henry Gao, 'Taking Justice into Your Own Hand: The TBI Mechanism in China' (2010) 44 *Journal of World Trade* 633, 650.

[60] Shaffer, *Defending Interests* (n 4) 6, 149.

As a striking contrast to the above-mentioned jurisdictions, the government in China commands a distinctively greater role in economic development and the overall operation of commerce. The economic sectors in China comprise a complex mix of controlled private companies, quasi-state enterprises and nationally, provincially and municipally controlled state-owned enterprises (SOEs).[61] The government therefore has a greater ability to intervene in the operations of foreign trade through state-owned enterprises, state-controlled industry representatives, or favourable support policies granted to privatised and strategic sectors.

3.1.3 Legislative, Institutional and Administrative Context

The legislative framework for handling WTO matters can be very different from country to country. There can be a constitutional set-up where all WTO matters are handled by a single ministry with separate departments handling investigation, private sector coordination and litigation work. Alternatively, different ministries may be responsible for the conduct of WTO matters. For example, in Brazil, the Ministry of Foreign Affairs is the central authority responsible for the settlement of trade disputes, though the Ministry of Trade and Industry has also recently assumed more powers in the field. In India, the Ministry of Trade and Commerce is responsible for the overall conduct of WTO disputes, but it has to conduct bilateral or multilateral consultations with other countries through the Ministry of Foreign Affairs. It also has to make a request to the Ministry of Law and Justice for the appointment of trade lawyers. On the other hand, China vests all WTO-related powers in the Ministry of Commerce (MOFCOM), which is responsible for the overall management of WTO disputes. MOFCOM, with the help of its internal departments (and externally hired professionals), performs its core functions relating to the protection of WTO rights.

Where a single official is responsible for deciding the appropriate course of action after consulting the affected industry, concerns regarding a potentially unfavourable outcome and allegations of corruption can 'weigh more heavily on individual decision-makers. . .'.[62] This is especially

---

[61] In the years 2010–2013, domestic private companies generated around 30% of the overall exports in China. The rest of the exports were generated by foreign and state-owned enterprises. Moreover, most of the strategic and wealthy economic sectors in China, such as steel, telecoms, oil, energy, and the financial industry are owned by the state.

[62] Jan Bohanes & Fernanda Garza, 'Going Beyond Stereotypes: Participation of Developing Countries in WTO Dispute Settlement' (2012) 4(1) *Trade Law and Development* 45, 83.

because the individual decision-makers may fear staining their character and career if they authorise an unsuccessful (and perhaps business-interest motivated) dispute. The responsible official can therefore employ a 'risk-averting' approach and that can influence the extent to which a government can protect its industries' interests through a privately funded action at WTO DSU. If decisions are made by multiple officials and departments, the shared risk of a possible failure and allegations of wrongfully launching a privately funded action may weigh less heavily on the government officials and that may make them more proactive in directly dealing with industries and making confident endeavours to protect their interests. However, a centralised system has its advantages. For example, the availability of a single dedicated department with expert officials responsible for the overall management of disputes can, to some extent, foster dispute settlement partnerships as it can make it easier for the industries to locate, approach and confide in the known officials.[63]

Moreover, for a coordinated management of disputes, it is important that the private sector confides in its government and believes that its government will protect and restore its infringed market access interests. However, it may not be possible in certain circumstances where '. . .a private company may be unwilling to give the government access to confidential information (sales data, identity of customers, internal accounting, etc.) that would be needed to effectively challenge [for example] an anti-dumping order in an export market'.[64] Hence, a legal provision that can provide participating stakeholders with the right to seek confidentiality of information and anonymity may have a positive impact on building a relationship of confidence. Additionally, a dedicated workforce, well-defined procedures of dispute management, and a forthcoming approach employed by the designated ministry can be instrumental in establishing and maintaining a relationship of trust and confidence between government and business community in a country.[65] However, the rotation of bureaucrats and the problem of 'brain drain' from government to the private sector can impede the formation of trusted and long-lasting government–industry relationships.

More experience in WTO litigation enables the government and industry to understand the requirements of WTO DSM and the actions that are required at the domestic level, and to develop appropriate arrangements for financing disputes and gathering information. Moreover, operation

---

63 Interview with an official, ICTSD, Geneva, Switzerland, 11 April 2012.

64 Bohanes & Garza (n 62) 83.

65 Interview with an official, ICTSD, Geneva, Switzerland, 13 April 2012.

of PPPs also depends upon the qualifications of government officials and their previous experience of dealing with a particular industry. The extent of resource exchange would also depend upon the legal expertise possessed by the concerned government department. If the government department (that is responsible for managing disputes in coordination with industries) possesses dispute settlement partnership experience and WTO litigation expertise, it can smoothly interact and seek the required information from non-state entities. It will also allow the government to prioritise the trade concerns of its industries, conduct meaningful consultations with the private sector, and lead the process of partnership at the domestic and international levels. The presence of in-house government lawyers with trade law expertise can also enable the government to oversee the working of trade lawyers and subject-specific consultants hired by industries for the preparation and presentation of a case. In-house or government-empanelled lawyers with knowledge and experience of WTO law can also directly engage with the affected private sector entities including companies, export promotion councils, trade associations, chambers of commerce and civil society organisations.

The bureaucratic structure of the government will also influence the effectiveness and operation of PPPs. The private sector will be more forthcoming if there is clarity, expeditiousness and non-complexity in locating and approaching the government officials that are responsible for negotiating with the offending country's government, coordinating with industries and the permanent mission, handling procedures of confidentiality of information, investigating trade barriers, and overseeing the overall conduct of disputes. In India, for instance, trade associations and companies are discouraged from approaching the government due to complex bureaucracy and multiple layers of decision-makers before a formal consultation or litigation is launched.[66] In Brazil, on the other hand, private stakeholders have benefitted from approachable and dedicated bureaucrats. A Brazilian private sector official observes the following: 'If we have a problem, we know whom to approach in the ministry and we can approach that government official by a phone call or an email or a visit to Brasilia.'[67]

These are some of the conditions that may influence PPP arrangements in a given country. However, the list of factors presented and discussed

[66] Interview with private sector representative, India-based trade association (audio conferencing), 15 June 2013.

[67] Interview with private sector representative, Brazil-based trade association, Sao Paulo, Brazil, 28 October 2013.

here is by no means exhaustive. There can be other domestic conditions that may have a significant bearing on the nature, suitability and performance of a PPP approach. For example, poor observance of rule of law in a country can impede the formation and functioning of effective PPP mechanisms. Conversely, a country with a system of rights and obligations regulating exchange of resources during WTO proceedings may be able to foster these partnerships. Hence, the effectiveness and suitability of PPP systems largely depend upon multiple factors including the political and economic climates, administrative cultures, and institutional and legislative set-ups prevailing in individual countries. In other words, the success or failure of any PPP strategy is subject to the national (that is, domestic) conditions of the country in which the strategy operates.

4.1 CONCLUDING REMARKS

With this conceptual background, the forthcoming chapters will explore the ways in which governments and industries can coordinate during the conduct of foreign trade disputes. A performance review of the existing PPP procedures in Brazil, India and China will provide practical insights to other developing countries (discussed in Chapters 4, 5 and 6). However, prior to the examination of the BIC's handling of trade disputes, the following chapter (Chapter 3) provides a brief overview of how the most active DSU users and the masters of the PPP approach (the US and the EU) identify and investigate trade barriers, engage in consultations, and prepare and litigate disputes at WTO. This is done in order to see if Brazil, India and China have derived any lessons from the successful dispute settlement experiences of these developed countries. The chapter also addresses the issue of whether other (non-BIC) developing countries could expand their understanding of the dispute settlement partnership approach and learn different ways of capacity-building by reviewing the experiences (negative as well as positive) of the US and the EU.

3. Handling of WTO disputes: the United States of America and the European Union

The United States of America (US) and the European Union (EU) are the most frequent users of WTO DSU. As of 20 January 2017, the US has acted as a complainant in 114 cases, as a respondent in 129 cases and as a third party in 136 cases at WTO DSU. The EU has acted as a complainant in 97 cases, as a respondent in 83 cases and as a third party in 161 cases. This frequent invocation of DSU provisions can directly be linked to the US's and the EU's gigantic market capitalisation size, overall share of world trade and absolute trading stakes. In addition, it can also be partly attributed to their well-established legal and institutional dispute management frameworks. This chapter enables readers to critically review these frameworks established for the management of foreign trade disputes in these two developed countries.

Readers are reminded that developed countries are not the focus of this work, and an examination of the US and the EU dispute settlement mechanisms in this chapter should not suggest that the domestic provisions of the US and the EU, however effective or workable in their respective jurisdictions, can be suitably adopted by developing countries. The conditions and needs of developing countries are different from those of developed ones, and therefore the laws, institutions and procedures of developed countries may not produce similarly positive results in developing countries. However, a review of dispute settlement mechanisms established by the US and the EU is vital as it illustrates different capacity-building approaches (with a special focus on the use of PPP arrangements) which have strengthened their participation at WTO DSU.

The importance of this chapter stems from the fact that both the US and the EU enjoy a wealth of dispute settlement partnership experience, so much so that they can truly be considered as the leaders of the dispute settlement partnership approach. They have established a massive set-up for public-private interaction during dispute settlement, which can be considered 'in principle' as a formal partnership mechanism because it is built on a system of legal 'rights and obligations'. The US and the EU are therefore important examples useful for understanding and examining the benefits and weaknesses of a formalised PPP arrangement as against an informal one. In particular, this chapter provides its readers with answers to the following pertinent questions:

i) Have the private sectors in the US and the EU frequently invoked the formal PPP provisions for the protection of their trade interests?
ii) Have these provisions been instrumental in the formation of public private coordination during the settlement of trade disputes?
iii) Are there any problems with the formal provisions that might deter their respective private sectors from approaching their governments? If so, what are these problems?
iv) Which features of the US's and the EU's formal systems have cost-effectively enhanced their dispute settlement capacity, and which ones have been ineffective or problematic? Can any of these capacity-building features be viably considered by developing Member States?

1.1 THE UNITED STATES

The United States is the first Member State under the GATT and the WTO trading system that has established detailed legal provisions on government-industry coordination aimed at the protection and expansion of trade in the US. It is also the first Member State that has granted direct petitioning rights to its private individuals in the event where a foreign practice impedes their market access interests. With the aim of sharing its dispute settlement partnership experience, the chapter's first part presents an overview of how the government departments and industries in the US have worked in coordination against foreign trade barriers. To begin with, the following section provides a brief description of the legal and institutional frameworks devised for the handling of foreign trade disputes in the US.

1.1.1 Institutional Framework

The United States Trade Representative (USTR) is the primary government authority responsible for the management of foreign trade disputes and overall WTO participation of the US.[1] It is an institutional interface

---

1 USTR is the competent authority under US Trade Act 1974, ss 301-310. It is obliged to function under the specific directions of the President. (Omnibus

between the government and the private individuals seeking to remove unfair trade barriers. It receives and examines trade barrier complaints from the private sector, investigates those that are legitimate, and decides the appropriate course of action for the removal of foreign trade barriers.

There are several advisory channels to enhance the communication and information exchange between USTR and the private sector. One such interface is the Private Sector Advisory Committee. The Advisory Committee provides commercial information and advice to the US government with respect to the private sector's bargaining position and negotiating objectives. The Industry Trade Advisory Center (ITAC) is another body that provides a forum where government officials can interact with trade representatives from different industries. Jointly managed by the US Department of Commerce and USTR, ITAC was established to strengthen government-industry consultation and inter-industry coordination.

The USTR employs an interministerial approach for handling trade disputes, which is also referred to as the 'whole-of-government' approach. With the establishment of the Interagency Trade Enforcement Center (ITEC) in 2012, USTR can benefit from the trade expertise and resources possessed by different government departments. ITEC can form multidisciplinary teams of experienced trade litigators, researchers, subject-matter experts, and economists to work together on specific trade matters. It therefore has the potential to serve as a forum for expertise-building, information-gathering and inter-agency coordination.

These public-private and intergovernmental procedures allow USTR to accumulate need-based information, advice or expertise with respect to different areas of trade law, as and when required, in a cost-effective manner. This institutional approach can be even more advantageous in developing countries as it can enable government officials to optimally utilise the available public and private resources, and as a result, build resource-capacity in a cost-effective manner. However, this may not be an affordable system for certain developing country governments as it may require enhanced human resources, expertise and finance.

1.1.2 Legal Framework

Multinational firms in the US monitor foreign trade practices that concern their trade interests. While trading across borders, they are often

---

Trade and Competitiveness Act of 1988, Public Law No 100-418, 102 Stat 1107 (23 August 1998), s 1601).

caught up in situations where a foreign trade practice injures their trade interests. In such situations, they commonly turn to USTR officials to seek the removal of trade impediments. The 'well-organised' private sector community in the US, represented by resourceful sector-specific trade associations, actively contributes to the process of dispute settlement at domestic as well as international levels. Section 301 procedure (Sections 301–310 of the US Trade Act 1974)[2] in the US provides a legal gateway for such business entities to access governmental processes. The provision enables individual entities to petition USTR if and when a foreign measure injures their trade interests.

A petition filed under Section 301 mechanism is regulated with the help of multiple legal provisions. These provisions are described sequentially in accordance with the different stages of dispute settlement.

1. *Administration and examination of petition*: Any interested person[3] (most commonly a commercial entity) can file a petition with USTR to convey to the government that its economic interest is being infringed by a foreign practice.[4] The petition will often urge USTR to investigate a matter and seek the removal of an alleged barrier. USTR may also identify a possible violation and initiate an investigation on its own.[5] It is legally obliged to administer and preliminarily examine the petitions filed under Section 301 procedure.[6]
2. *Investigation*: On the conclusion of preliminary examination, USTR may either decide to initiate an investigation in the matter or not.[7] USTR enjoys a discretionary power to determine whether an act, policy or measure merits an investigation and further pursuance of a matter.[8] The investigation can be conducted through various proce-

---

[2] Trade Act of 1974, Public Law No 93-618, 88 Stat 1978, 19 USC Ch 12, § 2411-2420 (As Amended through Public Law No. 112–208, enacted 14 December 2012). (Hereinafter referred to as Trade Act 1974). Full text accessed 15 October 2016 at <http://uscode.house.gov/download/pls/19C12.txt> accessed 15 October 2016.

[3] Trade Act 1974, s 301(d)(9) defines 'Interested persons' as those that '. . .includes, but is not limited to, domestic firms and workers, representatives of consumer interests, United States' product exporters, and any industrial user of any goods or services that may be affected by actions taken under subsection (a) or (b)'.

[4] Trade Act 1974, s 302(a)(1).

[5] Trade Act 1974, s 302(b).

[6] Trade Act 1974, s 301(a)(2).

[7] Trade Act 1974, s 302(a)(2).

[8] Trade Act 1974, s 302(c).

dures, which may include public hearings, solicitation with concerned industry and interministerial consultations.[9]

3. *Consultations upon initiation of investigation:* Upon the commencement of investigation under Section 302, USTR can launch a request for bilateral consultation with the offending Member States. If the matter is not resolved during the period of consultation (150 days from its commencement or as mentioned otherwise in the agreement), USTR can invoke the formal dispute settlement proceedings provided under the concerned agreement.[10]
4. *Publication, hearings and internal consultations*: USTR publishes its determination to initiate an investigation in the Federal Register. In the case of matters it decides not to pursue, a statement of reason for non-pursuance of a petition is published in the same manner.[11] It is also obliged to publish its determinations regarding the existence of a barrier and the appropriate action it has determined to undertake in the matter.[12] In order to prepare for formal consultations and dispute settlement proceedings, USTR seeks advice and information from the petitioner (if any) and appropriate expert committees established under Section 135.[13] USTR provides opportunities to the petitioners and other interested persons to present their views and provide information before it makes any determination upon the existence of a barrier.[14] If an expeditious action is required in a matter, public hearings and internal consultations can be carried out after the determinations are made under Section 304(a)(1).[15]
5. *Determination of appropriate course of action (Decision-making)*: After investigation and consultation, USTR determines whether a trade barrier exists or not, and whether it merits an immediate formal or a gradual action.[16] The determinations are made within a prescribed time limit, and they are subsequently published in the Federal Register.[17] Mandatory action requirements are imposed on the USTR officials in five alternative circumstances: (i) in cases where rights of the US under any trade agreement are denied; *or* (ii) in cases where an

---

[9] Trade Act 1974, s 302(a)(4)(A); s 302 (a)(4)(B); s 302(b)(1)(D).
[10] Trade Act 1974, s 303(a)(1); s 303(a)(2).
[11] Trade Act 1974, s 302(a)(3); s 302(a)(4).
[12] Trade Act 1974, s 304(c).
[13] Trade Act 1974, s 303(a)(3); s 304(b)(1)(B).
[14] Trade Act 1974, s 304(b)(1)(A).
[15] Trade Act 1974, s 304(b)(2).
[16] Trade Act 1974, s 304(a)(1).
[17] Trade Act 1974, s 304(a)(2).

act, policy or practice (hereinafter referred as a measure) of a foreign country violates any trade agreement; *or* (iii) in cases where a measure denies the US any benefits that should otherwise accrue to it as a result of any trade agreement; *or* (iv) in cases where a measure violates or is otherwise inconsistent with the international legal rights of the US; *or* (v) in cases where a measure is unjustifiable *and* it burdens *or* restricts US commerce.[18] In short, a USTR official is obliged to act in both violation as well as non-violation cases where a foreign measure violates the 'international legal rights' of the US or hampers its trade and commerce.

At the same time, USTR officials enjoy discretionary powers to determine the issue of action in non-violation cases (where no direct violation of a trade agreement or international legal right has been found) if a foreign practice is either 'unreasonable' *or* 'discriminatory' *and* if, as a result of that, it 'burdens' *or* 'restricts' US commerce.[19] The line of distinction between the situation required for discretionary action and the fifth situation (as enumerated above) under mandatory action requirement is very thin; the *former* covers measures that are 'discriminatory' or 'unreasonable' in nature, and the *latter* covers measures that are 'unjustifiable' in nature.

6. *Implementation of action*: The actions determined under Section 304(a)(1)(B) are implemented by USTR within a prescribed time limit.[20] USTR is obliged to undertake softer actions in certain cases that do not merit the invocation of formal dispute settlement procedures but nevertheless affect the exporting interests of a domestic industry.[21]
7. *Monitoring foreign compliance*: In order to ensure that US trade rights are enforced, USTR monitors the implementation of measures or agreements undertaken by foreign countries.[22] In the case where an offending country has not satisfactorily implemented a measure or agreement (including WTO Agreements), USTR will determine the appropriate course of action required to be undertaken against

---

[18] Mandatory action requirements are provided under Trade Act 1974, s 301(a).

[19] Discretionary action requirements are provided under Trade Act 1974, s 301(b). Section 301(c) lists the broad category of actions that USTR can undertake u/ss 301(a) and (b).

[20] Trade Act 1974, s 305(a)(1).

[21] Trade Act 1974, s 305(b).

[22] Trade Act 1974, s 306(a); monitoring and prioritisation of unfair foreign practices are listed in the Special 301 and Super 301 Reports produced annually by USTR.

the offending Member State.[23] Before making any determination upon such appropriate action, USTR consults the petitioners, other industry representatives and interested persons upon the matter.[24]

8. *Other related procedures*: After consultation with the petitioners, industry representatives and interested persons, USTR can modify or terminate the action being undertaken under Section 301.[25] USTR has other obligations that further facilitate the process of public-private solicitation, such as its obligation to provide information to the private sector on request,[26] and to issue regulations concerning the filing of petitions, investigation and hearings.[27] In addition, USTR must keep the petitioner informed of all determinations and developments made in a dispute that has originated from a petition filed under Section 301.[28]

These legal provisions create a system of 'rights and obligations', which directs the interaction and exchange of resources between USTR and the affected private stakeholders at nearly every stage of dispute settlement. In the words of Shaffer, it 'represents a process of public-private collaboration in fact-gathering, strategizing, negotiating, and (potentially) litigating over foreign trade restrictions'.[29] Section 301 mechanism can therefore be described as a specialised legal framework established for the management of foreign trade disputes with the help of public private coordination.

1.1.3 Dispute Settlement Partnerships in Practice: an Empirical Look

The nature of dispute management system established in the US can partly be attributed to the nature of its political economy. Owing to its democratic and highly capitalistic set-up, politics and economy are intricately interlinked in the US. The voting share of the ruling party's candidate generally increases with the increase in the gross national product (measured in or immediately before the election year) in the country.[30] The protection

---

23 Trade Act 1974, s 306(b)(1).
24 Trade Act 1974, s 306(c).
25 Trade Act 1974, s 307(a).
26 Trade Act 1974, s 308.
27 Trade Act 1974, s 309(1).
28 Trade Act 1974, s 309(2).
29 Gregory C Shaffer, *Defending Interests: Public-Private Partnerships in WTO Litigation* (Brookings Institution Press 2003) 30.
30 Alberto Alesina, John Londregan & Howard Rosenthal, 'A Model of the Political Economy of the United States' (1993) 87(1) *The American Political Science Review* 12, 13.

of business interests and expansion of foreign market access are always kept on the priority list of the Presidential Office. The business community in the US is very well-received by USTR officials, sometimes through presidential intervention because business entities are often involved in funding or managing electoral campaigns in the country.

The US Congress can also exercise significant influence over the functioning of USTR. Congress Committees can call USTR officials to justify their actions relating to the management of trade disputes. If they are unsatisfied with USTR's response or actions, Congress has the power to issue legislations to force USTR to act in a certain manner regarding international trade matters. This is possible mainly because, in accordance with the governance framework, the USTR depends upon Congress for the formulation of its policy goals and other operational requirements such as recruitment, funding and growth prospects. Hence, this huge interplay between the political and economic operations in the US influences the nature of the dispute management system and dispute settlement partnerships formed in the US. In short, its domestic environment nurtures and shapes public private interaction. This can be seen with the help of certain examples where USTR and business entities have jointly managed WTO dispute settlement proceedings.

Industries, in landmark disputes, have assisted USTR with information-gathering and fact-finding during investigation and litigation phases. For example, in *Korea – Alcoholic Beverages*,[31] the US distilled spirits trade association (DISCUS) assisted USTR with fact-finding and market research. It conducted field research and documented a comparative market analysis report, which was required to support the litigation. The report was subsequently used by USTR during Panel proceedings. In *EC – Bananas III (US)*,[32] Chiquita and its private lawyers were engaged in information-gathering and fact-finding activities. The information and evidential documents provided by Chiquita were extensively used by USTR during investigation and litigation of the dispute at the Panel stage.[33] Industries, in this manner, have been a constant driving force behind disputes that USTR has litigated at WTO.

---

31 Appellate Body Report, *Korea – Taxes on Alcoholic Beverages*, WT/DS75/AB/R, WT/DS84/AB/R, adopted 17 February 1999.

32 Appellate Body Report, *European Communities – Regime for the Importation, Sale and Distribution of Bananas,* WT/DS27/AB/R, adopted 25 September 1997.

33 Interview with international trade law scholar (audio conferencing) 9 September 2014; Mark A Pollack & Gregory C Shaffer, *When Cooperation Fails: The International Law and Politics of Genetically Modified Foods* (Oxford University Press 2009) 50.

Moreover, large multinational firms in the US have hired international law firms for the preparation and filing of Section 301 petitions. They have also hired law firms to assist USTR during investigation, consultations and litigation phases. On several occasions, these law firms have been directly involved in the litigation proceedings at Geneva. At other times, privately hired law firms have assisted the team of government lawyers presenting a case at WTO.[34] For example, in *Japan – Film*,[35] Kodak (the petitioner under Section 301) hired Dewey Ballantine LLP to assist USTR with the preparation of briefs and Panel submissions.[36] In *Korea – Alcoholic Beverages*, the US-based distilled spirit associations hired Michael Hathaway of Nall, Frazier & Hathaway to assist USTR in the matter. In the *EC – Bananas* case, Chiquita hired Carolyn Gleason of McDermott Will & Emery to provide USTR with overall legal assistance during preparation and litigation of the case.[37] Hence, USTR relies heavily on private resources for the investigation, preparation and litigation of trade disputes.

On several occasions, the industries have exerted congressional pressure to convince USTR to initiate an investigation or litigate a matter at WTO. For example, in *EC – Hormones (US)*,[38] the trade associations actively lobbied the congressional representatives to exert pressure on USTR to initiate a legal battle at WTO. Subsequently, they (most prominently, the American Meat Institute, the National Cattlemen's Beef Association and the US Meat Export Federation) were engaged in campaigns for gaining countrywide support to convince USTR to retaliate against the EC for its failure to comply with the WTO Appellate Body's ruling.[39] In the *Japan – Film* case, the rumour was that USTR would have preferred not to pursue the case but it was persuaded by the affected private company to litigate the dispute at WTO.[40] These examples show that the private sector in the US has been actively involved, through formal as well as informal procedures, in the government's handling of WTO disputes. This also goes

---

34 Interview with a scholar (n 33).

35 Panel Report, *Japan – Measures Affecting Consumer Photographic Film and Paper*, WT/DS44/R, adopted 22 April 1998.

36 Christian Tietje & Karsten Nowrot, 'Forming the Centre of a Transnational Economic Legal Order? Thoughts on the Current and Future Position of Non-State Actors in WTO Law' (2004) 5(2) *European Business Organization Law Review* 321, 338.

37 Shaffer, *Defending Interests* (n 29) 48.

38 Appellate Body Report, *European Communities – Measures Concerning Meat and Meat Products (Hormones)*, WT/DS26/AB/R, WT/DS48/AB/R, adopted 13 February 1998.

39 Shaffer, *Defending Interests* (n 29) 39.

40 Interview with a scholar (n 33).

to show that, in practice, the formal procedures of partnership in the US can sometimes be displaced by informal approaches such as lobbying and political campaigning.

1.1.4 Performance Review: Shortcomings and Benefits

With the legal and institutional provisions in place, and with an 'organized' business community able and willing to coordinate with the public sector, has the Section 301 mechanism been utilised frequently? Put differently, is the Section 301 mechanism a preferred means of coordination between USTR and industries?

Empirical works suggest that the Section 301 mechanism is neither a preferred means of partnership nor a frequently invoked provision. It has rather been considered as a 'weak', 'very infrequently invoked' and an 'ineffective' provision.[41] In practice, the private sector community has often preferred to approach USTR through informal means and procedures. USTR has also encouraged industries to make informal contacts with USTR officials to discuss the scope of their trade-related problems. The PPP arrangements formed in the US, in practice, may not be seen as strictly *formal* in nature as they are frequently shadowed and accompanied by informal exchanges. The US example reinforces the claim that the formal systems of PPP can overlap and converge with informal procedures of coordination, and it is therefore not possible to draw a clear line of distinction between the two.

Two key factors that seem to militate against the formal component of its dispute settlement partnership mechanism are the following:

1. *Mandatory action requirement*: The mandatory action requirement imposed on USTR officials has a very broad mandate as it can be invoked in both 'violation' as well as 'non-violation' matters. One of the reasons for USTR's preference towards informal means of engaging private stakeholders could be its possible inclination towards circumventing these mandatory obligations. USTR officials may not want to undertake an action under the 'orders' of business entities. That could be the USTR's key reason for not encouraging the industries to directly invoke the Section 301 mechanism.

   Industries also may not prefer to invoke this confrontational procedure. They may hesitate in filing Section 301 petitions as they may

---

[41] Interview with a trade lawyer, ACWL, Geneva, Switzerland, 11 April 2013; reaffirmed in interview with a scholar (n 33).

not want to convey to the USTR officials that '...we have a procedure that takes away your discretion to act and that you have to initiate the dispute for us if the matter meets the requirement u/s 301(a)'.[42] In most situations, industries may prefer to request the government for an action but not order the government to act. For these reasons, the mandatory action requirement of the mechanism may have discouraged the industries from invoking Section 301 provisions.

2. *Evidential requirements and resource dependency*: The provisions of Section 301 mechanism have imposed an evidential burden on the petitioners. The formal provisions have laid down specific requirements for the filing of Section 301 petitions. The petition has to be drafted in a given manner, and it must accompany the information and evidence required to support the allegations made. Presentation of factually supported and legally examined documents has become a 'pre-requisite' for the examination and investigation of Section 301 petitions. The difficulty of collecting the information and evidential documents at the preliminary stages of a dispute may therefore hinder the filing of formal petitions. The expense involved in preparing the petitions and the supporting evidential documents may also be substantial.

   The USTR officials have explicitly confirmed that a Section 301 investigation will mostly be set in motion if the affected industry is able and willing to support the process of investigation and dispute settlement. USTR's resource dependency upon the industry has been criticised by Sylvia Ostry. In her words, 'America does not have a trade policy. It has clients.'[43] Moreover, it is often alleged that the US government selectively protects the interests of wealthy business entities that can return this favour with substantial consideration. The *EC – Bananas* case is often cited as an example to support this strong allegation. Carl Lindner, Chiquita's president, was a major donor to the Democratic and Republican parties in 1998. He enjoyed congressional and executive support and this arguably made it easier for his company to convince USTR to litigate the case at WTO. Similar favourable protection has allegedly been accorded to the exporting interests of other powerful business interests in the US, such as Kodak's film, Cattlemen's beef and Pfizer's patents.[44] The discretionary powers of USTR to investigate a petition coupled with its

---

42 Interview with a trade lawyer (n 41).

43 Shaffer, *Defending Interests* (n 29) 23.

44 Ibid 24.

resource expectations, and its explicit practice of being funded by the private sector can exacerbate the possibility of USTR's discriminatory protection of special private interests.

These discussions confirm the arguments raised in the previous chapter; that is, the Section 301 mechanism can be used by the resourceful business actors, but the resource-constrained, non-influential and small-scale industries may not be able to utilise the mechanism in a similarly advantageous manner. This is because they may not be able to meet the evidential requirements at the time of petitioning the government. They may also not be able to provide additional resource assistance to the government during the conduct of dispute settlement proceedings. As a result, Section 301 mechanism could be seen as a tool prepared exclusively for the powerful, resourceful industries in the United States.

A similar situation of discriminatory protection of interests may also arise when the resources are exchanged in the absence of a formal law or regulation, but the informal nature of exchange may allow some flexibility, leniency and waiver in respect of the resource-demanding obligations imposed on the private complainants. Hence, the formalisation of evidential requirements may have a higher probability of hampering the resource-constrained business entities' access to government processes. However, it is possible to counter-argue that the chances of discriminatory protection of interests in the case of a formal PPP system could possibly be mitigated due to its in-built regulatory provisions that allow for constant supervision and monitoring of the USTR's handling of trade disputes.

The discussion shows that the formalised partnership mechanism has certain pitfalls; however, these disadvantages should not be allowed to conceal the multiple advantages it may have. The following paragraphs outline some of these advantages.

First, the provisions can guide petitioners and other interested non-state entities on how to approach the relevant government division through prescribed procedures and required documentation. With the publication and public hearing requirements, the formal provisions also have awareness-building potential, and they can arguably bring the public and the private sector together in a more transparent and unambiguous manner. Better transparency can be achieved as the public and private sector participants have a set of rights and obligations coupled with remedial provisions that are known to all participants and interested parties. The system can also reduce ambiguity and enhance predictability as the parties can refer to the statute whenever they need guidance in respect of dispute settlement procedures or coordination-related aspects.

Second, the formal provisions may also be advantageous because they confer a right to the industries to approach the government if their business interests are infringed by a foreign practice. The right can empower resource-constrained or otherwise uninfluential industries to approach or influence USTR officials to pursue their market access interests. They can even compel USTR to act in direct violation (and certain non-violation) cases under the previously discussed mandatory action requirement.

Third, the USTR's discretion to scrutinise, administer and investigate the petitions should arguably reduce the fears of mandatory action requirements. A mandatory action requirement would only operate if USTR in the first place decides to investigate the matter. Hence, it would not be entirely fair to say that USTR is dictated to by the industries in certain situations, as the former has the power to start an investigation or reject petitions (on several grounds including insufficient evidence and lack of industry support) before finding violations or other circumstances mentioned u/s 301(a).

Fourth, Section 301 has devised multiple transparent channels for interaction and information exchange between the government and affected industry representatives with the help of several provisions including private sector consultations,[45] publishing requirements,[46] and calls for public comments and public hearings.[47] Such public-private solicitation and transparency-enhancing provisions have strengthened the regulated exchange of resources between the two actors.

The above-mentioned benefits of this mechanism should be weighed against its possible disadvantages if the mechanism undergoes a process of review by the policymakers in the US, or if the strategy of formalised PPPs is considered by policymakers in other countries. This critical look at the dispute management experience of the US (especially in terms of the establishment of a formal PPP mechanism, litigation of landmark disputes with the help of formal as well as informal procedures, and the weaknesses and benefits of its formal procedures) can act as a catalyst for the future researchers and policymakers of developing countries which are aiming to strengthen their WTO participation capacity.

45 Trade Act 1974, s 303(a)(3); s 304(b)(1)(B).
46 Trade Act 1974, s 302(a)(3); s 302(a)(4); s 304(c).
47 Trade Act 1974, s 304(b)(1)(A).

2.1 THE EUROPEAN UNION

The European Union's PPP mechanism presents another example of a formal system which at times overlaps with informal procedures of coordination and exchange. The European Union is a political and economic partnership between 28 countries (as of 1 February 2017) from the European continent. One of the principal purposes for its establishment is the furtherance of economic cooperation and expansion of foreign market access through a single 'internal' market in the EU. In order to achieve its economic goals, and to work with the private sector for achieving these goals, the European Commission has devised various partnership procedures in accordance with its democratic inter-state nature. The partnership procedures are extensively coded in the EU regulations as the intergovernmental structure of the EU requires the Commission to function in a completely transparent, predictable and impartial manner. The following sections provide a brief description of the existing institutional and legal provisions in the EU that are established to manage foreign trade disputes.

2.1.1 Institutional Framework

The counterpart to USTR in Europe is the Directorate-General for Trade (DG Trade) at the European Commission. It is the primary government authority responsible for the management of foreign trade disputes. The WTO Dispute Settlement Unit at DG Trade is in charge of handling WTO disputes. It investigates trade-related complaints filed by private individuals, determines whether a legitimate complaint is being made, and whether it requires any further action.

Created in 1996, the EU's Market Access Strategy aims to ensure that multilateral and bilateral agreements signed by the EU are fully enforced, and the EU's foreign market access is protected and enhanced.[48] The Market Access Unit implements this strategy. The strategy has a clear commercial outlook, as it seeks to identify foreign trade barriers, prioritise them and devise procedures for their removal. On the operational side, the Market Access Database functions to ensure that information on tariffs, barriers, import formalities and documentary requirements is made readily available to business communities and the EU governments.[49] The online

---

48 European Commission, 'The Global Challenge of International Trade: A Market Access Strategy for the European Union' (Communication) COM (96) 53 final.

49 European Commission, Trade: Market Access Database, accessed 19 March 2017 at <http://madb.europa.eu/madb/indexPubli.htm>.

publication of this database has enabled the Commission, the Member States and the businesses to gather the most up-to-date information in a timely manner. In addition, the Market Access Advisory Committee performs an advisory function, and it comprises representatives from the EU Member States and the Commission.

Since its creation, the Market Access Strategy has undergone significant changes, and the main focus of the strategy now is the formation of market access partnerships between the Commission, Member States, and businesses to achieve better foreign market access.[50] The Commission has therefore proposed the adoption of a concerted approach of 'decentralized' partnership where local business communities and experts can help the Commission identify, analyse and eliminate the increasingly complex trade barriers. The proposal claims that 'trilateral discussions' at the local levels between public and private partners will result in better identification of trade barriers, the establishment of priorities for removal of barriers, cost-effective collection of databases and the creation of a network of specialists and experts. The proposal is grounded in the belief that the national embassies and businesses operating in foreign markets are best placed to identify trade barriers and conduct field research (including local searches), which may be required to investigate a barrier or to prepare for potential consultation and litigation.

With these reforms and proposals, the EU's PPP has gained a fresh momentum for stimulation and growth. The revised Market Access Strategy has reaffirmed that PPP has an indispensable role to play in the EU's future management of trade disputes.

2.1.2 Legal Framework

Dispute settlement partnerships between the Commission and industries can be formed via three alternative routes: (i) the traditional route of Article 207 of the Treaty on the Functioning of the European Union (TFEU);[51]

---

[50] Commission to the Council, the European Parliament, the European Economic and Social Committee and the Committee of the Regions of 18 April 2007 'Global Europe: a stronger partnership to deliver market access for European exporters' (Communication) COM (2007) 183 final; European Commission: External Trade, 'Global Europe: A Stronger Partnership to Deliver Market Access for European Exporters', 3, accessed 19 March 2017 at <http://trade.ec.europa.eu/doclib/docs/2007/april/tradoc_134591.pdf>.

[51] Treaty on the Functioning of the European Union [26/10/2012] OJ C326/49 [ex Article 133 of the Treaty Establishing the European Community].

(ii) the Trade Barrier Regulation (TBR) mechanism;[52] and (iii) informal coordination.

The Article 207 procedure is the 'traditional route' through which determinations over multilateral or bilateral actions for the removal of trade barriers are made. According to this provision, the Commission is obliged to work under the advisory supervision of the Consultative Committee appointed by the Council.[53] The Committee is known as the 'Article 207 Committee'. The provision requires the Commission to make recommendations suggesting appropriate actions, and to seek the prior approval (by qualified majority voting procedure) of the Council of the European Union to initiate an action. The procedure therefore makes it possible for the EU Member States to restrict the dispute settlement related activities of the Commission. At the same time, it also allows the Member States to represent private commercial interests by raising issues at the Council meetings. For this reason, making recommendations and winning the Council's approval by a qualified majority vote may require a considerable amount of time and political negotiations. The Article 207 process is therefore criticised for its politicised, complex and time-consuming approach as it can give rise to long-drawn political negotiations and economic trade-offs between the Member States before any trade negotiations, implementation actions or retaliatory measures can be initiated by the Commission.

The alternative legal route for the management of trade disputes is the Trade Barrier Regulation (TBR) established under the Council Regulation (EC) No. 3286/94. It provides individuals with the right to petition the Commission if and when their trade interests are infringed by a foreign practice. Under TBR provisions, the Commission can directly investigate an administered petition filed by a private entity and can invoke bilateral or multilateral dispute settlement mechanisms without seeking a prior approval from the Council.

The TBR Committee is the primary unit responsible for the overall management of the entire TBR procedure. Its key functions include the examination and review of complaints, investigation of allegations,

---

[52] Council Regulation (EC) No. 3286/94 [22 December 1994] amended by Council Regulation No. 356/95 [20 February 1995] and Council Regulation No. 125/2008 [12 February 2008] and EU Regulation No. 654/2014 of 15 May 2014 (laying down Community procedures in the field of the common commercial policy in order to ensure the exercise of the Community's rights under international trade rules, in particular those established under the auspices of the World Trade Organization) [1994] OJ L349. (Hereinafter referred to as 'Council Regulation').

[53] Treaty on the Functioning of the European Union, art 207(3).

bilateral consultations, and determination of an appropriate course of action. Unlike the Article 207 system, the Commission's determination of appropriate action under TBR provisions can only be altered if the Council overturns the Commission's decision by a qualified majority vote.[54] The TBR system is therefore seen as 'an instrument which effectively provides industry with an indirect access to the rights deriving from the WTO Agreements.'[55] Multiple legal provisions, as described below, regulate trade barrier complaints filed under the TBR mechanism.

1. *Filing TBR complaints*: Individuals, companies, associations or EU governments can file a TBR complaint.[56] A complaint must address three elements in order to be considered for investigation: (a) existence of a measure; (b) evidence that a measure is violating international trade rules; and (c) evidence of commercial injury.[57] The European Commission has prepared written guidelines to explain the process of filing TBR complaints. The guidelines contain a 'model TBR complaint' that shows different components that are required to be addressed in the complaint.[58]
2. *Admissibility review*: Once a TBR complaint is filed and accepted, the Commission has to determine whether or not it merits an investigation of the barrier complained of.[59] This procedure is known as 'admissibility review' and is mainly carried out to 'test the water' of the complaint.
3. *Consultation procedure*: Under the Council Regulations, an Advisory Committee is established for the purpose of internal consultations.[60] Consultations can be initiated at the request of a Member State or on the Commission's own initiative.[61] At this stage, the informa-

---

54 Council Regulation, arts 13 and 14.

55 European Commission, 'Trade Barrier Regulation: Opening Markets for European Exporters' (2008), 15, accessed 3 July 2016 at <http://trade.ec.europa.eu/doclib/docs/2005/april/tradoc_122567.pdf>.

56 See Council Regulation, art 2(5) and 2(6) for definitions of 'Community Industry' and 'Community enterprise'. Right to file a written complaint provided under Council Regulation, arts 3(1) and 4(1). An EU Member State's right to file a TBR complaint provided under Council Regulation, art 6.

57 Council Regulation, arts 3(2), 4(2) and 10.

58 Model complaint available at European Commission: Trade Barriers Regulation, accessed 3 July 2016 at <http://trade.ec.europa.eu/doclib/docs/2013/april/tradoc_150984.pdf>.

59 Council Regulation, art 5(4).

60 Council Regulation, art 7(1).

61 Council Regulation, art 7(2).

tion pertaining to a dispute is shared and exchanged between the Commission, Advisory Committee and the Member State(s). The consultation results are also referred to and supervised by the Article 207 Committee.[62]

4. *Notice of initiation*: If the examination concludes that a complaint forms a prima facie basis of a trade dispute and therefore merits investigation, a 'Notice of Initiation' of investigation is published in the *Official Journal of the European Union* (Official Journal). This marks the commencement of a formal TBR investigation. The Commission provides a window of 30 days (from the publication date of the 'Notice of Initiation') to private sector entities to register interests in the TBR procedure.[63]
5. *TBR investigation*: The TBR Committee investigates and determines whether a complained measure violates the rules of international trade or injures the commercial interests of its Member States.[64] The Commission communicates the investigation outcome and the determinations made at each stage to the complainants, and they are also subsequently published in the Official Journal.[65] At this stage, the Commission can coordinate with the EU Member States, the complainant(s), industry representatives and other economic operators to seek the required information and advice.[66] The Regulation contains a confidentiality provision which assures the complainant(s) that the business sensitive information provided by them to the Commission will remain confidential and will not be revealed without their prior approval.[67]
6. *Private sector consultation*: Upon a written request made by a private party, the Commission can hold public hearings to seek the views of the parties concerned. In addition, private sector meetings can also be organised by the Commission where concerned parties are given a forum to meet and present their views and share information.[68] The Commission, if required, can also seek additional information from the complainant(s) and other interested parties during the course

---

62 Council Regulation, art 7(2).
63 Council Regulation, art 8(1)(a).
64 Council Regulation, art 8(1)(c).
65 Council Regulation, art 8(4)(b) provides that the complainants and other interested persons can seek information and updates pertaining to the examination process from the Commission.
66 Council Regulation, art (8)(2).
67 Council Regulation, art 9.
68 Council Regulation, art 8(5) and 8(6).

of the TBR procedure. It is not necessary that the stage of private consultation follows the investigation stage or precedes the stage of decision-making. In practice, public private consultations can take place at any stage of the TBR procedure.

7. *Preparation of Examination Report*: Once investigations are concluded, the Commission prepares a report of its findings that is officially known as an 'Examination Report'.[69] The report is sent to the Advisory Committee (established under the Council Regulation) for consideration.
8. *Determination and implementation of action*: The Commission, through the TBR procedure, aims to remove the obstacles to trade as quickly and as effectively as possible. The TBR procedure therefore provides a time window to the Commission during which it can try to settle the dispute through informal or softer means. Examination or investigation procedures can be suspended or terminated if the offending Member State has taken steps to eliminate the practice, or if it has agreed to negotiate a settlement with the Commission.[70] If the matter is not mutually settled, the Commission can invoke WTO dispute settlement proceedings or other mechanisms provided under the concerned Agreement.[71] Such decisions are made by the Commission after taking into account the inputs provided by the Advisory Committee (established under the Council Regulation) and the concerned industry.[72] Unlike the mandatory action requirement imposed on USTR, the European Commission enjoys full discretion in deciding these matters.[73]

These are the key procedural stages which a formal TBR complaint can go through. The TBR procedure, with the given set of rules, provides for a

---

69 Council Regulation, art 8(8).
70 Council Regulation, art 11.
71 Council Regulation, art 12.
72 Council Regulation, art 14.
73 The Regulation (EU) 654/2014 has amended art 13 (relating to the decision-making procedures) of the Council Regulation 3286/94. The amendment does not affect the TBR procedures, and it is therefore not explained further in the book. Regulation (EU) 654/2014 of the European Parliament and of the Council of 15 May 2014 concerning the exercise of the Union's rights for the application and enforcement of international trade rules and amending Council Regulation (EC) No 3286/94 laying down Community Procedures in the field of the common commercial policy in order to ensure the exercise of the Community's rights under international trade rules, in particular those established under the auspices of the World Trade Organization [2014] OJ L189/50. (Hereinafter referred to as 'Regulation (EU) 654/2014').

public private solicitation mechanism aimed at the protection of the EU's foreign market access. These laws and institutions, shaped by the political environment of the EU and hence bonded together with stipulated time frames and procedures, provide another example of a formal system of PPP.

2.1.3 Dispute Settlement Partnerships in Practice: an Empirical Look

As discussed above, TBR as a legal instrument provides individual businesses with a right to file complaints relating to foreign market access issues. However, it is not the only route through which an EU industry can, in practice, approach the Commission. The latter can be indirectly approached through Article 207 process, or it can be approached rather informally through national trade units of the individual governments or through other divisions at the Commission. The national institutions of the EU Member governments (such as national trade gateways and concerned ministries) and the intergovernmental institutions of the EU (such as the European Commission), which function in a parallel, transparent and democratic manner, can occupy the position of key public sector participants in dispute settlement partnerships. Hence, business entities in the EU Member States generally have a choice of multiple public sector avenues to approach if they face a market access problem.

For initial informal discussion and guidance, firms and associations have frequently approached the subject-specific divisions, dispute settlement unit or the country-specific divisions at the Commission. The Market Access Unit of DG Trade has also been their first point of contact in a significant number of trade conflicts, and the Unit in such cases has gathered information and analysed the matters from economic and legal perspectives. For this reason, the Market Access Unit has often worked closely with the TBR Team while handling disputes and coordinating with the private sector. In practice, the Unit has functioned in a 'complementary' manner in almost half of the WTO cases that have been handled by the TBR Team.[74]

The Commission invites and encourages the potential TBR complainants to make an initial informal contact with the Market Access Unit.[75]

---

[74] Interview with an official, European Commission (audio conferencing) 3 June 2013.

[75] The guidance is available at European Commission: Trade, accessed 3 July 2016 at <http://trade.ec.europa.eu/doclib/docs/2013/april/tradoc_150984.pdf>. Another detailed guide is European Commission, 'Trade Barrier Regulation' (n 55). It provides guidance on the pertinent areas of TBR, such as: 'What is the

The Market Access Unit provides informal advice on the scope of the matter and the available appropriate options for dealing with the matter. If a matter necessitates filing a TBR complaint, the DG Trade's TBR unit can provide further assistance and guidance to the complainants on drafting and filing procedures. However, it remains unclear whether the TBR unit also provides assistance to the potential TBR complainants at the stages prior to drafting and filing a TBR complaint; that is, when the complainants are examining the barriers or when they are gathering required documentation.

The *Japan – Alcoholic Beverages II*[76] case is an example where an organised beverages industry worked closely with the Commission during pre-litigation and litigation stages. The key private participants included the United Kingdom's Scotch Whisky Association, French associations and the European Confederation of Producers of Spirits. They formed an alliance to work together for the protection of their converging market access interests. Jointly, they conducted market research and gathered information and documentary evidence to assist the Commission in litigating the case. The alliance was actively engaged in carrying out international campaigns with foreign industries, civil society organisations and foreign governments to generate pressure on Japan to remove the alleged barrier.[77]

Other landmark cases, for example, the *EC – Bananas III (US)*,[78] *EC – Export Subsidies on Sugar (Australia)*[79] and *EC and Certain Member States – Large Civil Aircraft*[80] cases are remarkable examples where industries have actively participated at all stages of dispute settlement. These examples illustrate public private coordination during WTO litigations wherein the Commission was acting as a respondent. Hence, these cases, to some extent, contradict the earlier observation (laid down in Chapter 2) that PPP arrangements may not work in defence litigations. In these

---

Trade Barrier Regulation?', 'Who can use the TBR?', 'How the system operates in practice', and 'How to prepare a complaint', along with a summary of past TBR complaints.

[76] Appellate Body Report, *Japan – Taxes on Alcoholic Beverages*, WT/DS8/AB/R, WT/DS10/AB/R, WT/DS11/AB/R, adopted 1 November 1996.

[77] Shaffer, *Defending Interests* (n 29) 84, 100.

[78] Appellate Body Report, *European Communities – Regime for the Importation, Sale and Distribution of Bananas,* WT/DS27/AB/R, adopted 25 September 1997.

[79] Appellate Body Report, *European Communities – Export Subsidies on Sugar*, WT/DS265/AB/R, WT/DS266/AB/R, WT/DS283/AB/R, adopted 19 May 2005.

[80] Appellate Body Report, *European Communities and Certain Member States – Measures Affecting Trade in Large Civil Aircraft*, WT/DS316/AB/R, adopted 1 June 2011.

cases, the industries provided the required commercial information to the Commission. The Airbus, the sugar associations and the banana producers also hired lawyers to assist the legal team of the Commission.[81] The private lawyers hired by the industry, unlike those in the US examples, were not directly involved in the litigation process. They were not invited by the Commission to join the delegation of lawyers during consultations or Panel proceedings. However, they provided indirect support and additional legal assistance to the Commission lawyers by engaging in legal research and preparing legal arguments and responses. The Commission lawyers vetted the arguments, evidence and legal analysis provided by the privately hired lawyers, and finalised the briefs and responses themselves.[82]

These examples confirm that, like USTR, the EU Member States and the Commission tend to rely on private sector inputs throughout the procedure of WTO dispute settlement. The concerned business communities remain active throughout and are heavily consulted by the Commission at every crucial stage of dispute management. But how and to what extent the private sector has participated has largely differed from case to case. The private sector's participation has ranged from meeting and discussing the disputes with the Commission officials, assisting the Commission to prepare actual drafts and responses to Panel questions, providing information and commercial evidence, to hiring of lawyers and financing the lawyers engaged by the governments and the Commission for litigating or defending a case.[83]

Notwithstanding these varied partnership dynamics, the Commission has constantly maintained its own 'policy line' and has not usually allowed the privately hired lawyers to dominate legal preparation or actual presentation of a case at WTO. An official representative at the Commission confirms that 'the official documents are drafted and finalised by the Commission and not by industry or their lawyers, though they can supply their drafts, information and suggestions which are almost always taken into account.'[84] A trade lawyer, who has worked as a privately hired lawyer

---

81 Interview with trade lawyer, White & Case (Geneva), London, United Kingdom, 16 May 2013. (The interviewee confirmed that the banana industry and the sugar associations in Europe were actively pursuing the case with their governments and the Commission.) For more information on the participation of Airbus in the *Civil Aircraft* dispute, see Ozgur Caliskan, 'An Analysis of the Airbus-Boeing Dispute from the Perspective of the WTO Process' (2010) 10(4) *Ege Academic Review* 1129, 1135.

82 Interview with a trade lawyer, London, UK, 26 June 2016.

83 Interview with an official, European Commission (n 74).

84 Ibid.

with the Commission lawyers on a landmark WTO dispute, confirms the observation and cites an interesting example to further explain the relationship between the Commission lawyers and privately hired lawyers:

> In one of the disputes where I was hired by an industry, it was always clear to me that the Commission would check the arguments that I was proposing to ensure that they were in line with their policy interests. Thus, the Commission does not simply puts [sic] its stamp on a draft or a brief prepared by a privately hired law firm or an industry.[85]

The Commission is the dominant partner in such partnerships, and it has led the process of dispute settlement with the help of its internal legal, political and economic expertise. There have, occasionally, been cases where the Commission has delegated the preparation and presentation of WTO case work to privately hired lawyers, but that has occurred on very rare occasions as the 'Commission does not want to be seen as a hired gun of private industry'.[86] The rationale behind the said dynamic of Commission-industry coordination during dispute settlement, as discussed before, is implicit in the nature of its political economy; that is, the EU's inter-state governance structure, the internal market demands and the Commission's consequent need to maintain full impartiality between different states and industries. In addition, three notable features of the EU's PPP emerge from the discussions above.

First, the PPP arrangements in the EU, as in the case of the US, are based on resource exchange, reciprocity and resource interdependency, and these elements can further be observed in the following statement made by an official representative of the Commission:

> [N]one of our disputes are brought without there being an industry that is adamantly behind it and pushing for the case to be taken to the WTO. Governments do not have the resources to monitor the observance of the rules, so they prioritise to take up cases that are strongly supported by private sector.[87]

Second, as discussed before, the TBR outcomes and determinations can be subjected to review at Council level or Advisory Committee level. A Commission official describes this process of review as follows:

---

85 Interview with a trade lawyer (n 81).
86 Ibid.
87 Interview with an official, European Commission (n 74).

> Capture may happen if the public interest is allowed to be substituted by the private interest in a trade dispute. But we have a system by way of which the Council of European Union, the Consultative Committee [Article 207 Committee] and the Advisory Committee established under the Council Regulation can ensure that both interests are balanced and protected.[88]

Decisions of the TBR can be reversed by the Council through qualified majority voting. The Examination Report of the TBR Committee is reviewed and approved by the Advisory Committee before an action can be initiated bilaterally or multilaterally. The determinations made under the TBR provisions are additionally supervised by the Article 207 Committee. These screening provisions allow dispute settlement partnerships to be fully supervised, as they seek to ensure that such partnerships continue to balance the interests of the nation with private commercial interests. These provisions seek to ensure that the Commission's handling of trade disputes remains immune from the potential regulatory threats outlined in the previous chapter.

Third, interaction between the public and private sectors in the EU has frequently occurred through informal channels of coordination. In the words of a Commission official, '[t]he TBR complaints have never been the private sector's preferred route to access the Commission. In practice, TBR has mostly been used where informal exchanges have not been satisfactorily effective or where the Commission has encouraged an industry to invoke it'.[89] In light of these observations, it may not be entirely accurate to portray the EU's PPP as a strictly formal mechanism as it is frequently shadowed by informal exchanges. The EU's formal PPP mechanism and the Commission's substantial inclination towards informal means of cooperation bring the EU model closer to the US partnership mechanism.

2.1.4 Performance Review: Shortcomings and Benefits

With a renewed commitment towards engaging the private sector, and the institutional and procedural reforms allowing the same, the TBR mechanism seems to be occupying a prominent position in the future handling of foreign trade disputes. However, any projections concerning its future performance would be baseless without an evaluation of its past performance. It is therefore important to raise the following questions: Are the provisions of TBR frequently utilised by the private sector? Is the

88 Ibid.
89 Ibid.

TBR mechanism a preferred means of coordination between industries and the Commission? Has it suffered from any drawbacks?

An official representative of the Commission observes that a very small number of cases have been pursued at Geneva via the TBR mechanism: 'The TBR mechanism is scantly used in practice, and it was last used five years ago [as of 1 March 2013].'[90] Moreover, from the year 1996 to 2008, only seven TBR-originating disputes were filed at WTO out of a total of 79 WTO cases filed by the EU as a complainant. The Commission has successfully managed and settled a majority of trade disputes without the TBR examination procedure. It therefore has little incentive and or reason to encourage the use of TBR provisions. Several reasons have been blamed for its infrequent utilization:

1. *Evidential burden imposed on complainants*: The Interim Evaluation Report on the TBR concludes that the provisions impose a high burden of evidential requirements on the complainant(s), and this is one of the key reasons for its underutilisation.[91] Past TBR users have observed that the information needed for establishing adverse trade effects, injury and causation, especially at the preliminary stages of a dispute, is the 'most burdensome' requirement of the TBR procedure.[92] There have been instances where industry associations and individual companies were discouraged from filing TBR complaints because of the substantial amount of information and evidential documents requested by the Commission officials for initiation of the examination procedure.[93] The expense, time and effort required to prepare the TBR complaints can therefore be substantial, and this can potentially result in the abandonment of the TBR procedure.

   Once a complaint is filed, the complainant cannot 'sit back and wait for the European Commission to take the initiative'.[94] The Commission can continue to seek input and resources from complainants throughout the process. Additional evidence, information,

---

[90] Interview with an official, European Commission (n 74).

[91] Council Regulation, arts 3(2) and 4(2) r/w art 10 impose evidentiary requirements on the petitioners. The Regulation also states that a petition can be rejected if these evidential requirements are not met by the petitioners.

[92] European Commission DG-Trade, 'Final Report: Interim Evaluation of the European Union's Trade Barrier Regulation (TBR)' (June 2005) 51, accessed 25 September 2016 at <http://trade.ec.europa.eu/doclib/docs/2005/october/tradoc_125451.pdf>.

[93] Ibid 44.

[94] Ibid 42, 51.

translations, economic analysis and legal assistance may be required at any stage by the Commission, especially in complicated and resource-intensive cases. In certain complex cases, additional resource assistance may also be required at each and every stage of the TBR procedure. Hence, the past users of TBR have experienced difficulties in meeting the additional information requests from the Commission before, during and after the conduct of examination procedures.

This seems to be a downside as it impedes the utilisation of the TBR mechanism by the private sector; however, it is important that such trade-related complaints contain sufficient information on the basis of which they can preliminarily be examined. Moreover, affected private stakeholders, as mentioned in the previous chapter, are best placed to gather and provide such inputs, which are required to investigate a barrier or prepare for consultation, litigation or compliance proceedings.

2. *Bureaucratic burden imposed on the Commission*: One of the factors contributing to the underutilisation of the mechanism could be the Commission officials' overt preference for informal procedures of coordination. An official representative at the Commission states that the TBR procedure is the Commission's least preferred option because it creates 'additional paperwork', imposes a 'bureaucratic burden' and entails 'procedural complications'.[95] The official further confirms that the 'support for the additional procedural complexity arising from the formal TBR mechanism remains low because the Commission has limited resources at its disposal'.[96]

   In the past, the Commission used to encourage the filing of TBR complaints in cases where intensive fact-finding was required. Gradually, however, this practice has been dropped. Its fact-finding utility has diminished with time as intensive investigation activities are now actively taken up by specialised divisions and local teams created under the Commission. In the words of an official, 'as the fact-finding is conducted automatically by various teams, there is practically nothing that cannot be done without the framework of TBR'.[97]

3. *Possible discriminatory impact*: Data shows that the TBR mechanism has been invoked mainly by the resourceful and well-organised industries in the EU.[98] This is because the resourceful companies and

95 Interview with an official, European Commission (n 74).

96 Ibid.

97 Ibid.

98 The data (covering 1996–2008) indicates that the following resourceful industry sectors have been repeat users of the TBR procedure: spirits and wine

trade associations in the EU are in a comparatively better position to meet the costs required for the invocation of the TBR mechanism. This could partly be attributed to the resource-demanding nature of the TBR mechanism, which can be an unaffordable option for certain business entities or SMEs that cannot afford to collect information or 'buy in' the external expertise required for preparation and filing of TBR complaints. The formalised TBR mechanism can therefore lead to a possible situation of discrimination between resourceful and resource-constrained business stakeholders in the EU. This possible outcome, as discussed in Chapter 2, is a limitation of the government-industry coordination approach.

4. *Lack of anonymity requirements*: One of the key discouraging factors for companies (and even trade associations) is that the TBR procedure does not contain strict provisions for maintaining the anonymity of complainants.[99] It is seen as 'one of the main reasons why companies, particularly SMEs, are hesitant to make more use of the TBR instrument'.[100] As discussed in Chapter 2, companies can be discouraged if the provisions do not grant a right to complainants to keep their identity anonymous. TBR complainants are clearly identified in the Notice of Initiations published in the Official Journal and the newspaper reports.[101] TBR complainants can therefore face a real threat of future adverse trade ramifications by the offending countries or trading partners as the latter can effortlessly locate the complainant's particulars. The use of TBR mechanism could possibly increase if the identity of complainant(s) under the procedure is made anonymous upon request.
5. *Complex and time-consuming procedures*: The companies, trade associations and industry federations in the EU have found it simpler to

(five), leather (twice), textiles (thrice), steel (twice), pharmaceuticals (twice), automobile (twice), fisheries, food products and agriculture (five). The quantity (in brackets) reflects the number of TBR complaints the industry has filed from 1996–2008. Data is obtained from: European Commission, 'Trade Barrier Regulation' (n 55) 17.

99 This is different from the confidentiality of information provided by complainants that is provided in Council Regulation, art 9.

100 European Commission DG-Trade, 'Final Report' (n 92) 46.

101 For example, see Official Journal of the European Union, Notice of Initiation of an examination procedure concerning obstacles to trade within the meaning of Council Regulation (EC) No 3286/94, consisting of measures imposed and practices followed by the Eastern Republic of Uruguay affecting trade in Scotch Whisky [2004] OJ C261/03, accessed 10 November 2016 at <http://eur-lex.europa.eu/LexUriServ/LexUriServ.do?uri=OJ:C:2004:261:0003:0005:EN:PDF>.

approach their national governments or trade gateways instead of invoking TBR procedures, which they have found to be complicated, time-consuming and costly. A report notes that '[t]he biggest gap between the expectations created in 1996 and the results achieved is in the time taken for the successful removal of trade restrictions even in the most clear-cut cases of breaches of multilateral or bilateral agreements'. It goes on to note that '[t]he private sector's interest in TBR has gradually diminished as it requires a whole procedure to be carried out before invocation of the WTO. You can add a whole year to an average WTO case that will be swallowed up by the TBR procedure.'[102] These remarks clearly suggest that businesses need quicker and more responsive actions to be undertaken in order to usefully invoke the TBR mechanism.

Time delays can happen on several occasions and for different reasons during the TBR complaints procedure. For example, delay can happen when the Commission officials need additional information for investigation or bilateral negotiation, or when TBR investigations are suspended, or when their determinations are reviewed or questioned by the Council or the Article 207 Committee.

Certain changes have been proposed to improve and simplify the procedures of registering, analysing and dealing with TBR complaints. The Commission has proposed to ensure:

a. that effective information-sharing between industries and the Commission should take place during the management of market access issues;
b. that all market access complaints should be registered in the Market Access Database, and the Database should be linked to other databases of the EU Member States;
c. that TBR cases should be given a 'unique case number' so that the developments and the status of each case can be tracked by private stakeholders in a regular and transparent manner;
d. that local Market Access teams and overseas EU business actors should work closely with the Commission during the management of market access issues;
e. that the Market Access Database should be simplified and be made more user-friendly to help private stakeholders identify and report problems in a timely manner; and

---

[102] European Commission: External Trade, 'Global Europe: A Stronger Partnership to Deliver Market Access for European Exporters' (n 50) 12.

f. that the reaction times to online, email and postal enquiries should be improved.

The above recommendations outline several practical procedures that can also be considered by developing countries that are keen to develop domestic procedures for the timely management of market access problems.

6. *Confrontational elements and fear of extra-WTO retaliation*: The general perception among the EU industries is that the invocation of TBR mechanism will give rise to a 'severe course of action' that will be handled litigiously by the Commission.[103] Industries therefore would normally prefer not to invoke any confrontational procedure that may compel the Commission to act in a given manner and follow a cumbersome procedure. The industries will instead prefer to request the Commission to look into their problem and determine a suitable course of action without a litigious framework. The TBR users have therefore referred to the TBR procedure as the 'last resort' or the 'nuclear option', which has seldom been used by industries facing market access problems.[104] Moreover, foreign governments have perceived TBR mechanism as 'confrontational' and 'aggressive'.[105] This negative overseas perception may lead to undesirable trade complications for the affected industries as it may further jeopardise their trade relations with private trading partners or their governments. Hence, fear of adverse extra-WTO retaliation, as discussed in Chapter 2, can also be considered as a discouraging factor for the prospective TBR complainants.
7. *Comparative ease of using other alternatives*: As mentioned earlier, TBR is not the only route for private stakeholders to approach the Commission. They also have informal, semi-formal and indirect avenues for addressing their market access problems. Enterprises and associations have in fact preferred to use these simpler, expeditious and cost-effective remedies.

   The comparative ease of using other alternatives can be considered as one of the reasons for the underutilisation of TBR, but it is, by no means, a shortcoming of the TBR mechanism. The industries should not be discouraged from pursuing the alternative routes for market access protection. The alternative options can at times be more suitable, especially in cases where barriers (complained of) are discrimina-

103 European Commission DG-Trade, 'Final Report' (n 92) 39.
104 Ibid.
105 Ibid.

tory or unfair but not illegal or where the disputes are perishable in nature. Hence, the alternative avenues have their advantages, and their use should be encouraged to further develop and complement the TBR procedure in the future.

There is one possible advantage which the TBR procedure could have over other informal and formal channels of partnership; that is, its potential to be used as a threatening or a pressurising tool against the offending Member States. Much like the notorious mechanism of Section 301 in the US, TBR can be used to pressurise the offending countries to reduce or eliminate the barriers complained of before the commencement of WTO litigation. However, the Commission claims that it has not used the mechanism as a threatening or punitive weapon against any trading partner. 'The EU has been impartial and objective in its use of the TBR' as it has not targeted any particular trading partner or a specific area of trade barrier.[106] Unlike the Section 301 procedure of the US, the TBR mechanism does not even have the advantage of exerting pressure on offending Member States. Therefore, with the availability of 'softer' or informal options, there is hardly anything that cannot be done outside the framework of TBR. In that case, should the TBR procedure be abandoned altogether? To this question, industries seem to have responded negatively; they have opined that TBR is a desirable instrument even though it requires substantial reforms before it can be seen as an attractive option.[107] Past TBR users have seen several advantages in the system.

First, the TBR mechanism empowers industry. It provides a right for private stakeholders to approach the Commission if and when their trade interests are infringed by a foreign practice. It becomes particularly useful for 'industries which have no or marginal political or financial traction to attract the attention of their national government or the Commission'.[108] The mechanism can help such industries secure a share of government's or the Commission's resources for resolving their market access problems. Furthermore, the mechanism is beneficial in situations where other softer or informal options (such as lobbying) have failed to persuade the Commission to act.

Second, similar to the US's Section 301 mechanism, TBR provides for well-defined procedures of dispute management. These unambiguous procedures are advantageous for encouraging and guiding private-public

---

106 European Commission DG-Trade, 'Final Report' (n 92) 38.
107 Ibid 63.
108 Interview with a trade lawyer (audio conferencing) 26 June 2016.

solicitation and resource exchange in a transparent, predictable and well-established manner.

Third, as discussed earlier, TBR has its inbuilt system of regulatory governance. The regulatory checks by the Advisory Committee, the Article 207 Committee and the Council can ensure that the national interests of the EU Member States are not captured and displaced by special private interests.

The revised institutional framework of the 2007 Market Access Strategy has provided an interesting case study for the developed and developing world. The revised Strategy has also reinforced the commitment of the Commission, governments and industries towards the formation of effective partnerships for the resolution of market access problems. In the light of the changes suggested in the Interim Review and the 2007 Strategy, it can be anticipated that the Commission, in the future, will strive to increase the utilisation and effectiveness of its TBR mechanism. In doing so, the Commission officials should review the mechanism in light of the problems discussed in this section.

3.1 THE US AND THE EU EXPERIENCE: A COMPARATIVE LOOK

There are several features that the partnership arrangements in the US and the EU have in common. *First*, both systems confer a legal right on individuals to access their respective governments for the protection of their trade interests. The government entities (USTR and the Commission) have a corresponding obligation to administer and examine legitimate market access complaints filed by the private sector. Put differently, they have a duty to protect the market access interests of their respective industries. Hence, the US and the EU have in place a formal ‘rights and obligations’ system for the formation and functioning of dispute settlement partnerships.

Second, they have established a dedicated institutional framework for the management of disputes and coordination with the private sector. Specialised and independent focal points have been created for the enhancement of public private solicitation during dispute settlement proceedings.

Third, industries in the EU and the US have integrated and coordinated their efforts with the help of trade associations, cooperatives and federations. Most commonly, business entities have approached USTR or the Commission with the help of their trade associations or confederations of industry. Both developed countries undoubtedly realise that an indispensable requirement for an effective PPP mechanism is the presence of an organised private sector community which is willing and able to partner the government during the management of foreign trade disputes.

Fourth, formal partnerships in the US and the EU have frequently been accompanied by informal procedures such as lobbying, political campaigning and pressure-building techniques. As described by an EU Commission official, '[t]he initial interaction, in practice, takes place through an informal process . . . the channel through which industry contacts the Commission is not necessarily formal, and is often not formal. It can simply be through an email, a letter, or a meeting'. As discussed previously, the industries and the government departments both in the US and the EU have shown an inclination towards informal procedures over formal ones. At the same time, their formal systems of PPP, though infrequently used, have not been completely abandoned. This is mainly because they have certain undisputable benefits as compared to the mechanisms that lack a system of 'rights and obligations'.

Amidst these commonalities, it is important to note that the EU's TBR is different from the US's Section 301 procedure in many respects. *First*, as the European Commission is a member-driven commission, its Member States can interfere and impede the Commission's endeavours relating to investigation or litigation of a trade barrier through qualified majority voting at the Council. On the other hand, the US Congress Committees can call on the USTR officials to justify their actions and proceedings relating to the management of trade disputes. They can, in very rare situations, issue legislation to force USTR to act in a certain manner if they are not satisfied with USTR's justification. Hence, the different nature of political frameworks in the US and the EU results in varied regulatory procedures.

Second, Shaffer observes that the US business entities are, as compared to the EU business entities, more 'aggressive' while approaching and persuading USTR and Congress to act for the protection of their economic interests.[109] Moreover, USTR, as compared to the Commission, is much more explicit in receiving assistance from the affected industries and overtly relying on their resources throughout the dispute settlement proceedings. As initially seen in the previous chapter, this can mainly be attributed to the state of the political economy in the US.

Third, USTR is under a mandatory obligation to initiate a formal bilateral or multilateral action in cases of violations (and sometimes

---

[109] Shaffer, *Defending Interests* (n 29) 102.

in non-violation cases as well) where no agreement or settlement has been reached within a stipulated time limit. No such mandatory action requirement is imposed on the European Commission, and it has complete discretion on the issues of initiating, terminating or suspending actions.

Fourth, the Special and Super 301 procedures, with the help of their 'Watch List' or 'Priority Watch List', are allegedly used unilaterally by the US as pressurising devices against offending Member States engaged in unfair, unreasonable, discriminatory or illegal foreign trade practices. The TBR procedure, on the other hand, has no such compelling or pressurising impact. Hence, unlike the Section 301 mechanism, TBR is not notoriously known and criticised for its unilateralism.

Notwithstanding these differences, transatlantic partnerships have frequently been formed between the two developed countries. Overlooking their own trade rivalries, the EU and the US have formed public-private or private-private cross-border partnerships to challenge the practices of third party countries wherever their interests have coincided. Although their national governments have shown some reluctance to working together, private stakeholders in these countries have formed frequent alliances to protect their overlapping and converging interests.[110] For example, during the cases of *Japan – Alcoholic Beverages* and *Korea – Alcoholic Beverages*, the US spirits association (DISCUS) was coordinating and working together with the European-based Scotch Whisky Association during pre-litigation, litigation and post-litigation stages of dispute settlement.

The US and EU private law firms have also worked together during the investigation, preparation and litigation of WTO disputes. Additionally, private firms and trade associations have, at times, 'bypassed' their national governments to form partnerships with public authorities in foreign jurisdictions. For example, certain US trade associations have established foreign offices in Brussels to lobby and informally coordinate with the Commission officials at Brussels. These cross-border interactions have led to the formation of transatlantic public private partnerships between the public and private sector entities in the EU and the US. Transatlantic partnership strategy does not fall within the scope of this book, and hence it will not be discussed in the following chapters. However, it is an interesting capacity-building approach that deserves attention by researchers and policymakers in the future.

---

[110] Ibid 139. (The author notes that 'large firms have interests that extend well beyond the domestic sphere'.)

4. Handling of WTO disputes: China's experience

China presents the contrast of being an emerging world leader in international trade and a developing country beset with challenges that are similar to those of other developing countries. This developing superpower is one of the most active DSU users among developing country members of WTO. From January 1995 to January 2017, China has acted as a complainant in 15 cases, as a respondent in 39 cases, and as a third party in 135 cases. These numbers show that China, in different capacities, has participated in 189 cases out of a total of 520 cases filed at WTO DSU during this period. Hence, in one way or the other, it has participated in over 36 per cent of the cases filed at WTO.

It is the first and the only developing Member State which has, through legal, institutional and procedural reforms, established a formalised mechanism of PPP. The formalisation of public private coordination, along with other strategies including recurring participation as a third party participant and building of domestic trade law expertise, affirms China's commitment towards building WTO dispute settlement capacity at the domestic level. Its perception and approach towards resolving trade disputes by way of negotiations vis-à-vis WTO litigations has also undergone a radical change. This transitioning outlook of the government and industry in China also contributes in making this chapter an attention-grabbing part of the book.[1]

With the advent of 'marketisation' and 'open door policy' in China, its government has realised the need to coordinate with its private sector for the effective management of trade disputes, and this has been evident since the very first year of China's accession to WTO. In 2002, an official from the Ministry of Commerce (MOFCOM) expressed this transitioning outlook as he observed that '. . . the government and firms should actively

[1] Xiaojun Li, 'Understanding China's Behavioral Change in the WTO Dispute Settlement System: Power, Capacity, and Normative Constraints in Trade Adjudication' (2012) 52(6) *Asian Survey: University of California Press* 1111.

collect information on the developments in foreign trade policy as well as trade-related measures currently in force or which might be adopted.'[2] The statement shows that government-industry cooperation has become 'an important pre-condition' in China's 'battle against trade barriers'.[3] There is an increasing perception amongst government officials that public private cooperation has the potential to improve the domestic analytical skills and litigation capacity that are required for defending the country's WTO rights.[4]

In short, the combination of China's expanding foreign trade, its developing nature, the evolution of its dispute management approach and the legal and institutional transformations it has undergone to enforce its WTO rights has made China a very interesting case study from the perspective of this book. This chapter provides readers with an analysis of different dispute settlement strategies employed by the government and industries in China. In particular, it provides readers with answers to the following pertinent questions:

1. How has China strengthened its WTO DSU participation?
2. What have been the benefits of engaging the private sector in the intergovernmental process of WTO dispute settlement?
3. What has been the nature and extent of dispute settlement partnership arrangements formed in China? In other words, how have the industries and the government exchanged resources during the management of trade disputes?
4. Are there any problems with China's dispute management approach that might impede the formation and functioning of effective PPP arrangements? If so, what are these problems?
5. Which features have cost-effectively enhanced China's dispute settlement capacity, and which ones have been ineffective or problematic? Can any of its capacity-building features be viably considered by other developing countries?

---

[2] Wang Shichun, 'Yingdui Maoyi Bilei de Duice Jianyi' ('Strategies for Dealing with Trade Barriers'), *Renmin Ribao* (*People's Daily*) 27 May 2002. (As cited in Henry Gao, 'Taking Justice into Your Own Hand: The TBI Mechanism in China' (2010) 44 *Journal of World Trade* 633, 636).

[3] Ibid.

[4] Interview with an official, Permanent Mission of People's Republic of China to WTO, Geneva, Switzerland, 17 September 2013; interview with an international trade law scholar, Xiamen Academy of International Economic Law (audio conferencing) 6 December 2013.

1.1 LAWS, PROCEDURES AND INSTITUTIONS: MANAGEMENT OF FOREIGN TRADE DISPUTES IN CHINA

1.1.1 Legal Framework

China is a unique example of a national emerging economy that has undergone a transition from being a centrally planned to a market economy. From being a closed and state-run economy, it has become the largest recipient of foreign direct investment among developing countries and the most rapidly emerging player in international trade.[5] Since its accession to WTO in 2001, China has lowered its trade barriers and opened its market with a series of sweeping economic reforms that include the creation of non-state-owned models of organisation, the emergence of joint-venture business models, and wholly foreign and private enterprises.[6] However, its single-party governance, engrained with the remnants of authoritarianism and socialism, continues to interact with and regulate the industries.

In an effort to reduce state intervention in business affairs and pursue the objectives of its 'open door policy', China has moved from a highly centralised to a decentralised form of political governance. This has been done by vesting more powers in its provincial, state and local authorities and reducing the powers of the central government. However, the increasing political power of local authorities in China has created another problem; that is, the local governments have received extensive powers to intervene and control the affairs of industries.[7] To reduce this intervention, the central government has recentralised some of its powers. Hence, when it comes to the management of foreign trade issues, China has employed a mixed approach. The approach is partly centralised because it confers all powers of investigation and decision-making relating to WTO disputes on the Ministry of Commerce. However, the management of issues relating to trade defence remedies, foreign direct investments and

---

[5] For discussion on China's 'open door policy' and economic reforms, see Lawrence J Lau, 'Gain Without Pain: Why Economic Reforms in China Worked' in Gungwu Wang & John Wong (eds), *China's Political Economy* (Singapore: Singapore University Press 1998) 43.

[6] For a discussion on China's economic reforms and the nature of its political economy, see Hiroki Takeuchi, 'Political Economy of Trade Protection: China in the 1990s' (2013) 3 *International Relations of the Asia-Pacific* 1, 2–3.

[7] For discussion on objectives of political decentralisation and need for recentralisation in economic affairs, see Zheng Yongnian, 'Will China Become More Democratic? A Realistic View of China's Democratisation' (1998) *China's Political Economy* 167, 181.

other related matters are decentralised as the powers to handle them are allocated among national, state, provincial and local authorities.

The remnants of Confucianism in China have created a psychological divide between the government officials (who were often referred to as 'masters' or 'rulers') and private individuals (who were referred to as 'subjects'). Due to this artificially created psychological fence, private entities in China may still find it difficult to approach the government, more so in the absence of a well-defined procedure of interaction. China has tried to minimise the impact of this impediment with the establishment of the Trade Barrier Investigation Mechanism[8] (TBIM), as it confers a right on the individual[9] to petition MOFCOM[10] if its trade interests are infringed by a foreign practice.[11] The Rules, on the other hand, impose a legal obligation on MOFCOM to administer and examine such petitions, and investigate those that are legitimate.[12] In this manner, China has followed the PPP approach developed and practised by the US and the EU.

Domestic firms or associations that are affected by a foreign measure may file a petition with MOFCOM.[13] The ministry can launch a trade barrier investigation on either being petitioned by an individual or on its own initiative.[14] Once a petition (along with its supporting documents) is received, MOFCOM becomes obliged to examine the petition and make a determination on pursuance or non-pursuance of the matter within 60

[8] Officially known as PRC Investigation Rules of Foreign Trade Barrier, the mechanism was introduced in 2002 as the Provisional Rules. Revised rules were issued on 1 July 2004 and were known as the 'Rules on Foreign Trade Barrier Investigation'. They took effect on 1 March 2005. (Hereinafter, referred to as the 'TBI Rules'). Full translated text accessed 15 October 2016 at <http://co2.mofcom.gov.cn/aarticle/chinalaw/foreigntrade/200503/20050300029747.html>. The relevant arts are arts 1–37 of the Investigation Rules of Foreign Trade Barrier (2005).

[9] They are referred to as applicants, and they can either be legal or natural persons, domestic enterprises, domestic industries or organisations. Details provided in TBI Rules, art 5.

[10] It was originally known as the Ministry of Foreign Trade and Economic Cooperation (MOFTEC). It was restructured in 2003 as the Ministry of Commerce of the People's Republic of China (MOFCOM).

[11] See TBI Rules, arts 5 and 6.

[12] TBI Rules, art 10 states that 'Ministry of Commerce *should* examine the application materials and make the decision on starting an investigation or not within 60 days at the receipt of the application letter and relevant evident materials' (emphasis added). Art 4 states that the 'Ministry of Commerce *may* place the case on file for trade barrier investigation on its free will as it deems necessary' (emphasis added).

[13] TBI Rules, art 5.

[14] TBI Rules, art 4.

days.[15] A trade barrier investigation, if launched, is normally concluded within six months (with the possibility of extension for three additional months) from the date of determining its launch.[16] If the investigation concludes that the foreign measure in question constitutes a trade barrier, MOFCOM will determine the appropriate course of action for the removal of the barrier. In such circumstances, MOFCOM may decide to initiate bilateral consultations with the offending Member State, or may invoke the provisions of WTO DSM, or may even raise the issue at the WTO Committee meetings, or employ any other appropriate measure.[17]

China's TBIM contains certain provisions similar to those of the EU's TBR and the US's Section 301 mechanism. These provisions guide the private applicants and government administrators in discharging their rights and obligations. Some of these provisions are of the following nature:

1. Certain provisions guide the applicants on the procedure of filing petitions.[18]
2. A number of provisions guide the administrators on receiving and examining the petitions, and investigating those that are legitimate.[19]
3. One of the provisions relaxes the standard of evidential proofs and documents required of the applicants as it gives them the option to request a waiver in the case of inability to provide the required evidence.[20]
4. There are provisions that require the government to maintain confidentiality if the same has been requested by the applicant.[21]
5. A provision allows the investigating unit to constitute an expert consultative committee for seeking advice and assistance during investigations.[22]
6. Other provisions lay down procedures for termination of proceedings, publication of determinations, issuing statement of reasons, withdrawal of complaints, launch of actions, decision-making and determination of the appropriate course of action.[23]

---

15 TBI Rules, art 10.
16 TBI Rules, arts 18 and 32.
17 TBI Rules, art 33.
18 TBI Rules, arts 6, 7 and 8.
19 TBI Rules, arts 10, 11, 12, 13 and 16.
20 TBI Rules, art 8.
21 TBI Rules, arts 23 and 24.
22 TBI Rules, art 20.
23 The relevant provisions are TBI Rules, arts 1–33.

The TBIM has therefore provided a formal route for the private sector to approach its government if and when its interests require protection. It has built a legal interface between the two sectors, which in a way also facilitates the government to approach the concerned industry in situations where access to additional resources is required.

1.1.2 Institutional and Procedural Framework

Multiple public and private sector institutions are responsible for the management of foreign trade disputes. For example, while the Bureau of Fair Trade for Import and Export (BOFT) is primarily responsible for conducting trade barrier investigations, the Department of Treaty and Law under the Ministry of Commerce is responsible for coordinating with the private sector, for decision-making and for the preparation and litigation of WTO cases. A diagrammatic illustration of the existing institutional framework is provided in Figure 4.1.

As shown Figure 4.1, it is MOFCOM that is chiefly responsible for the management of foreign trade disputes. Under MOFCOM, the two concerned units are the Department of WTO Affairs and the Department of Treaty and Law. MOFCOM, with the help of these departments (and externally hired professionals), performs its core functions relating to the protection of WTO rights. These functions may include, but are not limited to: international negotiations, monitoring of trade barriers, internal and external consultations, preparation and presentation of WTO cases, and determination of appropriate actions. The Department of WTO Affairs is responsible for conducting multilateral and bilateral trade negotiations, along with other international trade-related functions. Concurrently, it also functions as China's WTO Notification and Inquiry Center.

The WTO Law Division, under the Department of Treaty and Law, is specifically responsible for managing China's participation at WTO DSM. The lawyers working at the WTO Law Division are responsible for preparing and litigating cases at WTO. Depending upon the subject matter of the case, the Division coordinates with subject-specific public sector departments during different stages of dispute settlement. Interestingly, the lawyers at the Division have developed a practice of working in pairs with the externally hired (mostly overseas) legal counsels during the preparation and presentation of WTO cases. MOFCOM has consistently hired overseas law firms and required them to work with its domestic lawyers. For example, in *China – Intellectual Property Rights*, MOFCOM hired Hogan Lovells

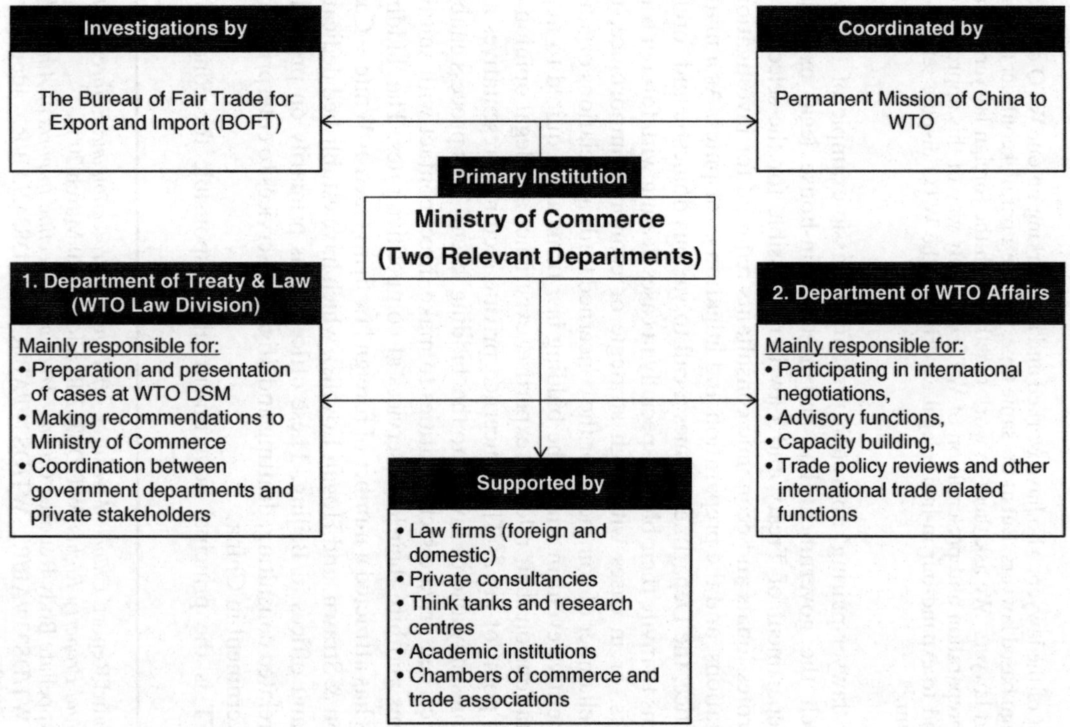

Figure 4.1 Institutional framework in China

(US-based law firm) and King & Wood (China-based law firm).[24] In *China – Auto Parts*, Steptoe & Johnson (US-based law firm) and Hylands Law Firm (China-based law firm) were hired in parallel by MOFCOM.[25] This strategy is explained by an official representative in the following words.

> Most of the lawyers who have worked and are working on our WTO cases are foreign based lawyers. But at the same time, we give a parallel contract to China based lawyers. We ask them to work together with the foreign lawyers during the preparation and presentation of WTO cases. By way of this approach, we intend to expand our in-house legal expertise in the WTO dispute settlement system.[26]

This 'lawyer-pairing' approach presents a classic example of the way in which the government has enhanced its in-house legal expertise. The Department of Treaty and Law is responsible for the selection of legal professionals and economic consultants required for investigations, consultations, and the preparation and litigation of disputes. As a matter of practice, the Department issues a call to various domestic and foreign law firms to invite their bids. Especially in cases dealing with foreign trade remedies, or in cases with high strategic or economic importance, the related chamber of commerce or the concerned trade associations organise a competitive event in which the bidding law firms are required to make presentations on their relevant expertise, experience and legal opinion on a given point of law.[27] The concerned private sector representatives and companies may also be invited to the 'bidding' event. This process enables the concerned private sector entities to make direct contact with suitable law firms and hire their legal services at competitive rates. The 'bidding' process has attracted a number of foreign law firms (such as White & Case, Winston & Strawn, and Hogan Lovells), which have established dedicated teams and offices in Beijing. These offices focus primarily on providing WTO-related consulting, drafting and litigation services to enterprises and the government in China.

BOFT is the principal government unit responsible for conducting

---

[24] Panel Report, *China – Measures Affecting the Protection and Enforcement of Intellectual Property Rights*, WT/DS362/R, adopted 20 March 2009.

[25] Appellate Body Reports, *China – Measures Affecting Imports of Automobile Parts*, WT/DS339/AB/R, WT/DS340/AB/R, WT/DS342/AB/R, adopted 12 January 2009.

[26] Interview with an official, Permanent Mission of China to WTO (n 4).

[27] Pasha L Hsieh, 'China's Development of International Economic Law and WTO Legal Capacity Building' (2010) 13(4) *Journal of International Economic Law* 997, 1023.

foreign trade barrier investigations. BOFT investigates the foreign trade measures that infringe business interests of the complaining or affected industries. It conducts trade barrier investigations through a combination of methods: it collects information through questionnaires; it conducts public hearings, private sector consultations, expert consultations and field research; and it organises joint public-private workshops. It is therefore considered as a focal point, responsible for conducting investigations and consultations with private stakeholders.

The Permanent Mission of China to WTO also plays an active role as it provides the government with relevant information concerning substantive WTO rules and procedures. It helps the government to understand the substantive requirements of cases in light of the WTO provisions and precedents, and it advises the government on the potential difficulties it may face while litigating the issue or conducting consultations. It also serves as a focal point of contact between its government, the government of other Member States involved in the matter, the WTO Secretariat, and the WTO Dispute Settlement Body. As compared to a number of other developing countries, China's WTO Mission is relatively well-staffed, forthcoming and responsive.[28]

The establishment of think tanks in China has also facilitated the process of public-private exchange. Some of these prominent think tanks are the Shanghai WTO Affairs Consultation Centre, the Beijing WTO Affairs Centre, the Shenzhen WTO Affairs Centre, and the China-WTO Dispute Settlement Mechanism Centre. These centres provide training in WTO laws, and also offer advisory services to small and medium-sized companies concerning the use of government resources. They organise seminars and conferences for the dissemination of WTO knowledge among students and trade officials working with the government and industries. They also assist private companies and the government in monitoring and identifying trade barriers and conducting domestic legal proceedings such as anti-dumping or anti-subsidy investigations.

WTO-related scholarship and teaching have also gained momentum in China.[29] The Chinese Society of International Economic Law at Xiamen University, for example, has been instrumental in disseminating international trade-related legal training to practitioners, government

---

[28] Observed during the discussions and semi-structured interviews the author has conducted with Mission officials.

[29] Interview with an international trade law scholar (n 4). (The interviewee notes that the 'WTO courses have occupied a significant place in the discipline of law, and doctoral research is being promoted by the Academy in trade related disciplines.')

officials, private sector entities and students. Moreover, academics from prestigious learning and research institutions are often invited by the government to present their opinion and analysis relating to international trade matters. WTO-related training activities are also conducted by the Ministry of Justice and the Supreme People's Court of China with the aim of disseminating WTO awareness and expertise. These training sessions are conducted jointly by foreign and domestic experts, and they are mainly focused on the country's academic development in respect to WTO laws.[30]

The government has also strengthened its legal expertise and understanding through its third party participation in WTO litigations. As a third party participant in 135 disputes out of a total of 520 disputes filed at DSU (as of January 2017), it has closely observed WTO consultation and litigation proceedings, and as a result, obtained a better understanding of how the disputes are adjudicated by the Panels and the Appellate Body. This 'learning by observation' approach has further enhanced the WTO law expertise within the government departments and local law firms in China.

2.1 PUBLIC PRIVATE COORDINATION: ANALYSIS OF SELECTED TRADE DISPUTES

This section introduces and analyses two trade disputes that were conducted through TBIM in China. It describes the manner in which the public and private sector agencies coordinated in these disputes, and the extent to which they acted in accordance with the TBIM provisions. It also identifies the characteristics of TBIM that have contributed to the building of dispute settlement capacity in a cost-effective manner.

2.1.1 Japan – Quotas on Laver

The first attempt of the private sector to approach MOFCOM through TBIM is noted in *Japan – Quantitative Restrictions on Laver*. In this dispute, China accused Japan of maintaining a discriminatory quota regime on the importation of laver (a type of edible seaweed). China alleged that Japan's practice disqualified its laver exports from entering the laver markets in Japan. After receiving a petition from the laver industry, trade barrier

---

30 Han Liyu & Henry Gao, 'China's experience in utilising the WTO Dispute Settlement Mechanism' in Gregory C Shaffer and Ricardo Melendez-Ortiz (eds), *Dispute Settlement at the WTO: The Developing Country Experience* (Cambridge University Press 2010) 145.

investigations were formally launched in the matter. The DSU provisions were not invoked in the present instance as Japan withdrew the challenged measure during bilateral consultations.[31]

The main TBI applicant in this matter was the Jiangsu Laver Association. The Association was established to pool the resources possessed by the affected companies, and to represent the business interests of these companies to the government in an integrated manner. The Association challenged the laver import quota system of Japan on the ground that it violated the WTO non-discrimination obligations. It petitioned MOFCOM and urged that an investigation in the matter should be launched. On receiving the petition, MOFCOM examined the legitimacy of the complaint and initiated its first formal trade barrier investigation in February 2004.[32]

An investigation was subsequently carried out by BOFT. It notified the formal launch of investigation to the applicant and the government of the offending Member State.[33] The notice of launch was subsequently published in the Official Gazette. Through this notification, BOFT sought comments and inputs from the interested parties. It collected the relevant information from the government and the private sector entities through questionnaires, field investigations and hearings. During investigation, it often sought expert opinion from the Bureau of Fisheries of the Ministry of Agriculture, the China Chamber of Commerce of Import and Export of Foodstuffs, Native Produce & Animal By-Products, and the China Aquatic Products Processing and Marketing Association.[34] Alongside, MOFCOM organised several consultative meetings with its counterparts in Japan. It was directly assisted by the Jiangsu Laver Association during these bilateral consultative meetings. Notably, the national delegation of China during bilateral consultations comprised officials from both MOFCOM and the Jiangsu Laver Association.[35]

---

[31] MOFCOM Announcement No 10 of 2005 (as cited in Liyu & Gao (n 30) 162).

[32] The launch of trade barrier investigation was formally announced in Announcement No 16 in line with Interim Rules for Foreign Trade Barrier Investigation on 22 April 2004. (MOFCOM, Network Center, accessed 9 October 2016 at <http://english.mofcom.gov.cn/sys/print.shtml?/newsrelease/significantnews/200503/20050300021005>. Details about the applicant, application filed by the applicant, the investigation procedure and termination of the investigation are available at FDI: Invest in China <http://www.fdi.gov.cn/1800000121_39_1019_0_7.html> accessed 9 October 2016.

[33] MOFCOM Announcement No 65 of 2004 (as cited in Liyu & Gao (n 30) 162).

[34] Gao 'Taking Justice into Your Own Hand' (n 2) 645, 646.

[35] Zhongguo Maoyi Bao, 'Japan Applies Discriminatory Measures against Chinese Laver Products. Chinese Producers Vow to Fight to the End' *China Trade*

Throughout the investigation and consultation meetings, the Jiangsu Laver Association (along with the affected private firms) supplied the required information, evidence and data sheets to MOFCOM. The Association also sent its representatives to Korea and Japan for conducting field research and gathering additional information required by MOFCOM. At the conclusion of its field research, it compiled the information and prepared a detailed factual report. This report was sent to MOFCOM for assisting the process of investigation. The Association also formed an in-house team of trade lawyers to help the participating private entities understand and follow the dispute. These privately hired lawyers also assisted the government lawyers at MOFCOM with legal analysis and investigation of the matter.[36]

Subsequently, on 21 February 2005, Japan announced the replacement of its challenged quota regime with the Global Quota System. This enabled the laver exports from China to enter the markets in Japan. Shortly after this announcement, MOFCOM terminated its trade barrier investigations on 22 April 2005.[37] The termination of the investigation and restoration of China's laver market access together constitute an important landmark as, for the first time in China, the industry utilised the provisions of TBIM and was subsequently successful in resolving the dispute through informal consultations with Japan. The PPP arrangement in this instance better enabled the MOFCOM to negotiate a mutually agreed settlement with Japan, and hence, to self-enforce its WTO rights under the 'shadow of a potential WTO litigation'.[38] TBIM's contribution towards strengthening MOFCOM's conflict-resolution capacity in this case provides a strong inference in favour of the formalised TBIM. In addition, the dispute outlines certain interesting features of the TBIM-enabled PPP arrangements.

First, the industry in the present instance utilised its right to petition the government, and the government departments discharged their respective obligations throughout the process of petitioning, investigation and consultation.

Second, the establishment of the Jiangsu Laver Association and the instrumental role it has played in the present example goes to show that

---

Daily 21 September 2004. (As cited in Gao, 'Taking Justice into Your Own Hand' (n 2) 646).

[36] Interview with an official, Permanent Mission of China to WTO (n 4).

[37] MOFCOM Announcement No 10 of 2005 (cited in Liyu & Gao (n 30) 162).

[38] The instance is referred to as 'litigotiation' by Galanter. For details, see M Galanter, 'Contract in Court; or Almost Everything You May or May Not Want to Know About Contract Litigation' (2001) 3 *Wisconsin Law Review* 577, 579.

an organised private sector is a vital requirement for PPP to function effectively.

Third, the industry in the present instance utilised the representational authority of the government (China being a member of WTO and therefore having the authority to litigate disputes at WTO DSM) for the protection of its exporting interests. On the other hand, MOFCOM enjoyed wider access to the informational resources and legal expertise required for the smooth conduct of investigation and bilateral consultations. Hence, resources were exchanged on a reciprocal basis to eliminate a trade barrier, and the exchange was effective as it enabled MOFCOM to mobilise resources and thereby restore an industry's lost market access.

Fourth, this interaction also demonstrates that the affected private stakeholders are a vital source of commercial information that may be required to investigate a trade barrier. The private sector often has the capacity, motivation and the required pragmatic approach to gather information, for example, through field trips, questionnaires, symposia and global commercial alliances. Hence, PPP approach can be seen as a cost-effective method for gathering information that is required for settling complex trade disputes. However, evidence shows that the benefits of this approach have not been able to stimulate a significant level of interest amongst the industries in China. Until 2010, *Japan – Laver* was the only instance where an industry had invoked TBIM to convey its trade grievances to the government. However, following on, a further TBI application was filed in 2011 by a different industry for a different trade dispute. This is discussed in the following section.

2.1.2 US – Countervailing Measures (China)

The second noted dispute in which the provisions of TBIM were invoked is the *US – Countervailing Measures (China)* case.[39] The China Chamber of Commerce for Import and Export of Machinery and Electronic Products, together with the China New Energy Chamber of Commerce of the All-China Federation of Industry and Commerce, filed a TBI application in October 2011.[40] In November 2011, MOFCOM launched its trade barrier investigation against the US support policies and subsidy programmes which were allegedly granting beneficial treatment to the US local renewable

[39] Appellate Body Report, *United States – Countervailing Duty Measures on Certain Products from China*, WT/DS437/AB/R, adopted 16 January 2015.

[40] Henry Gao, 'Public-Private Partnership: The Chinese Dilemma' (2014) 48(5) *Journal of World Trade* 983, 985.

energy industry. The investigation was conducted by MOFCOM with the assistance of BOFT. MOFCOM found that the US practices supporting wind, solar and hydroelectric energy programmes were in the nature of 'prohibited subsidies' and were therefore violating the WTO Subsidy and Countervailing Measures Agreement and GATT 1994. It also found that the US authorities had imposed countervailing duties on Chinese solar imports. This triggered the dispute further, and the Chinese government immediately launched a formal WTO challenge against the US.

The WTO dispute was known as *United States – Countervailing Duty Measures on Certain Products from China*. China in this dispute alleged that the US practices were in violation of the provisions of GATT 1994, the Agreement on Subsidies and Countervailing Measures (SCM Agreement), and the Protocol of Accession of China to the WTO. China's main contention was that the US anti-subsidy duties were affecting $7.3 billion of exports of solar panels, thermal paper, wind towers and steel wire from China, and thereby violating the WTO rules. The Panel upheld some of China's allegations regarding the inconsistency of the US measures with the SCM Agreement. However, most of the claims made by China against the United States Department of Commerce's (USDOC) findings were fully or partially rejected by the Panel. Both Member States appealed this decision. The Appellate Body Report was issued in favour of China as it reversed those findings of the Panel that recommended that China had not established the alleged WTO-inconsistent practice of USDOC with respect to the SCM Agreement.

This case is an important instance where the concerned industry was visibly active in partnering with the government through the TBI gateway. Trade barrier investigations were launched by MOFCOM on the basis of a written application filed by the local industry associations. The affected companies and associations actively supplied the commercial information to MOFCOM.[41] The companies, through their trade associations, often interacted with MOFCOM and the hired lawyers, as it allowed them to track the progress and legal position of the case. The associations conducted a commercial and legal analysis of the dispute with the help of their technical experts and in-house lawyers. They were therefore fully equipped to provide the government with information, commercial inputs and legal analysis as and when required during investigation and litigation.

Alongside the investigation, the CEOs of the China-based four largest photovoltaic companies established the Solar Energy Promotion Alliance.

---

41 Interview with an official, Permanent Mission of China to WTO (n 4).

The Alliance provided a discussion and information-exchange forum to the affected companies which were looking to restore and expand their depleted exporting interests.[42] The formation of the Alliance by the largest energy companies during the dispute reinforces the argument that an organised private sector is vital for effective protection of economic interests. It also presents a sound example of how affected companies can form alliances and reduce the burden of cost imposed on each of them for the protection of their common exporting interests.

3.1 POTENTIAL CHALLENGES AND LESSONS LEARNT: A CRITICAL LOOK

The investigation results show that the TBIM provisions have only been invoked twice from the year 2002 to 2013;[43] but this marginal utilisation of TBIM should not suggest that the businesses in China have not engaged with MOFCOM in the handling of disputes. On the contrary, a government official confirms that the '. . .private sector through the import and export chambers of commerce and trade associations has frequently participated with the government in the process of dispute settlement.'[44] Gao further confirms that China has increasingly been seeking and receiving assistance from the private sector during the management of trade disputes.[45] These findings indicate that the private sector in China has often approached the government in ways other than the provisions mentioned under TBIM. Several domestic factors lie behind the suggested infrequent utilisation of TBIM.

1. Due to China's non-litigious culture, the route of petitioning the government in a formal manner has often been the last option for business communities in China.[46] The non-litigious culture is very much engrained in the mindset of the entities engaged in doing business and government officials. Litigation, according to the Confucianist-

---

42 Johan Mathews & Hao Tan, 'China's renewable energy revolution has global implications' Clean Technica website article 8 April 2014, accessed 12 June 2014 at <http://cleantechnica.com/2014/04/08/chinas-renewable-energy-revolution-global-implications/>. (The article notes that 'China's energy revolution [. . .] underpins its transformation into the world's largest manufacturing system'.)

43 Gao, 'Public-Private Partnership' (n 40) 984.

44 Interview with an official, Permanent Mission of China to WTO (n 4).

45 Interview with an academic, Singapore Management University (audio conferencing) 24 June 2013.

46 Li, 'Understanding China's Behavioral Change in the WTO Dispute Settlement System (n 1) 1111.

philosophy, . . . causes irreparable harm to relationships and should be pursued as a last resort, or better still, [be] . . . avoided.'[47] Therefore, it has often been observed that an exporter facing trade barriers would prefer to find a new market or a new product, or give up the trade, or change the location of business, or perhaps approach the government in an informal manner, especially if it is losing its market substantially.[48]

China has demonstrated a strong preference towards avoidance of litigation during the initial years of its WTO membership. In the first seven years of its WTO membership (2001–2008), China's participation as a complainant was limited to only three WTO disputes. Moreover, out of 13 complaints filed against China during the same period, eight complaints were settled through negotiations and agreements or were terminated or kept in abeyance. However, the following seven years (2009–2016) tell a very different story, as China has filed 12 WTO complaints during this period. Moreover, from the year 2009 onwards, with an evident increase in China's WTO-related legal capacity, most of the challenges launched against China have also been strongly litigated. This shows that the non-litigious mindset of the government has undergone a radical change.

2. The provisions of TBIM have also imposed an evidential burden on its applicants. Like the EU's TBR complaints and the US's Section 301 petitions, TBI applications have to be drafted in a given manner, and they must accompany the information and evidence required under the Rules.[49] The difficulty of collecting the information and evidential documents at the preliminary stages of a trade barrier dispute has served as a hindrance to the filing of formal TBI petitions. The expense involved in preparing a TBI application and its supporting evidential documents may also be substantial. Hence, in accordance with the findings of the previous chapter, a formal procedure may impose an evidential burden, and hence it may become an unaffordable option, especially for the minimally organised or resource-constrained business entities.

   Hiring external lawyers and consultants for the initial preparation of applications and documents might substantially escalate the cost, and make TBIM an unaffordable and unviable option for most

---

47 X Jiang & S Tan, 'Non-Litigation Tradition in China' (2008) 4 *Legal System and Society* 239.

48 Interview with an official, Permanent Mission of China to WTO (n 4).

49 TBI Rules, arts 7 and 8.

businesses in China. However, Article 9 of the TBI Rules allows MOFCOM to eliminate or reduce this evidential requirement in cases where a legitimate request for waiver is made by the applicant. This can be seen as an effort to strike a balance between the government's need to access information and the industries' need to maintain control of expenditure. This burden-reducing provision can also be considered as a possible solution to minimise the high evidential requirements associated with the EU's TBR and the US's Section 301 mechanisms.

3. Not all industries in China are well-organised. Gao confirms that one of the main reasons for the infrequent utilisation of TBI rules in China is 'the lack of industry associations truly representing the interests of private firms in China'.[50] The country's socialist market economy and nationalistic framework means that both state-owned and non-state-owned enterprises in China continue to be regulated and controlled by the government at national, provincial and local levels. Accordingly, the industry representatives and trade unions in China are also governed and controlled by public sector authorities.

   Most of the industry representative associations are fully constituted and regulated by the provincial or state authorities, and some trade associations and chambers of commerce, though recognised as independent legal entities, are semi-governmental in nature.[51] This is largely because they require the endorsement and constant supervision of certain government authorities for the purposes of registration and functioning. Most industry associations are often staffed with retired government officials who commonly are disconnected from the operational realities of business. Their primary obligation is to assist the government in gathering required resources and regulating the industry. Hence, the nature and composition of trade organisations and the extent of government intervention in their functioning have discouraged private enterprises from joining the representative organisations and turning to them when their trade interests are infringed.

   By contrast, 'new generation' industry associations have now emerged in China with the help of private sector initiatives (the Jiangsu Laver Association being one such association). However, these privately owned associations have different problems. *First*,

---

[50] Gao, 'Taking Justice into Your Own Hand' (n 2) 650.

[51] Regulation on Registration and Administration of Social Organizations [1998] State Council Order No 250, arts 3, 9, 27, 28. For details, see Hao Qian, 'Trade Associations and Private Antitrust Litigation in China' (16 April 2013) 4(1) *CPI Antitrust Chronicle* 2.

they can be dominated and practically governed by a handful of resourceful and influential firms in the sector. *Second*, if they are established by small and medium scale industries, then their activities might get paralysed due to insufficiency of funds or lack of sufficient members willing to make annual contributions. Hence, strategies need to be devised for overcoming these obstacles and for integrating and organising the industries in China.

4. The government has tried to create new avenues for interaction with business entities, but a traditional cultural barrier still draws an invisible line between the government officials and the rest of the people in China. Private individuals still believe that government officials are 'unapproachable entities' as they are equivalent to 'masters' or 'lords'. Unlike governance systems based on 'rule of law', China is closer to the governance model of 'rule by law'. The political climate in China is heavily influenced by its predominant tradition of Confucianism. It means that political and bureaucratic officials cannot be controlled by any institutions and procedures. They control everything. One of the impediments to the utilisation of TBIM is this divide between the rulers and the ruled, which often makes government officials 'non-receptive' to private sector requests.[52] Due to these cultural and psychological impediments, the private sector in China has preferred to find alternative business solutions in situations where foreign practices have diminished their business interests.
5. The private sector may also be discouraged because of the level of discretion granted to MOFCOM in launching investigations under the TBI Rules. The TBI Rules, under Article 4, state that the government *may* initiate the investigations if 'it deems necessary'. Hence, the required investment of resources combined with an element of uncertainty caused by possible governmental discretionary intervention can act as a major deterrent to the filing of formal TBI complaints. However, the government is the guardian of national interests, and it should therefore be able to scrutinise and pursue legitimate applications that it thinks are in the best interest of the nation. In the absence of a similar provision, the government may at times be compelled to pursue disputes that might favour a narrow business interest and infringe upon the wider economic or social interest of the nation.

On the positive side, the government's existing obligations under the TBI Rules to issue a statement of reasons (in case of non-pursuance of an application) and publication of determinations may

[52] Gao, 'Taking Justice into Your Own Hand' (n 2) 649.

offset the discouraging impact of MOFCOM's discretionary right of pursuance or non-pursuance.[53] In addition, a call for public opinion and public hearings (on request) can also be introduced to further counter the problem of the private sector's lack of confidence in the government.[54] Also, a precise description of possible circumstances and reasons for non-pursuance of a matter, set out clearly in a legal text or a rule book, might also enable private stakeholders to develop more confidence and predictability in relation to TBI provisions.

6. Empirical research suggests that the Chinese government, at times, has maintained an element of secrecy in respect of its domestic proceedings and actions taken at WTO. For instance, in the case of *China – Auto Parts*,[55] a legal researcher's request to access the official briefs (filed in the case) was denied by MOFCOM, despite the fact that the WTO Panel had by that time released its Report.[56] The secrecy-favouring approach of MOFCOM, as argued in Chapter 2, can act as a serious deterrent as industries might be unwilling to share their trade knowledge and information with government entities that might act covertly in relation to such matters.
7. The lower status of Foreign Trade Barrier Investigation Rules in China's hierarchal legal system can also be considered as a weakness of the mechanism. The Constitution of the People's Republic of China is the supreme and first tier of the legal system in China.[57] The second tier constitutes the laws enacted by the National People's Congress and its Standing Committee.[58] The third hierarchal tier comprises the regulations issued by the State Council. This is followed by the local

---

53 TBI Rules, arts 14, 17, 26, 29.

54 A similar provision is provided under US Trade Act 1974, ss 302(a)(4) and 305(b)(1)(A) (right to request for public hearings); and also Council Regulation, art 8(6), which states that: 'the Commission shall, on request, give the parties primarily concerned an opportunity to meet, so that opposing views may be presented and any rebuttal argument put forward'. Currently, the TBI Rules do not oblige MOFCOM to hold such public hearings during investigations.

55 Appellate Body Reports, *China – Measures Affecting Imports of Automobile Parts*, WT/DS339/AB/R, WT/DS340/AB/R, WT/DS342/AB/R, adopted 12 January 2009.

56 Liyu & Gao (n 30) 165.

57 Law on Legislation 2000 (promulgated by the Standing Committee of the National People's Congress, 15 March 2000, effective on 1 July 2000) Standing Committee National People's Congress Gaz. 112 (PRC), art 78 (as cited in Junrong Song, 'A Comparative Study on the Trade Barriers Regulation and the Foreign Trade Barrier Investigation Rules' (2007) (4) 41 *Journal of World Trade* 799, 802).

58 Law on Legislation 2000, art 79.

laws and regulations issued by the local People's Congress and its Standing Committee.[59] The lowest tier consists of the local laws issued by the local governments. The regulations issued by the departments of the State Council occupy an equivalent status to that of local laws issued by local governments.[60]

Since MOFCOM is a department of the State Council, the Foreign Trade Barrier Investigation Rules (as they are promulgated by MOFCOM) are subordinate to the Constitution and to the laws and regulations issued by the national government and the State Council. The Rules therefore have to give way to the superior laws in cases where they conflict with the higher hierarchal sources of laws.[61] This arguably reveals an unimportant positioning of TBI Rules in the overall legal system of China, and this situation might also be a contributing factor to the infrequent utilisation of TBI Rules. The hierarchal status can also be seen as a probable reason for the lack of support the TBI Rules receive from other government departments and political institutions.

In addition to these impediments, there are other problems associated with China's DSU participation and the utilisation of TBIM, such as the lack of common law and litigation experience, language constraints, and inadequate internal capacity to ensure compliance with WTO commitments. If these problems impede the functioning of TBIM, how and what made it function effectively in the cases of *Japan – Laver* and *US – Countervailing Measures (China)*? It may be recalled that the case of the Laver Association was exceptional. The seaweed industry had the required political influence on the government. The industry had personal and professional contacts with senior government officials, and it was one of China's main exporting sectors. These favourable circumstances are likely to have enabled the partnership to flourish. In the case of *US – Countervailing Measures (China)*, TBIM could again be invoked as the solar enterprises and other enterprises dealing with renewable energy products in China are equally (or even more) resourceful and influential.[62]

---

59 Law on Legislation 2000, art 80.

60 Law on Legislation 2000, art 82.

61 In cases where the TBI Rules conflict with the higher hierarchal laws, the issue of prevailing law is decided by the State Council. Law on Legislation 2000, art 86.

62 Interview with an official, Permanent Mission of China to WTO (n 4).

4.1 CONCLUDING REMARKS

The evolution of partnership provisions, institutions and procedures in China provides an interesting case study for the developing world. China has learnt from the experiences of active WTO Member States (such as the US and the EU), as it has tried to evolve a formalised PPP mechanism for the management of trade disputes. Its TBIM has enabled MOFCOM to successfully negotiate trade conflicts and conduct trade litigations at WTO DSU. Hence, one could view TBIM as an effective government-industry coordination mechanism. However, it is difficult to reach any definite conclusions regarding its effectiveness as it has not been invoked and utilised frequently. Nevertheless, other capacity-building strategies employed by China and its increasing participation at WTO DSU testify to the fact that China is willing to protect and expand its foreign trade with the help of WTO adjudicatory provisions. China's experience of building legal expertise through third party participation, the bidding process for the selection of lawyers, and the pairing-up of foreign and domestic trade lawyers, can also act as a catalyst for policymakers in other developing countries.

5. Handling of WTO disputes: Brazil's experience

Brazil has emerged as a global leader in international trade. As a part of major trading alliances including WTO, MERCOSUR,[1] G-20,[2] Cairns Group[3] and BRIC,[4] it has played a significant role in bilateral and multilateral trade negotiations. After the United States (US), the European Union (EU) and Canada, Brazil is the fourth most active complainant at WTO DSM, making it the most frequent complainant among developing country members of WTO. From January 1995 to January 2017, it has in different capacities participated in 154 out of 522 cases filed at WTO DSU. Hence, it has participated, in one way or the other, in over 29 per cent of the cases filed at WTO. Moreover, Brazil has gained international repute not only for the quantity but also for the quality of its participation at WTO DSU.

Brazil has witnessed landmark WTO disputes where industries have actively worked with the government during pre-litigation, litigation and post-litigation stages. Unlike the Section 301 mechanism in the US, the TBR process in the EU and the TBIM in China, there is no legal provision in Brazil that confers a right to petition on the individual and imposes a corresponding duty to examine such petitions upon the Brazilian government.[5] For this reason, the nature of PPP formed during WTO

---

1 It is a regional trading bloc in South America. For more information, see MERCOSUR, accessed 8 July 2016 at <http://www.mercosur.int/>.

2 It is an international alliance of economies that collectively accounts for almost 80% of world trade. For more information, see John J Kirton, *G20 Governance for a Globalised World* (Ashgate 2013) 1.

3 It is a coalition of agricultural exporting countries. For details, see The Cairns Group, accessed 8 July 2016 at <http://cairnsgroup.org/Pages/default.aspx>.

4 It is a trading alliance of major emerging market economies. For more information, see The BRICS Post, accessed 10 November 2016 at <http://thebricspost.com>.

5 Interview with an official, Permanent Mission of Brazil to the WTO, Geneva, Switzerland, 16 September 2013. ('The private sector does not have a piece of legislation or regulation or a list of guidelines to follow or to refer to while approaching the government for the protection of its trade interests.')

litigations in Brazil is largely informal. However, it may not be entirely accurate to label it as 'purely informal' as the government has created a framework to facilitate such partnerships with dedicated institutions and procedures. The Brazilian PPP arrangement may therefore be described as a system which has the elements of both a formal mechanism (as it resembles the US, the EU and China's PPP in respect of its defined institutional procedures) and an informal coordination (as it operates without a legal or a regulatory framework).

An examination and review of this 'semi-formal' or 'imperfectly informal' form of partnership in Brazil makes this chapter an indispensable part of this book as it introduces readers to a different form of partnership system.[6] By analysing the characteristics, weaknesses and the capacity-building potential of a PPP approach that is not based on a system of 'rights and obligations', the present chapter expands the horizons of this investigative work. In particular, this chapter provides readers with answers to the following pertinent questions:

1. How has Brazil established a 'semi-formal' form of dispute settlement partnership system?
2. How is this system different from the ones examined in the previous chapters?
3. How have the industries and the government in Brazil, in practice, coordinated during the management of trade disputes?
4. Which features of its PPP system have cost-effectively enhanced Brazil's dispute settlement capacity, and which ones have been ineffective or problematic?
5. Can other developing countries learn anything from the Brazilian dispute settlement partnership experience?

1.1 INSTITUTIONAL AND PROCEDURAL FRAMEWORKS: MANAGEMENT OF FOREIGN TRADE DISPUTES IN BRAZIL

Brazil enjoys a presidential representative democracy with a multiparty system of governance. It is run by a federal government, along with multiple states, federal districts and municipalities. However, it is important

---

[6] This chapter is adapted from Amrita Bahri, 'Handling WTO Disputes with the Private Sector: The Triumphant Brazilian Experience' (2016) 50(4) *Journal of World Trade* 641.

to note that Brazil, before becoming a democracy, followed an authoritarian form of governance with a largely state-owned or state-controlled economic sector. In the past three decades, it has undergone a huge transition from being an authoritarian to a democratic nation. Although it has moved from a closed and protected economy to an open market economy with a capitalistic set-up, the remnants of its pre-1990s socialistic framework and its 'Import Substitution Industrialisation' policy are still visible in the existing regulations governing international trade.[7] The Brazilian government continues to control many strategic sectors of the economy, including power generation and telecommunications. Highly complex and detailed sets of rules still govern the registration and operation of businesses.[8] However, at the same time, the left-wing governments (which have led the country since 2003 and were originally known for their state interventionist and nationalist policies) have used 'privatisation' and 'deregulation' as tools to move towards a moderately free market economy.[9]

Brazil has expanded its economy through international trade activities pursued mostly by private business entities, while the government has retained some powers to regulate foreign trade to achieve the ends of overall development and national welfare. This shift from the 'Import Substitution Industrialisation' policy to 'export-oriented' trade-liberalising policies, which coincided with the establishment of WTO in the 1990s, created new challenges and opportunities for the country. In response to these changes, the government underwent a massive reorganisation. In particular, to respond to the demands of multilateral trade obligations after the establishment of WTO, and more particularly, to manage foreign trade disputes under the rule-oriented WTO DSM, Brazil established a specialised 'three pillar' dispute settlement mechanism.

---

[7] 'Import Substitution Industrialisation' (ISI) was the cornerstone economic policy of the country since the 1930s. Its aim was to protect the domestic industry through local production of high value goods and services and reduction of importation. It was facilitated through state-owned industries, infrastructure investment and subsidies granted to domestic firms. For details, see Carlos Pio, 'Brazil: Political and Economic Lessons from Democratic Transitions' (June 2013) *Civil Society, Markets and Democratic Initiatives* 1, accessed 9 July 2016 at <http://i.cfr.org/content/publications/images/csmd_ebook/PathwaystoFreedom/ChapterPreviews/PathwaystoFreedomBrazilPreview.pdf>.

[8] For example, the Labor Laws regulate the operation of businesses in Brazil as they seek to protect the welfare of workers. (Consolidated Labor Laws (CLT) Decree-law 5452 (1943), arts 578 and 591). Also see the Constitution of the Federative Republic of Brazil, arts 7 and 8.

[9] Pio (n 7) 4.

Shaffer's work indicates that the Brazilian 'three pillar' dispute settlement mechanism 'consists of a specialized WTO dispute settlement division located in the capital, Brasilia (the "first pillar"), coordination between this unit and Brazil's WTO mission in Geneva (the "second pillar"), and coordination between both of these entities and Brazil's private sector, as well as law firms and economic consultants funded by the private sector (the "third pillar")'.[10] Coordination between these three pillars has better enabled the government to manage trade disputes with the help of public private coordination. A more detailed and comprehensive illustration of this institutional framework is provided in Figure 5.1.[11]

The Ministry of Foreign Affairs appears at the heart of this illustration. Since the pre-WTO era, it has been responsible for managing international trade matters, as the 'Union' (which is the official expression used to refer to the Federal Government) under the Constitution of Brazil oversees all international affairs.[12] The Ministry's long-standing interest and expertise accumulated over the past decades in international trade are the main reasons behind its continued central position in WTO matters including dispute settlement. A specialised dispute settlement established under the Ministry, the 'General Coordination of Disputes' (CGC), is responsible for seeking coordination with the private sector, initial examination of disputes, and presentation of cases at WTO DSM. The private sector in Brazil assists CGC during various stages of dispute settlement, mainly with the help of trade associations, consultancies and law firms.

The dispute settlement process is most commonly initiated when a company, either through its trade association or on its own, approaches the Ministry of Foreign Affairs or the Ministry of Trade and Industry (or its subject-specific ministry) to convey or informally discuss a foreign trade barrier. Companies and trade associations, with the passage of time, have realised the importance of approaching the government with a well-researched and documented application (or legal memorandum) to request a governmental action in a matter.[13] This practice of filing well-documented

---

[10] Gregory C Shaffer, Michelle Raton Sanchez Badin & Barbara Rosenberg, 'The Trials of Winning at the WTO: What Lies Behind Brazil's Success' (2008) 41(2) *Cornell International Law Journal* 383, 423.

[11] For detailed procedural analysis, see PDM Veiga, 'Trade Policy-making in Brazil: Changing Patterns in State-Civil Society Relationship' in Mark Halle & Robert Wolfe (eds), *Process Matters: Sustainable Development and Domestic Trade Transparency* (Geneva, IISD 2007) 143, 178.

[12] The Constitution of the Federative Republic of Brazil, art 21.

[13] Interview with an official, Permanent Mission of Brazil to the WTO, Geneva, Switzerland, 16 September 2013.

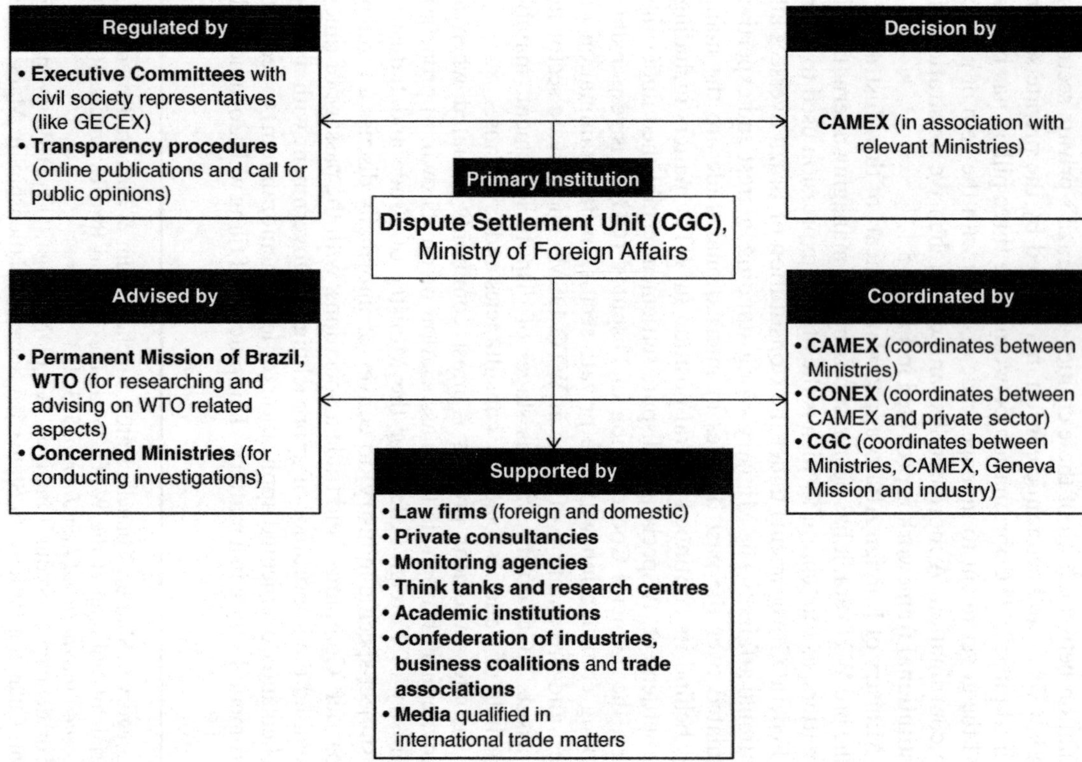

Figure 5.1 Institutional framework in Brazil

and substantiated applications by affected private stakeholders and the government's initiation of investigation upon receiving such complaints draws similarities between the Brazilian PPP arrangements and the ones formed between the European Commission and the affected European businesses with the help of their formal TBR mechanism.

On administering a complaint from the private sector, or on identifying a barrier *suo moto*, CGC conducts an initial examination of the legal and economic viability of pursuing a dispute. Based on the findings of the preliminary examination, CGC refers the dispute to the concerned unit within the Ministry of Foreign Affairs, and to other concerned ministries, such as the Ministry of Development, Industry, Trade, Agriculture, or others. It is at this stage that the concerned ministries carry out a detailed investigation, wherein they further examine in detail the legal, economic and political viability of pursuing the dispute. They prepare an investigation report, along with their recommendations and relevant information, which is subsequently forwarded to an interministerial department known as the Inter-Ministerial Foreign Trade Chamber (CAMEX).[14] Based on the recommendations provided by the ministries, CAMEX decides whether the government should pursue the dispute at all, and if so, bilaterally or multilaterally. If dispute settlement provisions under any of the concerned trade agreements are invoked, CAMEX decides the appropriate course of action required at the pre-litigation, litigation and post-litigation stages of a dispute.[15]

Once CAMEX decides to pursue a dispute, CGC becomes obliged to launch consultations with the offending Member State(s), and if required, to prepare and present a given case at WTO. From this stage onwards, CGC officials work closely with the private counsels (frequently hired by the industry) and the concerned private sector representatives. Moreover, CGC 'encourages companies to hire counsel' and it often has 'conditioned the pursuit' of filing a WTO complaint on the private sector's willingness to finance the counsel's fees.[16] It also shares updates and information about the settlement of disputes with the concerned ministries and the officials at its Permanent Mission to WTO. In this manner, CGC serves as a contact point for the government, the Permanent Mission of Brazil

---

[14] CAMEX is the counselling chamber of the government, and it is also known as the Foreign Trade Chamber. It comprises several government departments and is assisted by a common secretariat. For more information, see Ministry of Development, Industry and Foreign Trade, CAMEX, accessed 24 August 2016 at <http://www.mdic.gov.br/sitio/interna/interna.php?area=1&menu=1920>.

[15] Interviews with two officials, Permanent Mission of Brazil to the WTO, Geneva, Switzerland, 16 September 2013.

[16] Shaffer, Badin & Rosenberg (n 10) 431.

to WTO, participating business entities and private counsels working towards the removal of a trade barrier.

CAMEX is constituted under the Ministry of Development, Industry and Foreign Trade, along with several other ministries.[17] It interlinks these departments and coordinates issues relating to trade (including the settlement of foreign trade disputes) among different government departments. This interministerial approach allows the Brazilian government to act in a concerted, integrated and informed manner. An institutional link between CAMEX and the business community is provided with the establishment of the Private Sector Consultative Council (CONEX), a unit situated within CAMEX. It comprises around 20 private sector representatives, and they mainly focus on trade policy issues for export promotion. CONEX gathers required information from the concerned business entities as and when required during various stages of dispute settlement.[18] This development is similar to the EU's creation of the Market Access Advisory Committee, which provides an institutional interface between the EU Commission and the business communities in Europe.

The private sector in Brazil has also organised itself with the help of well-funded trade associations and large individual companies. The emergence of strong trade associations is an exemplary development, which is closely supported by the Brazilian Constitution. The Brazilian Constitution and the Consolidated Labor Laws contain various favourable provisions supporting the functioning of trade associations. For example, they provide for an annual tax, known as 'Union Contributions', which is mandatorily levied on employers.[19] The union contributions are distributed among trade associations and confederations with the purpose of funding their representative activities. The compulsory statutory provisions for financing trade associations have established 'some of the wealthiest business associations in Latin America'.[20]

---

17 Other ministries are: Ministry of State Chief of Staff; Foreign Affairs; Farm, Agriculture, Livestock and Supply; Planning, Budget and Management; Land Development.

18 World Trade Organization, 'Trade Policy Review: Brazil' Report of the Secretariat [WT/TPR/S/140] 1 November 2004, 19, 37, accessed 6 July 2016 at <http://www.wto.org/english/tratop_e/tpr_e/tp239_e.htm>.

19 It is provided in Consolidated Labor Laws (CLT) Decree-law 5452 (1943), arts 578 and 591; Constitution of the Federative Republic of Brazil, art 8. For details, see CNI: Contributions from Industry, accessed 22 October 2016 at <http://www.cni.org.br/portal/data/pages/FF80808121B629230121B62A6BCF0345.htm>.

20 S Haggard, S Maxfield & BR Schneider, 'Theories of Business and Business-State Relations' in S Maxfield & BR Schneider (eds), *Business and the State in Developing Countries* (Cornell University Press 1997) 36, 45.

Think tanks and research centres in Brazil also play an important role in matters of international trade. Some of them have been created by entrepreneurs for advising, informing and assisting the government and industry on various trade issues. For instance, one of the leading think tanks in Brazil is the Institute of Studies on Trade and International Negotiations (ICONE), which provides technical analysis and research support relating to agriculture and agribusiness to the government and the agriculture industry. Some of the think tanks are directly linked to universities and are run by academics. For example, the Brazilian Center for International Relations (CEBRI), founded by a group of academics, government officials and businessmen, is a non-profit-based think tank that seeks to achieve coordination between public and private entities. It is mainly engaged in sponsoring research programmes, commissioning studies on international issues, and organising roundtables, symposia and debates. It is also interesting to note that the Center is fully sponsored by exporting companies, trade associations and private law firms in Brazil.

Think tanks, trade associations and law firms have created several internship opportunities for students, trade lawyers, private sector and government officials. These internships are offered at various locations. The Ministry of Foreign Affairs, in association with the Law Firm Study Center, offers a four-month internship programme at the Brazilian WTO Mission to private lawyers, government officials and to the officials from trade associations. Similar internship programmes have been introduced by the National Missions at Geneva and Washington DC, various government departments and prominent consultancies and research centres in Brazil. A Mission official confirms the following:

> The Permanent Mission of Brazil at Geneva had organised an internship program in the year 1994 with more than 200 participating lawyers. Most of these lawyers, after the internship program, returned to Brazil and served industries and the government. Therefore, it has gradually become easier for the government to analyse private claims and disputes. The provision of internships has also helped our industries in approaching these trained lawyers to investigate barriers and prepare applications for registering their trade grievances with the government.[21]

These internships have enabled law students and professionals to gain experience and expertise in WTO laws. The rise in the number of interns and young professionals has in turn assisted the private sector and the government to conduct disputes in a cost-effective manner as they have

---

21 Interview with an official (n 13).

gained enhanced access to legally marshalled information and evidence at a comparatively affordable rate. This trend has further increased the enthusiasm and demand for courses in international economic law at universities, leading to an overall enhanced trade law expertise and awareness in the country.

Finally, the growing interest of the Brazilian media in international trade affairs has served as an important information interface between the government, business community, academia, think tanks, law firms and other interested parties. As journalists in Brazil are increasingly being trained in WTO-related aspects, their improved understanding of trade issues has resulted in effective and intelligible reporting of WTO-related issues.[22] This development suggests that national media has an instrumental role to play in raising awareness and disseminating information in respect to international trade among citizens of a developing country. An educated and free media can also discharge watchdog functions by monitoring the activities of the government and the interaction between the public and private sector entities. In particular, the importance of media can mainly be realised in democratic countries where democratically elected governments are particularly responsive to the needs of individuals and they seek to achieve public support, and hence political advantage, through media reports.

2.1 PUBLIC PRIVATE COORDINATION: ANALYSIS OF SELECTED TRADE DISPUTES

This section introduces and analyses four WTO disputes that were conducted through varied forms of coordination between the government and private stakeholders in Brazil. With the help of these cases, the section analyses the way the public and private sector entities have coordinated, and the extent to which they have acted in accordance with the above-mentioned institutional and procedural frameworks established for dispute settlement coordination. The primary purpose of this analysis

---

22 See, for example, 'EU Violates WTO Rules With Out-Of-Quota Sugar Exports, Say UNICA' *UNICA News* 17 December 2011, accessed 12 June 2016 at <http://www.unica.com.br/news/7064751920334804993/eu-violates-wto-rules-with-out-of-quota-sugar-exports-por-cento2C-says-unica/>; 'Brazilian Sugarcane Industry Association Calls on European Commission Not to Authorize Sugar Exports Above WTO Ceiling' *7KPLCtv.com* Sao Paulo, 25 January 2014, accessed 13 June 2016 at <http://www.kplctv.com/story/11878241/brazilian-sugarcane-industry-association-calls-on-european-commission-not-to-authorize-sugar-exports-above-wto-ceiling>.

is to identify those characteristics of PPP strategies that have strengthened Brazil's WTO dispute settlement capacity.

2.1.1 The Aircraft Cases

The *Canada – Aircraft*[23] and *Brazil – Aircraft*[24] cases were a wake-up call for the government of Brazil as they outlined the need to expand its domestic dispute settlement capacity. These disputes are significant as they have changed the outlook and approach of the government towards the handling of WTO disputes. They neatly illustrate the potential role that can be played by the affected industries in WTO litigation, and therefore the capacity-building potential of PPP mechanisms.

Bombardier and Embraer are the leading manufacturers and exporters of aircraft, respectively speaking, in Canada and Brazil. WTO challenges were initiated by Canada and Brazil (against each other) to protect the interests of these respective aircraft exporters. Canada, in the *Brazil – Aircraft* case, challenged the export subsidies granted to foreign purchasers of Embraer aircraft with the contention that these subsidies were inconsistent with the Subsidies and Countervailing Measures (SCM) Agreement.[25] The pursuit was shortly followed by a similar challenge from Brazil in the *Canada – Aircraft* case against certain subsidies that were granted by the Government of Canada to support the export of its civilian aircraft. Brazil also contended that these measures were inconsistent with the SCM Agreement. The Panel and Appellate Body in these cases substantially upheld the challenges and found that both Brazil and Canada were acting in violation of their commitments under the SCM Agreement.

The private and public sector entities in Brazil had overlapping interests in litigating as well as defending these disputes. Embraer was seeking the removal of subsidies granted to its competitor so that it could maintain a profitable business of manufacturing and exporting aircraft. For the Brazilian government, successful litigation of the case against Canada and strong defensiveness to the challenge from Canada were important for political and economic reasons. Embraer, a state-owned company until 1994, was privatised during the period when many state-owned enterprises in Brazil were being privatised. Shortly after its privatisation,

---

23 Appellate Body Report, *Canada – Measures Affecting the Export of Civilian Aircraft*, WT/DS70/AB/R, adopted 20 August 1999.

24 Appellate Body Report, *Brazil – Export Financing Programme for Aircraft*, WT/DS46/AB/R, adopted 20 August 1999.

25 Agreement on Subsidies and Countervailing Measures (15 April 1994) LT/UR/A-1A/9, arts 3, 27, 27.4, 27.5.

Embraer began to emerge as a leading aircraft provider (for commercial, corporate and military use) in the international market. Brazil therefore had an important technological sector to protect as it was preparing itself for international competition. In addition, it became politically important for the Brazilian government to win these disputes as the national and international media was extensively covering their developments. These cases were discussed in Brazilian newspapers just as a 'soccer match' is covered and discussed in Brazil.[26] Mass awareness created a political pressure on the government, which was at the same time planning its re-election campaign.

During the two aircraft disputes, the strategies and nature of partnership formed between the government and the aircraft industry in Brazil were very similar. In both disputes, Embraer hired foreign-based lawyers and economic consultants. The Permanent Mission of Brazil to WTO worked closely with the privately hired lawyers and economic consultants during the litigation and post-litigation stages of the disputes. Moreover, the privately hired lawyers were, for the first time, allowed to join the national delegation and participate directly in the WTO adjudicatory proceedings. Hence, unlike earlier cases where only diplomats were allowed to present and respond to legal arguments, the present cases witnessed a new era where private lawyers were presenting the cases at the formal WTO hearings. The private lawyers were closely monitored and guided by the government officials. Therefore, these cases could aptly be seen as a turning point as the government arguably began to delegate the WTO litigation work to private sector entities.

The gradual delegation of functions performed by government officials to privately hired service providers, accompanied by transfer of resources from the private company (Embraer) to the government, resulted in the evolution of PPP in Brazil. However, the smooth interaction in this case should be seen with a caveat; that is, the company was originally state-owned and the government, after the company's privatisation, continued to retain some control in its functioning. This meant that the officers in control of the company were either public officials or private officials working under the close supervision and guidance of the public officials. This state of affairs resulted in open channels of communication, which in turn helped to foster a relationship of confidence between the government and company officials. Hence, the case suggests that smooth conduct of dispute settlement procedures requires a relationship of confidence and trust between government and industry, and this can possibly be estab-

---

[26] Interview with an official (n 13).

lished if there are effective channels of communication and information exchange between the two.

2.1.2 EC – Export Subsidies on Sugar (Brazil)

The *EC – Export Subsidies on Sugar (Brazil)*[27] provides another striking example of coordination between the CGC, the Permanent Mission of Brazil to WTO, the sugar industry, and lawyers and economic consultants in Brazil. In this case, Brazil challenged the EC's provision of export subsidies to its sugar industry. Brazil alleged that the EC's Common Agricultural Policy[28] provided subsidies to sugar and sugar-containing products above the agreed commitment limit specified in the Schedule of Concessions. It was therefore contended that the EC's export subsidies were in violation of the Agreement on Agriculture,[29] the SCM Agreement,[30] and GATT 1994.[31]

In addition, collateral challenges were initiated against the EC's subsidisation of its sugar sector by Australia and Thailand. Owing to the common nature of these challenges, a single Panel was composed. With respect to these three cases, separate but identical reports were recommended by the Panel. The Panel found that the EC's practices were inconsistent with WTO rules as they violated the Agreement on Agriculture. The Appellate Body upheld the findings of the Panel. It also gave its observations on the claims filed under the SCM Agreement as they were not addressed in the Panel report.[32]

The CGC and CAMEX provided an institutional gateway for the sugar industry in Brazil to approach the government for the protection of its exporting interests. Creation of these public sector institutions transformed the nature of informal coordination formed during the previously litigated *Aircraft* disputes into an institutionally prescribed partnership.

---

27 Appellate Body Report, *European Communities – Export Subsidies on Sugar, Complaint by Brazil*, WT/DS265/AB/R, WT/DS266/AB/R, WT/DS283/AB/R, adopted 19 May 2005.

28 Council Regulation (EC) No 1260/2001 of 19 June 2001 on the Common Organization of the Markets in the Sugar Sector [2001] OJ L178/1.

29 Agreement on Agriculture (15 April 1994) LT/UR/A-1A/2, arts 3.3, 8, 9.1(a), (c), and 10.1.

30 Agreement on Subsidies and Countervailing Measures (n 25) arts 3, 27, 27.4, 27.5.

31 General Agreement on Tariffs and Trade 1994 (15 April 1994) LT/UR/A-1A/3, arts III:4 and XVI.

32 For details, see WTO Dispute Settlement: Dispute DS266, accessed 23 October 2016 at <http://www.wto.org/english/tratop_e/dispu_e/cases_e/ds266_e.htm>.

With the help of these institutions, lawyers and economic consultants assisted the government during the investigation, preparation and litigation of the dispute. Their services were paid for by the industry; that is, the sugar cane associations (mainly the Brazilian Sugarcane Industry Association (UNICA)).[33]

Several meetings were held between the ministries, lawyers, economic consultants and private sector representatives during the dispute settlement proceedings. A Mission official confirms that '. . . lawyers were not preparing the case on their own, but they were helping the government and the private sector to prepare the case'.[34] The lawyers and consultants were marshalling the legal and commercial arguments; the ministries were vetting, editing and finalising them; and the industry representatives were being consulted extensively by the ministries throughout the entire process.

The above-mentioned description usefully outlines a possible composition of PPP arrangements. The Ministry of Foreign Affairs, the Ministry of Agriculture, the Permanent Mission of Brazil to WTO, UNICA, Sidley Austin (a US-based law firm) and Datagro (Brazil's main independent agricultural consultancy) were the key participants involved in the overall litigation process. The arrangement also clearly reflects that although the dispute was financed by the sugar industry, the government was the leading partner in the dispute as it was closely monitoring and coordinating the work of the privately hired service providers and private sector representatives.

During the disputes, Pedro de Camargo and Elisabeth Serodio, both former government officials, worked as consultants with UNICA. Their past experience in the field and pre-established contacts with government officials helped the association to coordinate with the government.[35] They enabled the industry and the government to confide in each other as they provided a trustable channel of interaction between the industry associations and the ministries. Moreover, national and international media played an important role in this dispute. The case was extensively covered by journalists, and this initiative made the public aware of the ongoing international trade developments. As a result, successful litigation of the case became very important for the political leadership. Positive outcome of the litigation was exhibited as one of the main achievements of the

---

33 See UNICA: Sugarcane Industry Association, About Us, accessed 7 November 2016 at <http://english.unica.com.br/>.

34 Interview with an official (n 5).

35 Shaffer, Badin & Rosenberg (n 10) 67, 80.

democratic government during electoral campaigns that were concurrently taking place in the country. This finding reaffirms that media in democratic countries, through its awareness-enhancing role, can play an instrumental role in the domestic management of trade disputes.

2.1.3 US – Upland Cotton

US – Upland Cotton[36] is a landmark case that exemplifies how a resource-constrained private sector and a developing country's government can successfully litigate a complex and a long-drawn-out WTO case with significant international ramifications. Brazil initiated this WTO dispute against the US on the grounds that the US was granting prohibited subsidies, actionable subsidies and other forms of assistance to the US producers, users and exporters of upland cotton. It contended that the US subsidies to the upland cotton industry were inconsistent with the SCM Agreement, the Agreement on Agriculture, and GATT 1994. The Panel upheld the challenge. At the appeal stage, the Appellate Body substantially upheld the Panel's findings.[37]

The actual expenditure incurred in the dispute was approximately two million US dollars.[38] In order to meet these costs, the Brazilian government and cotton industry collected financial resources from various sources. A newspaper has reported that the main sources of funding the dispute included the affected private companies, the Export Promotion Agency, the government's budget, and the proceeds from a lottery sale.[39]

The CGC worked closely with the Ministry of Agriculture during the initial examination and investigation of the dispute. The information and statistical analysis was provided by the cotton industry, which was mainly led by the Brazilian Association of Cotton Producers (ABRAPA).[40] CGC

---

[36] Appellate Body Report, *United States – Subsidies on Upland Cotton*, WT/DS267/AB/R, adopted 21 March 2005.

[37] For details, see WTO dispute Settlement: Dispute DS267, accessed 25 October 2016 at <http://www.wto.org/english/tratop_e/dispu_e/cases_e/ds267_e.htm>.

[38] Calculations based on empirical investigation conducted in Shaffer, Badin & Rosenberg (n 10) 460.

[39] PC Mello, 'Cotton producers are raffle to fund the WTO panel' *PC Estado De Sao Paulo* 18 September 2003, accessed 28 October 2016 at <http://www.scielo.br/scielo.php?script=sci_nlinks&ref=000166&pid=S0104-44782007000100006000016&lng=es>.

[40] Interview with an official (n 13); Venilson Ferreira & Angelo Ikeda, 'U.S. suspends compensation to Brazilian producer' *Economia & Negocios* (Brasilia & Sao Paulo, 8 August 2013), accessed 28 October 2016 at http://www.estadao.com.br/noticias/impresso,eua-suspendem-indenizacao-a-produtor-brasileiro-,1061750,0.

shared the information (provided by the industry) with the Ministry of Agriculture, and hence it served as a communication link between the government departments and the industry. Besides that, ABRAPA hired a former official of the Ministry of Agriculture to work as a consultant.[41]

The complex nature of the case made it difficult for the government to collect the required factual and financial resources. It therefore reached out to the industry (producers, manufacturers, and exporters of varying sizes) to convince them to 'coordinate and pool their resources through a trade association' in order to help pay for outside legal and economic consultants and gathering of information.[42] The cotton industry at this stage was insufficiently resourced to finance the litigation.[43] A government official confirms that 'the cotton industry was fragile and not very organized during these years.'[44] The cotton industry therefore incurred only a part of the initial costs spent on hiring lawyers, consultants and gathering information during the initial stages of the dispute. Due to the fact that the litigation lasted for several years (2002–2005), and the post-litigation proceedings were even more protracted (2005–2012), the cotton industry 'ran out of their available yet limited funds' and eventually discontinued its resource support to the government.[45]

With the available funding, the industry (together with the government) hired the US-based law firm, Sidley Austin. It also hired a US-based economist to conduct the economic analysis. The economist was hired to explain and interpret the economic formulas and calculations used for providing subsidies to the US cotton industry. The litigation work, that is, preparing briefs and submissions, attending hearings, assisting the government to answer the issues raised during adjudication, analysing the legal and economic position of the case, marshalling commercial and legal arguments, and related tasks, were jointly performed by the law firm and the economist. Their work was closely supervised and guided by the CGC lawyers.

Furthermore, considerable support from voluntary organisations (such

---

htm. (The news article notes that ABRAPA paid the cost of litigation that was incurred during the Panel proceedings.)

41 Pedro de Camargo Neto, Former Deputy Minister in the Ministry of Agriculture (Shaffer, Badin & Rosenberg (n 10) 449).

42 Ibid 459.

43 Interview with an official, Government of Brazil (details withheld). (The interviewee observes the following: '. . . the cotton producers allegedly were concerned about the cost of the case and asked the government to fund it, but the government refused, stating that it lacked funds'.)

44 Interview with an official (n 13).

45 Ibid.

as Oxfam) was given during the post-litigation phase. Oxfam was engaged in international campaigning, which helped to generate some pressure on the US to remove its subsidies. They also monitored the implementation performance of the US and helped the Brazilian government in gathering evidence on non-implementation for the compliance proceedings.[46] The voluntary sector therefore played an important role through campaigns, monitoring and research, especially during the post-litigation stage

It is also worth mentioning that the collaborative work of the team of lawyers, economists and subject-specific consultants provided the government with strong and comprehensive arguments. It may not be possible for legal experts to comprehend and translate commercial data and economic formulas from the legal point of view. Similarly, it may not be possible for economic and technical experts to interpret and incorporate commercial information and analysis into the legal texts. A successful litigation may therefore require a team consisting of lawyers, economists and subject-specific experts, especially where the matter being litigated is of a highly complex or technical nature. Collaborative work by different experts ensures that the gaps between legal analysis, economic explanations and commercial evaluation are not left unfilled.

The case was a long-fought battle between a developed and a developing country, the latter with a resource-constrained industry at stake. It puts into focus a situation where the government had to finance the later stages of the dispute (mainly the stages of appeal and compliance) as the industry fell short of the required funds. This seems to suggest that governments in developing countries, when litigating disputes at WTO, should be careful to avoid relying entirely on private funding or whatever (invariably small) amount may be available from their own budgets. This is particularly true for complex disputes with expected longer time frames for settlement. Additional financial arrangements should be made to finance the litigation that can possibly go beyond a calculated time frame. To this end, the governments can create an contingency fund or a standing budget for meeting such additional expenses.[47]

Finally, the case also confirms that an organised private sector is an essential requirement for the formation of effective PPPs. The cotton industry, for instance, was insufficiently organised, and formed an initial partnership with the government only after establishing its trade association (ABRAPA). However, due to inadequate financial means within this newly constituted association, and the complexity and length

46 Shaffer, Badin & Rosenberg (n 10) 463.

47 Interview with a trade lawyer, ACWL, Geneva, Switzerland, 11 April 2013.

of the case, ABRAPA could not provide resources to the government throughout the Panel, Appellate and Compliance stages of proceedings. The case indicates that developing country governments can face severe constraints in enforcing their WTO rights if they lack an organised business community or if a trade barrier affects the interests of a less-organised industry. The phenomenon of less-organised industries with limited resources is more prevalent in developing countries. Therefore, it is important to devise ways for organising business interests in developing countries for the effective formation of PPPs and the successful conduct of WTO disputes.

2.1.4 EC – Measures Affecting Soluble Coffee

In *European Communities – Measures Affecting Soluble Coffee*,[48] the Brazilian government, at the request of its soluble coffee industry, launched formal consultations with the EU. Brazil's main contention was that the EU's Preferential Tariff Scheme (under the Generalised System of Preferences (GSP)) was injuring the exporting interests of the Brazilian soluble coffee industry, and the practice was inconsistent with the Enabling Clause and Article I of GATT 1994. The dispute did not reach the Panel stage as it was settled between the parties during consultations.[49]

The industry association partnering the government in this matter was the Brazilian Soluble Coffee Industry Association (ABICS). The cost incurred during the investigation and consultation stage was mainly borne by the coffee industry. It provided information and commercial evidence to the government during the investigation and preparation of consultation requests. In addition, ABICS employed the services of a Brazilian private law firm (Veirano Advogados) to assist the government in carrying out the legal analysis of the dispute.[50]

Shortly after the commencement of formal consultations, the EU made a conditional proposal. It proposed lifting the alleged tariff from the Brazilian coffee exports on the condition that Brazil would not proceed

---

[48] *European Communities — Measures Affecting Soluble Coffee*, WT/DS209, in consultations on 12 October 2000.

[49] For details, see WTO Dispute Settlement: Dispute DS154, accessed 12 October 2016 at <http://www.wto.org/english/tratop_e/dispu_e/cases_e/ds154_e.htm>; Marislei Nishijima & Maria Sylvia Macchione Saes, 'Tariff Discrimination on Brazil's Soluble Coffee: An Economic Analysis' (2010) 30(2) *Brazilian Journal of Political Economy* 293.

[50] Shaffer, Badin & Rosenberg (n 10) 491.

with the dispute.[51] The condition was accepted by the Brazilian government and the EU subsequently removed the alleged tariff from coffee exports, thereby granting the Brazilian coffee industry a larger market access. The seemingly favourable concession was accompanied with an understanding that the '. . . "sensitive" farm imports will continue to be restricted through quotas and other non-tariff barriers. These products include sugar, cereals, dairy products, tobacco, meat and some fruits – all of which are Brazilian exports.'[52]

The coffee industry managed to restore its lost market access in the EU with the help of privately funded intergovernmental consultations. On the other hand, the Brazilian government allegedly chose to selectively defend the exporting interests of its coffee industry in a situation where the EU's protectionist policies were also injuring the interests of Brazil's other exporting sectors. No manifest attempts were made by the government to protect the interests of the other affected sectors as Brazil was implicitly restrained from further challenging the EU's GSP scheme.

The present dispute exemplifies the possibility of certain regulatory threats that such partnerships can face. It illustrates an instance of a possible clash of interests; that is, a conflict between the special economic interests of the soluble coffee industry versus wider economic interests of various farm-based sectors, where the former prevailed over the latter. This instance could also be seen as a case of 'private capture' where the coffee industry captured, to some extent, governmental authority for the purpose of protecting its own market access interests. Regulatory problems of this nature are especially noticeable in countries with high levels of corruption and poor observance of 'the rule of law'. As noted in Chapter 2, this is a potential limitation of the PPP approach, since the capture of national interests by a handful of profit-motivated organisations or individuals can never be a desirable situation. Effective PPP arrangements should always try to balance such competing interests in the best interests of the nation and industry.

---

[51] M Osava, 'EU lifts tariffs on Brazilian soluble coffee' *Third World Network* (Rio de Janeiro, 11 July 2001), accessed 5 July 2016 at <http://www.twnside.org.sg/title/soluble.htm>; European Commission, 'The EU and Brazil solve dispute over soluble coffee' IP/01/987 (Brussels, 11 July 2001), accessed 24 October 2015 at <europa.eu/rapid/press-release_IP-01-987_en.pdf>.

[52] Osava (n 51).

3.1 BRAZILIAN DISPUTE SETTLEMENT PARTNERSHIPS: FURTHER ANALYSIS

3.1.1 Nature and Elements of PPP

The PPP in Brazil is *flexible*, *semi-formal* and *dynamic* in nature. It is *flexible* as the government and the private sector can coordinate and exchange resources through varied procedures and channels, depending upon the requirements of each case. The private sector can either approach the Dispute Settlement Unit or the subject-specific ministry through a trade association or on its own. Government officials can approach private sector representatives and seek their assistance in any way and at any stage of dispute settlement. Moreover, there are no fixed guidelines for financing litigation as issues of financing mostly depend upon multiple factors including the nature of a dispute.[53] A government official confirms that 'it has been possible to adjust and revise our approach and financing procedures with every case we have conducted'.[54]

The PPP arrangement is *semi-formal* in nature as it is guided and facilitated by specialised procedures and institutions established for the management of trade disputes. In other words, the Brazilian PPP is institutionalised, but unlike the EU's TBR or the US's Section 301 mechanism, it is not entirely formalised, because:

1. It does not confer a right on the private sector to file trade grievances in the form of written complaints.
2. It does not impose any obligation on the government to examine and consider such complaints from the industry.

It is *dynamic* as the procedures have gradually evolved according to the changing domestic conditions and the nature of disputes litigated and defended by the government. Different strategies of dispute settlement and PPPs have evolved at different times. Strategies that have introduced effectiveness to the process include: the creation of business coalitions; the creation of think tanks, academic networks and research groups working on international trade law; the direct participation of privately hired counsels in WTO hearings; the creation of specialised and dedicated institutions and procedures; and the development of domestic legal expertise through the provision of internships and training. These features have

53 Interview with an official (n 13).
54 Ibid; interview with an official (n 5).

facilitated effective exchange between the government and industries, and hence they have played a capacity-building role. These developments can therefore be considered by other developing countries that are seeking to establish flexible, ad hoc and semi-formal PPPs.

It is the combination of a 'professionalised Ministry of Foreign Affairs', an 'inter-ministerial Chamber', a 'specialised Dispute Settlement Unit', and a 'relatively well-organised business sector' with 'large, export-oriented companies' and trade associations that has enabled Brazil to become a leading developing country at WTO DSM.[55] As mentioned before, the Ministry of Foreign Affairs has specialised in handling foreign trade matters. Its officials are experts in the area of international trade and they are appointed through a competitive selection process. With the creation of specialised units having dedicated and well-qualified staff members, the ministry has been able to tap into and retain relevant expertise and experience in international trade law it has developed over time.

CAMEX, an interministerial institution established for the management of foreign trade concerns, is another interesting development as it has enabled the government to consolidate its approach on trade matters and achieve expertise with optimum utilisation of available resources. A professionally qualified, well-staffed and responsive Permanent Mission of Brazil to WTO can also be seen as one of the key reasons for its success at WTO. Brazil has utilised its WTO Mission to enhance its organisational and cultural knowledge of WTO; this has partly been done by the appointment of its Foreign Affairs Ministers as the Ambassadors to WTO and through the secondment of its government officials and lawyers at the Mission.

Brazil's WTO participation is further strengthened with the help of its wealthy and large industries such as oil and aircraft, as large entrepreneurial enterprises with significant trading stakes can better participate in the management of disputes. Moreover, its 'pluralistic' private sector community, which consists of strong trade associations, confederations of industry, multinational private companies, well-resourced business coalitions, private consultancies and law firms (accompanied by various supporting agencies such as monitoring institutions, think tanks and research networks), has also strengthened the dispute settlement capacity of Brazil. One of the most widely proposed reasons for Brazil's success at WTO DSM is its 'organised private sector', which is indeed a vital requirement for the establishment and smooth functioning of dispute settlement partnerships.

---

55 Shaffer, Badin & Rosenberg (n 10) 404.

3.1.2 Regulatory Threat: A Possible Shortcoming

Dispute settlement partnerships have frequently been formed between the government and different industry sectors in Brazil and they have often enabled their participants to achieve their respective goals. Different industries in Brazil, such as coffee, sugar, poultry and aircraft, have managed to restore their lost market access. On the other hand, the government, partially with the help of these successful litigations, has gained the status of an emerging global economy having an effective system of governance.[56] However, the partnership has not been able to survive when an industry has fallen short of resources, such as in the *US –Upland Cotton* case, where the partnership disappeared after the initial stages of the dispute due to a shortage of resources in the private sector. The government, especially after the Panel stage, had to finance the case and gather additional information on its own. Moreover, small scale industries (such as the ones dealing in footwear and wood products) in Brazil have not been able to approach and partner the government in any WTO litigation.[57] These observations lead to a possible inference that PPP arrangements may create a situation of discrimination between the 'haves' and the 'have nots' industries in Brazil. As discussed in Chapter 2, this is a potential limitation of the PPP approach.

One possible counterargument to this alleged limitation could be that such economic sectors often do not have the potential to operate at the international level and therefore would have had no or only insignificant concerns relating to international trade. Alternatively, the small or unorganised industries may not be able to afford investigation and litigation of disputes as they may not have the required resources and capacity to survive for the duration of dispute settlement proceedings at WTO. It has also been observed that 'the smaller companies and industries often require immediate results and they mostly expect financial compensation as an effective remedy due to the size of their businesses'.[58] Immediate

---

56 'Globalisation and Emerging Economies' (March 2009) Organisation for Economic Co-operation and Development Policy Brief, accessed 30 October 2016 at http://www.oecd.org/tad/tradedev/42324460.pdf.

57 Rajshri Jayaram & Peter F Lanjaw, 'Small Scale Industry, Environment Regulation and Poverty: The Case of Brazil' (2004) 18(3) *The World Bank Economic Review* 443, 447; Matleena Kniivila, 'Industrial Development and Economic Growth: Implications for Poverty Reduction and Income Inequality' in Department of Economic and Social Affairs, *Industrial Development for the 21st Century: Sustainable Development Perspectives* (United Nations 2007) 295, 316–317.

58 Interview with an official (n 5).

results and financial compensation are their desired outcomes, but they cannot possibly be achieved through remedies provided under WTO DSU. For these reasons, it may be argued that WTO DSM might not be an appropriate and viable avenue for small businesses.

There may be companies in Brazil that are facing economic problems due to China's growing export market and diminishing prices of products. Some of these companies may not even be able to come to Brasilia to speak with government officials. This may either be because their stakes are small, or their trade concerns are perishable and nonlitigable in nature, or because they have insufficient resources (such as evidence) to approach the government. Hence, one could argue that no purpose would be served by formalising PPP and giving all (including such companies) a legal right to approach and petition their government. However, as discussed in Chapter 3, there are clear benefits that can arise from the formalisation of PPP.

A PPP arrangement without any accountability, supervisory and transparency enhancing provisions can create conditions suitable for corruption. Amidst the stark wealth inequality in Brazil, its PPP arrangement can fall short of granting an equal right of access to all economic sectors because the treatment of the 'rule of law' remains 'tilted' in favour of wealthy and politically influential businesses in Brazil.[59] Hence, as initially seen in Chapter 2, and subsequently illustrated in this chapter, it is important for a partnership arrangement (especially in countries with poor observance of the 'rule of law' and high rates of corruption) to have established regulatory provisions for the elimination or reduction of discrimination and for ensuring that the government makes strategic choices in the best interests of the nation. It is also important that the government should always take the leading role in such partnerships, and it should be able to filter and prioritise claims and disputes in relation to their potential scope, overall impact, and their harmony with the wider economic, social and environmental interests of the nation.

The European Commission's Guidelines for Successful Public Private Partnerships acknowledge that 'the development of effective regulatory and watchdog mechanisms' is a vital condition for an effective regulation of PPP arrangements.[60] Brazil has also realised the need to deal with potential regulatory challenges, and this is evident from several transparency-enhancing provisions and practices employed by the government.

---

59 Pio (n 7) 4.

60 European Commission, 'Guidelines for Successful Public-Private Partnerships' (March 2003) 39, accessed 29 July 2016 at <http://ec.europa.eu/regional_policy/sources/docgener/guides/ppp_en.pdf>.

Transparency practices devised for regulating such partnerships in Brazil include: (a) seeking public opinion on proposed policies, bilateral negotiations, disputes and resolutions;[61] (b) online publication of resolutions, regulations and trade proposals; and (c) appointment of representatives from civil society and social service agencies to various committees, including the Management Executive Committee (GECEX) of CAMEX. These provisions have, to some extent, enhanced transparency in Brazil's management of trade disputes. Developing countries with similar domestic circumstances (such as the high levels of corruption and disregard for the 'rule of law') should consider the proposed PPP approach in light of these regulatory concerns and the discussed transparency-enhancing practices that can regulate such partnerships.

3.1.3 Formal versus Informal PPP Arrangements

The issue of informal versus formal PPP arrangements also deserves a mention. It has been seen that a flexible arrangement of PPP in Brazil has worked well in various WTO cases. Nonetheless, the Brazilian government is discussing the potential benefits and viability of introducing formal procedures of PPP.[62] The question of whether a formal mechanism of PPP (similar to the ones in the US and the EU) will be more effective than the present informal means of PPP is difficult to answer. A government official has observed the following:

> The private sector is satisfied with the present informal ways of coordination, and they have had almost no problems with it. We receive applications from the private sector very often, they identify barriers, assist us in various tasks, and the issues are resolved in close coordination with them. Seven different Ministries compose CAMEX, and each ministry has close contacts with their industries. Therefore, industries know the right channel and authority to contact when they are faced with a foreign barrier. Hence, it is difficult to find a concrete reason for establishing formal provisions of PPP in Brazil. But the debate is still very much ongoing.[63]

Unlike the formalised PPP arrangements we have seen in the previous chapters, informal partnerships provide industries with an opportunity

---

[61] A recent example is the call for public comment: CAMEX, 'Secex opens public consultation on negotiating agreements with the EU and Canada' (26 September 2012), accessed 29 October 2016 at <http://www.camex.gov.br/noticias/ler/item/218>.

[62] Interview with an official (n 13).

[63] Ibid.

to express their interests to the government in a non-litigious and flexible manner. A private sector representative from Brazil states that '... approaching the government officials for such matters is not a difficult task as we live in a highly democratic society. If we have a problem, we may approach the government officials by a phone call or an email or a visit to Brasilia, to which they are often very responsive.'[64] Moreover, as seen in Chapter 3, there are clear disadvantages to a litigious complaints procedure that is based on a system of 'rights and obligations'. On the other hand, its benefits are numerous, and they can possibly counterbalance some of its disadvantages in certain situations.

It is difficult to provide a definite answer to the dilemma of whether Brazil should follow in the footsteps of the US and the EU by establishing a formal PPP mechanism for the future management of trade disputes. It is also difficult, and rather meaningless, to address the issue of whether a formal PPP system is more effective than an informal system of coordination. This is because the dispute settlement partnerships, as initially discussed in Chapter 2, are deeply embedded in the domestic environment of a country. Hence, multiple domestic factors operating together in a given country can determine whether a particular kind of arrangement would be effective or ineffective in harnessing privately owned resources for the settlement of disputes in that country.

4.1 CONCLUDING REMARKS

With its qualified and experienced ministries, strongly represented industries, institutional developments and an export-oriented economy beset with challenges common to the developing world, the semi-formalised set-up in Brazil seems to be providing the required flexibility of procedures on one hand and the capacity-building advantage on the other. The institutional framework fosters public private collaboration. At the same time, it also benefits from the inherent flexibility of an informal set-up as no legal obligation to provide financial or evidential resources to the government is imposed on the affected industries. Hence, this quasi-formal arrangement provides a unique example of an in-house dispute settlement strategy to the developing world.

Developing countries can 'learn lessons' by peer reviewing the dispute settlement partnership experience of Brazil. They can observe how Brazil has gradually overcome the problems (at least to some extent) that they

---

64 Interview with private sector representative, 28 October 2013.

face today at WTO DSU. Dispute settlement partnerships can either be formed with the help of laws and regulations, or with an institutional framework devised at the domestic level. Private stakeholders can also be engaged without a legal, regulatory or an institutional framework, as long as the procedures of partnership and dispute management are robustly defined to enhance the transparency and predictability of rules. The following chapter presents a classic example of how such partnerships can be formed without a legal, regulatory or an institutional interface.

6. Handling of WTO disputes: India's experience

India, increasingly seen as one of the emerging superpowers of the world, is an enthusiastic participant in the multilateral trading system. As a founding member of GATT 1947 and an original member of WTO, India has played a redefining role in shaping the WTO jurisprudence through negotiations and litigations. It has participated numerous times in the WTO dispute settlement process as a complainant, respondent and third party. Since January 1995 to January 2017, India has acted as a complainant in 23 cases, as a respondent in 24 cases, and as a third party in 126 cases. These numbers show that India, in different capacities, has participated in 173 cases out of 520 cases filed at WTO DSU during the same period. Hence, in one way or the other, India has participated in over 33 per cent of the cases filed at WTO.

India's significant participation at WTO DSU has not been hurdle-free. As with other developing countries, it has faced various challenges during identification and investigation of barriers, preparation and presentation of factually supported legal arguments, and seeking compliance in cases of victory. These challenges can be directly attributed to the paucity of finance, trade lawyers, economists, monitoring agencies and information-gathering channels – to name a few – at the domestic level. However, as it will be shown in this chapter, India is now on the path of capacity building.

India's participation impulse and strengthened dispute settlement capacity can be evidenced from the number of times it has filed complaints against the world's superpowers (such as the US and the EU). Out of 23 complaints India has filed at WTO DSU, ten were filed against the US and seven against the EU. Additionally, it has not wavered in litigating disputes against its economic and political allies such as Brazil and Turkey. This should not however suggest that India gives preference to litigation over negotiation. India has withdrawn or settled (with or without invoking WTO's consultation provisions) 16 out of 24 complaints filed against its trade practices or policies by different Member States. At the same time, it has not shied away from displaying a strong defence in the remaining eight complaints that were litigated, even though six of them were filed by the US and the other two by the EU. Hence, from a pragmatic point of view, it will be interesting for readers to see how India has strengthened its ability to self-enforce its multilateral trading rights both as a complainant and as a respondent.

There is no formal provision or procedure (like the EU's TBR, the US's Section 301 mechanism or China's TBIM) or a dedicated institution (like Brazil's CGC) that allows an industry to register a trade grievance with the Government of India if and when its trade interests are vitiated. However, this should not suggest that Indian industries have not been active participants during the settlement of disputes. On the contrary, industries with high exporting interests in India, such as textiles, clothing and steel, have coordinated with the public sector through undefined, ad hoc and casual procedures. This chapter's review of India's dispute settlement partnership experience therefore introduces a fresh dimension to this work of investigation as it examines a different form of dispute settlement arrangement.

The chapter reviews and analyses the characteristics, weaknesses and capacity-building potential of a purely informal and ad hoc PPP approach.[1] The findings provided in this chapter are almost exclusively based on empirical research conducted by the author. Hence, its readers benefit from the first-hand insights received from the public and private sector officials directly involved in the handling of WTO disputes. Moreover, it provides readers with answers to the following pertinent questions:

1. Do the public sector institutions in India engage industries in the handling of trade disputes?
2. How is the nature of government-industry partnership in India different from the partnerships examined in the previous chapters?
3. In practice, how and to what extent have the industries and the government worked together for the better management of trade disputes?
4. Which features of its PPP system have cost-effectively enhanced India's dispute settlement capacity, and which ones have been ineffective or problematic?
5. Can other developing countries learn anything from India's dispute settlement partnership experience?

---

1 This chapter is adapted from Amrita Bahri, 'Public Private Partnership: Enabling India's Participation at WTO Dispute Settlement Mechanism' (2016) 8(2) *Trade, Law and Development* 151.

1.1 INSTITUTIONAL AND PROCEDURAL FRAMEWORKS: MANAGEMENT OF FOREIGN TRADE DISPUTES IN INDIA

India is a parliamentary democracy. It enjoys a dual polity system of governance, with central and state governments discharging their functions in accordance with the constitutional provisions. From 1947 (the year of independence) until the early 1990s, India followed a socialist and closed model of economy which was largely controlled by the central government. During this period, the policy of 'License Raj' was employed to control and regulate business endeavours, and the policy of 'export promotion import substitution' was created to protect domestic industries against international competition.[2] Dominant state-owned industries in a mixed economy and discretionary powers of the government over the regulation of trade and commerce made India one of the most controlled economies in the 'non-communist' world.

In the early 1990s, India's political economy underwent a major transition. In 1991, India applied to the International Monetary Fund (IMF) for emergency aid, to which the IMF responded with several conditionality requirements. The conditions required India to open its economy to foreign trade, competition and investment, reduce state intervention in the operation of trade and commerce, and abandon its licensing requirements and eliminate subsidies.[3] In an effort to satisfy these requirements, and with the coinciding advent of WTO, India started to liberalise its economy. In the following years, India moved towards an export-oriented market economy with lower trade barriers, deregulation, globalisation and a capitalist framework. To prepare itself for this new economic climate and to meet the multilateral obligations it had undertaken under the

---

[2] 'License Raj' was abolished with the 1991 economic reforms. It was an economic policy in India that aimed to create a state-controlled, state-owned and state-regulated economy. The 'export promotion import substitution' policy aimed to achieve favourable balance of trade and economic development through expansion of exports and minimisation of imports. For a detailed discussion on these policies, see Aseema Sinha, *The Regional Roots of Developmental Politics in India: A Divided Leviathan* (Bloomington: Indiana University Press 2005); Jagdish Bhagwati, *India in Transition: Freeing the Economy* (Clarendon Press 1993).

[3] For details on the IMF requirements, see Francine R Frankfurt, *India's Political Economy 1947–2004: The Gradual Revolution* (Oxford University Press 2005) 603; for a discussion on the nature of India's economy pre- and post-1990s, see Shalendra D Sharma, 'From Central Planning to Market Reforms: India's Political Economy in Comparative Perspective' (1997) 23 (1/2) *Humboldt Journal of Social Relations* 175.

WTO agreements, India had to reorganise its approach regarding the management of international trade. The following subsections depict these re-organisation efforts in the form of institutional and procedural developments.

1.1.1 Institutional Framework

The country needed a new institutional set-up to manage international trade, as it was gradually becoming the backbone of the Indian economy. As a result, multiple public and private sector institutions were established to handle the liberalising economic climate, changing trade barrier dynamics and a new rule-based era of foreign trade conflicts. India's current institutional framework is illustrated in Figure 6.1.

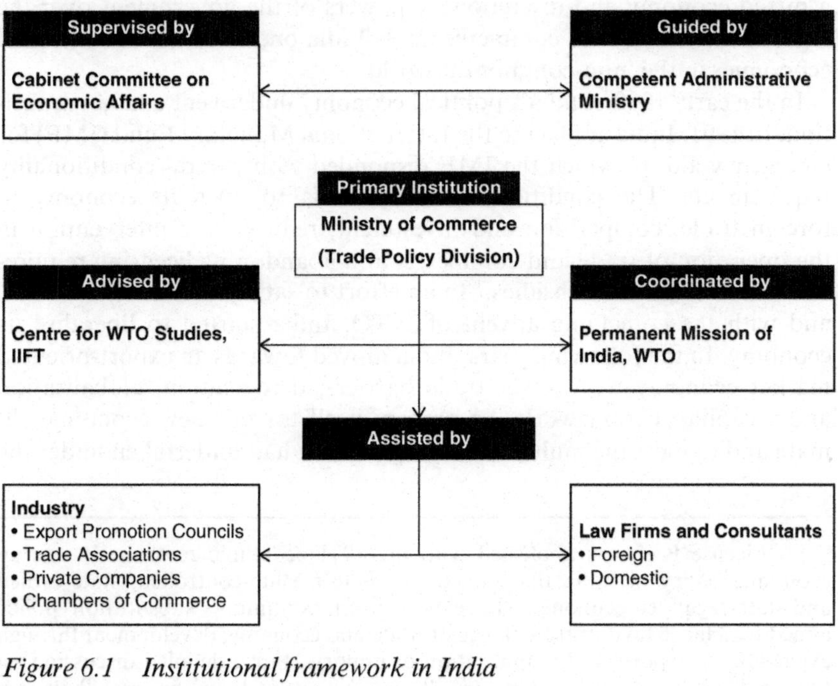

Figure 6.1 Institutional framework in India

As shown in Figure 6.1, the key public sector entity in India for handling international trade issues including the settlement of foreign trade disputes is the Ministry of Commerce. More precisely, its Trade Policy Division (TPD) is responsible for identifying and investigating disputes and litigating them at WTO.

Other ministries that deal with the subject matter of the case at hand also play an important role. They are officially known as 'Competent Administrative Ministries'. The TPD officials are expected to perform their tasks in coordination with the Competent Administrative Ministries, as these ministries are expected to provide expert assistance to TPD during the investigation of trade barriers and preparation of cases. The Permanent Mission of India (PMI) to WTO also plays an active role in the management of foreign trade disputes as it provides the government with information on WTO rules, especially with respect to substantive, procedural and administrative requirements.

The Centre for WTO Studies, Indian Institute of Foreign Trade (IIFT) works as a think tank for the Ministry of Commerce. It gathers information and evidence, organises outreach programmes and consultative meetings with the private sector, monitors foreign practices and analyses the legality and scope of trade disputes.[4] The Centre often works in close coordination with law professionals and expert consultants hired by the government or the private sector, depending upon the nature and requirements of each case.

Export Promotion Councils (EPCs) play an important role in the settlement of disputes as they are expected to serve as an interface between the concerned private entities and the government units. They are established and sponsored by the Government of India, and they finance their activities through membership subscription fees, governmental aid and other payments received from industry members. Amidst increasing privatisation of industries in India, EPCs are, on one hand, made responsible for presenting the government's viewpoints and decisions to the private sector, and on the other, they serve to integrate the interests of the private sector and represent them to the government on a sectoral basis.[5]

Industries in India are also represented by various other private sector representatives, such as trade associations and chambers of commerce. However, many sectors of the Indian economy have trade associations that are insufficiently resourced and influential, and so the business interests of the entities in those sectors are under-represented. Micro, small and medium enterprises (MSMEs) play a very important role in the Indian economy, and their numbers have grown rapidly during the past

---

[4] Details of the outreach and training programmes provided by the Centre are available at Centre for WTO Studies: Indian Institute of Foreign Trade <http://wtocentre.iift.ac.in/ORP6.asp> and http://wtocentre.iift.ac.in/SHC.asp, accessed 19 September 2016.

[5] A list of all export promotion councils in India is available at Ministry of Commerce, Government of India http://commerce.nic.in/aboutus/aboutus_epc.asp, accessed 9 September 2016.

few years. To promote decentralised economic development in various states of India, the state governments have encouraged the formation and growth of small businesses. They have also encouraged these businesses to participate in foreign trade activities; as a result, MSMEs account for more than 40 per cent of overall exports from India. However, they remain insufficiently organised and represented.[6]

The establishment of the abovementioned public and private sector institutions has resulted in the creation of a set of informal procedures that are employed in an ad hoc fashion on a case-by-case basis. A description of these procedures is provided in the following section.

1.1.2 Procedural Framework

1.1.2.1 As a complainant

Individual exporters or their representatives (such as trade associations, chambers of commerce or export promotion councils) can approach the Ministry of Commerce and/or their subject-specific ministry when they face a foreign measure infringing their trade interests. Once private concerns reach the government, or if the government identifies a barrier on its own, the Ministry of Commerce can choose to follow a set of procedures which can broadly be categorised under the following eight stages of dispute settlement.[7]

Figure 6.2 shows that a trade dispute in India can go through *eight* potential procedural stages, wherein one stage may lead to another. The given procedural stages resemble the dispute settlement model illustrated in Chapter 2. These stages may not occur in the order shown above. It may happen that the stage of cost-benefit analysis coincides with the stage of private sector consultations, or vice versa. Furthermore, each trade barrier identified by the government or the private sector may not go through all eight stages. This is because some barriers may simply be removed, or an understanding may be formed between the complaining and the responding governments during the course of informal consultations or during

[6] For details on MSMEs in India, see Sultan Singh Jaswal, 'Problems and Prospects of Micro, Small and Medium Enterprises (MSMEs) in India' (2014) 3(5) *Innovative Research and Studies* 1.

[7] The prevailing set of procedures has been described by various officials working with the Trade Policy Division, Ministry of Commerce, Ministry of Law & Justice, PMI to WTO, Centre for WTO Studies, IIFT, and private sector organisations (that is, from TEXPROCIL, MPEDA and SEAI). Interviews with these official representatives from the public and private sectors were conducted on different dates and through different modes by the author.

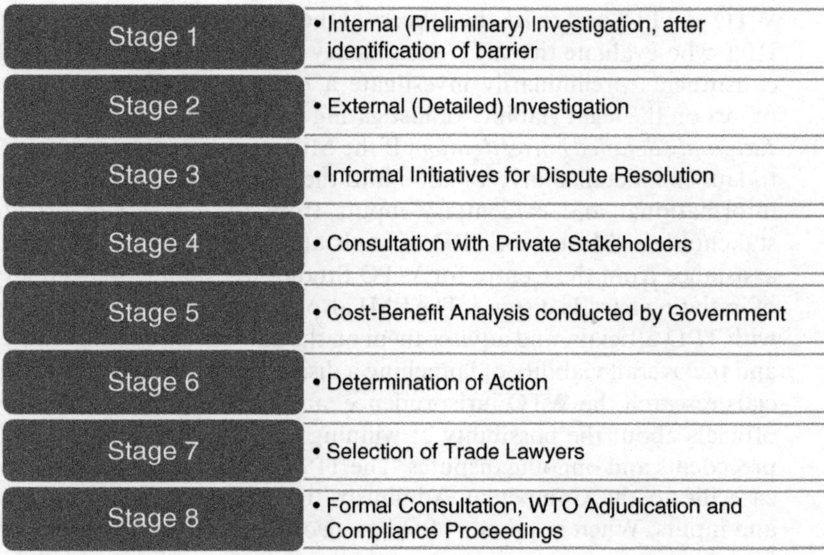

Figure 6.2 Potential procedural stages for dispute settlement (as complainant)

WTO Committee Meetings. Moreover, several disputes may die or fade out due to other economic, diplomatic or political reasons. Therefore, depending upon the nature and requirements of each case, the stages illustrated in Figure 6.2 may arrive in a different order, or may overlap each other in a few instances, or may not even arise in the lifecycle of a dispute at all.

The procedures that may be employed at each stage are described below:

1. *Internal (preliminary) investigation*: When a complaint is received from the private sector, or when a barrier is identified by the Ministry of Commerce or by a different department, the TPD initiates the process by examining the prima facie legitimacy of the barrier, its consistency with WTO laws and its impact on the affected industry. This is mainly done based on information provided by the industry. Based on their judgement following a preliminary examination, the TPD officials decide whether further investigations should be launched in the matter or not. Three key officials are normally involved during preliminary examination: *first*, the officer who is handling that subject-specific WTO Agreement at TPD; *second*, the officer who is handling the foreign trade disputes and broader rules of

WTO at TPD; and *third*, the officers at the Centre for WTO Studies at IIFT who evaluate the WTO-consistency of the measure. These three constituents preliminarily investigate a barrier and prepare a brief report on the legal viability of instigating a dispute.

2. *External (detailed) investigation*: If the Ministry of Commerce decides to launch a detailed investigation into the matter, it may seek further informational and evidentiary inputs from the concerned private stakeholders. Moreover, TPD officials at this stage can seek further assistance from the Centre for WTO Studies to examine the viability of initiating a trade dispute. The PMI also remains in constant contact with TPD officials, and advises them on the administrative procedures and the overall viability of launching a dispute at WTO. The PMI officials research the WTO jurisprudence, and they apprise the ministry officials about the possibility of winning a case in the light of WTO precedents and ongoing disputes. The TPD is also obliged to refer the case file to the Competent Administrative Ministry for its opinion and inputs. When required, TPD has also sought assistance from law firms and economic consultants at this stage for intensive analysis and investigation of the barrier.[8]

The depth and scope of the investigation carried out at this stage is comprehensive, as the matter is analysed from several different perspectives.[9] The investigation mainly seeks answers to the following key questions: Is the barrier legally inconsistent with WTO law? What impact is the barrier having on the economic interests of the industry, and to what extent? What are the prospects of winning the case at WTO? What are the costs involved in litigating the dispute, and are sufficient resources available for the same? Is the affected private sector willing and able to assist the government in bringing a challenge against the offending Member State? Is it diplomatically and politically viable to launch the dispute? What might be the systemic implications of launching the dispute? What are the chances of com-

[8] For example, the Ministry of Commerce approached an India-based law firm, Luthra & Luthra, to seek its legal opinion during investigations in the matter of *India – Solar Cells* (Appellate Body Report, *India – Certain Measures Relating to Solar Cells and Solar Modules,* WT/DS456/AB/R, adopted 14 October 2016). Similar advice during investigation was sought from ACWL in the *EC – Tariff Preferences* case (Appellate Body Report, *European Communities – Conditions for the Granting of Tariff Preferences to Developing Countries*, WT/DS246/AB/R, adopted 20 April 2004).

[9] These concerns were expressed during interviews with two officials from the Ministry of Commerce, an official from the Ministry of Law & Justice and an official from the Centre for WTO Studies, IIFT.

pliance in this case, and would it be viable to pursue the case up to the stage of retaliation in the event of noncompliance?

Once these issues are addressed, TPD prepares a report in which it recommends the further course of action. Depending upon the TPD's recommendation, the Ministry of Commerce can either discontinue the pursuance of the matter at this stage or initiate informal bilateral consultations with the offending Member State(s).

3. *Informal initiatives for settlement of dispute*: The government will usually prefer to exhaust all informal means of dispute resolution before launching a formal complaint at WTO. Hence, the Ministry of Commerce, in consultation with the PMI, may initiate informal consultations with an offending Member State. It may also, in close coordination with the PMI, raise the issue at the concerned WTO Committee. Once the Ministry of Commerce has exhausted the informal means of conflict resolution, and if a settlement has not been reached, the dispute will enter its next phase where internal discussions on the systemic viability of launching a formal dispute will be conducted. A dispute may also be discontinued or held in abeyance at this stage if the offending Member State has withdrawn the measure, or has given an assurance of withdrawing the same within a mutually agreed time frame. In most cases, government officials prefer to gradually scale up the dispute to the formal stages of settlement if their informal initiatives have failed to deliver the desired negotiated results.
4. *Consultations with private stakeholders*: If the government fails to reach a settlement through informal initiatives, it will usually apprise the affected private stakeholders of the situation and discuss with them the implications of escalating the dispute to the next level. The government can also discuss the possibility of seeking resource assistance from the private sector, if required, for conducting consultations and possible litigation. A TPD official makes the following observation:

> The model of PPP is inherent in almost every dispute we litigate. The government will finally consult the industry before making a determination on the initiation of a dispute. There will rarely be a case where the government will proceed to the formal stages of settlement without engaging with the private sector.[10]

---

10 Interview with an official, Ministry of Commerce, Government of India, Delhi, India, 12 June 2013; also confirmed in the written response to the Right To Information application filed by the author on 17 September 2013 (under India's

A dialogue with private sector representatives can be established at any stage of dispute settlement. The consultation meetings with the private sector are mostly organised before a decision on the initiation of a formal dispute is made. But the private sector can also be consulted during or before informal initiatives for dispute resolution are undertaken. Based on the feedback and additional resources received from the private sector, TPD conducts the cost-benefit analysis of launching a formal complaint at WTO.

The lead coordinator during the consultative meetings with the private sector is one of the leading chambers of commerce in India.[11] The lead coordinator, in consultation with TPD, decides the date and place of the meeting, and is responsible for making other administrative and organisational arrangements. Additional participating private sector representatives can be other chambers of commerce, export promotion councils, trade associations, affected private companies, NGOs and consumer organisations.[12]

5. *Cost-benefit analysis*: The final task before launching a formal challenge is usually the cost-benefit analysis conducted by the government. With the feedback received from the private sector, and the investigation report prepared with the assistance of lawyers, the Centre for WTO Studies and the PMI, the Ministry of Commerce calculates and compares the expected cost of litigation with the expected benefits from the removal of the questioned measure. If the expected benefits from its removal are higher than the anticipated cost of dispute settlement process, the case would normally progress from the cost-benefit analysis stage to the stage of final decision-making. This analysis is not conducted entirely on the basis of quantifying the benefits *versus* the costs, but it is largely based on the 'systemic evaluation' of these anticipated factors, along with other factors considered during the investigation stage.

Right to Information Act 2005). The RTI reply was received from the Ministry of Commerce on 5 December 2013 vide Document No. 1/27/2013-TPD.

[11] Examples of chambers or federations include the following: Federation of Indian Chambers of Commerce and Industry (FICCI), Confederation of Indian Industry (CII), Associated Chambers of Commerce and Industry of India (ASSOCHAM), Federation of Indian Export Organisations (FIEO), and Federation of Indian Micro and Small & Medium Enterprises (FISME).

[12] Details on recent consultations with private stakeholders, lead coordinators, venues, and dates for the consultative meetings held in recent years and those planned for the future, can be accessed at Centre for WTO Studies: Indian Institute of Foreign Trade http://wtocentre.iift.ac.in/SHC.asp, accessed 18 September 2016.

The cost-benefit analysis is carried out by a team comprising three main constituents: the officer handling the subject-specific WTO Agreement under TPD; the officer handling the foreign trade disputes and broader rules of WTO at TPD; and the export promotion council(s). Other participants could be officials from various concerned ministries, advisers from the Centre for WTO Studies, and representatives from private companies, trade associations and chambers of commerce. Following this analysis and the private sector consultations, the team submits its report suggesting the appropriate course of action to the Ministry of Commerce.

6. *Decision-making*: The internal, external and consultative reports are synthesised by TPD, and a recommendation is prepared to make a decision on whether to initiate a formal case at WTO. If TPD recommends that the government should launch a formal challenge against a foreign measure, the Union Minister of Commerce would normally approve such recommendation. Usual practice dictates that the case file is signed by the Commerce Secretary; however, if the dispute is particularly important, the Commerce Secretary will refer the case file to the Minister of Commerce for final approval. In cases with substantial strategic implications or in cases that are politically sensitive in nature, the file may further be referred to the Cabinet Committee on Economic Affairs or the full Cabinet for final approval.[13] Hence, there could be alternative decision-makers for such actions in India. Once the file is signed, it is sent to the PMI at Geneva for further coordination of tasks. In addition, a request is made to the Ministry of External Affairs to launch formal consultations with the offending Member State(s).
7. *Selection of trade lawyers*: The selection of lawyers for the preparation and litigation of disputes is also based on a flexible and needs-based procedure. The appointment of lawyers depends upon several factors, including the nature of a case, availability of relevant in-house expertise and capacity, availability of government resources, and past experiences of dealing with the available legal experts. An official states that 'in some cases, we may bank upon the expertise of new trade lawyers, and in other cases, we may prefer lawyers with whom

---

13 WTO case files have only been referred twice or thrice to the Cabinet Committee. Hence, it is not a practice, but more of an exception. (Interview with an official, Ministry of Law & Justice, Government of India, Delhi, India, 3 June 2013).

we have had some previous experience'.[14] The decision to engage a lawyer in a matter is taken by the Ministry of Commerce. In cases where an industry is participating actively, the decision is made after consulting the participating industry representatives.

Over the past few years, the procedure for the selection of trade lawyers has become somewhat 'systemic' in nature. The Ministry of Commerce issues a call of interest to the Government of India empanelled law firms that have expertise in the relevant subject matter. The law firms that respond to the call are asked to analyse a given trade matter and submit their legal opinion on the same. They are simultaneously asked to provide information about their team of trade lawyers and their relevant experience in the subject matter. The TPD examines their credentials and the extensiveness of their legal analytical work reflected in their written opinion. Based on this examination and other specified factors, the decision to engage an appropriate law firm is made by the officials at TPD.

At times, the empanelled law firms are also hired on a rotational basis. 'As a practice, the Panel stage work generally is allocated to the same lawyer who assisted the government at the time of the consultation. The same sequence of action is envisaged at the Appellate stage as well, if any.'[15] However, there have been cases in India where a different set of lawyers was hired for different stages of dispute settlement. For example, in *EU – Seizure of Generic Drugs in Transit*,[16] Luthra & Luthra (a New Delhi-based law firm) provided the initial opinion relating to the legal viability of launching the dispute but Mr Venugopal, Mr Abbot and Mr Tiwari were subsequently hired for the formal consultative meetings.

The selection process employed by the government is described by a trade lawyer as a 'learn to swim or sink' strategy.[17] The lawyer states that the government has, in the past, hired law firms based in India with no previous WTO experience, and has asked them to prepare and present a case at the WTO Panel on their own. However, the same interviewee comments that this strategy 'enhances the potential and

---

[14] Interview with an official, Ministry of Commerce, Government of India, Delhi, India, 12 June 2013.

[15] Written response to RTI Application (n 10).

[16] *European Union and a Member State – Seizure of Generic Drugs in Transit*, WT/DS408, in consultations on 11 May 2010.

[17] Interview with a trade lawyer, Luthra & Luthra, Delhi, India, 21 June 2013.

brings out the best in domestic law firms',[18] which suggests that the selection process works sufficiently well.

8. *Consultations, litigation and compliance proceedings*: The main constituents responsible for preparing consultation requests and legal briefs for the WTO adjudicatory hearings are: the officials from TPD, the officials from the Department of Regional and Multilateral Trade Relations, law officers from PMI, advisers from the Centre for WTO Studies, and the lawyers and consultants engaged for the dispute. The national delegation at the consultation meetings, Panel and Appellate Body hearings, and compliance proceedings is composed of these public and private sector officials, but it can vary as per the requirements of each case. The roles of these public and private representatives are not clearly defined or demarcated during these stages. They are expected to work together and in close coordination with one another. However, TPD continues to be the lead coordinator and it is responsible for coordinating tasks among these officials.

The Ministry of Commerce employs a slightly different approach when it acts as a respondent or as a third party during the settlement of WTO disputes.

1.1.2.2 As a respondent

On receiving a formal consultation request from a WTO Member State, the Ministry of Commerce refers the matter to its TPD for detailed investigation. While acting as a respondent in a WTO case, the key public sector participants involved in preparing the defence are largely the same, but the scope of their role changes. The TPD, PMI and Competent Ministry are together responsible for preparing a defence. Together, they decide the course of action, the appropriate response to the challenge, the lawyers to be engaged and the channels for gathering information and evidence. While defending a case, or participating in consultations as a respondent, the national delegation would normally comprise the first legal secretary from PMI, the Indian Ambassador to WTO, director level officials from TPD, officials from Competent Ministries, and lawyers.

Each participating constituent has a defined role while the country is acting as a respondent. The TPD, with the assistance of lawyers, is responsible for investigating the legality of a challenge and the WTO-consistency of a measure that is challenged. It is also responsible for preparing the defence briefs, determining the legal positions of the country at different

---

[18] Ibid.

stages of a dispute, and determining the legal procedures to be followed. The Centre for WTO Studies investigates and analyses the scope of a dispute, including the implications of the continuance or discontinuance of a challenged measure(s). On being approached by the government or otherwise, the export promotion councils, trade associations, chambers of commerce and relevant government departments usually provide information, evidence and commercial arguments to help the government prepare a sound defence. They provide practical insights on the commercial situation of the challenged measure and the implications of its removal for the affected industry. The Ministry of Commerce, after consulting the Competent Ministry and relevant stakeholders, determines whether to withdraw the challenged policy and resolve the matter with the complainants during the consultation stage, or to allow the matter to proceed to the Panel stage of proceedings. The PMI guides TPD while preparing the timelines for policy removal, deciding the dates for filing responses, and other procedural issues that have to be determined in conformity with WTO rules.

The procedures employed for the selection of lawyers here is also different from the cases where India acts as a complainant. In 2010, the Department of Commerce, together in consultation with the Department of Legal Affairs, enlisted 17 law firms onto its panel for defending India's interest in WTO disputes. 'The work related to these disputes is allocated to these law firms on a rotation basis subject to their expertise in the relevant field'.[19] With certain exceptions, the same law firm is hired for initial investigations, consultation meetings, subsequent litigation and compliance proceedings.

1.1.2.3 As a third party

The procedure for filing a third party request is simple. If the Ministry of Commerce, in consultation with the Competent Ministry, decides to join a specific WTO case as a third party, the Ministry of Commerce will send the request to PMI. PMI files the formal application with the consulting members and DSB requesting to join a dispute as a third party.

Together, these procedures have been employed, generally on an ad hoc and flexible basis, by the government and private sector during the handling of trade disputes. These procedures are neither codified nor detailed in a rulebook; hence, the public and private entities do not have a document to refer to while they are jointly managing a dispute. As these

---

19 Written response to RTI Application (n 10).

procedures are not prescribed anywhere, this chapter's description of them is based on the recollections of Indian officials from the Ministry of Foreign Affairs, PMI to WTO, Centre for WTO Studies, and various industry associations. It should be noted that the procedures do not constitute a set of hard and fast rules that must be complied with, and it is possible for the government and industry officials to depart from them on a case-by-case basis.

2.1 PUBLIC PRIVATE COORDINATION: ANALYSIS OF SELECTED TRADE DISPUTES

In this section, three WTO litigations shed light on the nature and characteristics of informal partnership arrangements commonly formed between the government and industries in India either in an ad hoc manner or through repeated instances of coordination.

2.1.1 EC – Tariff Preferences

In the case of *EC – Tariff Preferences*,[20] India challenged the tariff concessions granted by the EU (the then European Communities) to twelve developing countries.[21] These tariff concessions were granted through a preferential tariff arrangement under the EU's 'Generalised System of Preferences' Scheme, which allows developed countries to provide favourable market access to the exports from developing countries.[22] India alleged that the tariff concessions granted under this arrangement violated the provisions of Most Favoured Nation (MFN) and the Enabling Clause.[23] The Panel and the Appellate Body upheld the challenge as they

---

20 Appellate Body Report, *European Communities – Conditions for the Granting of Tariff Preferences to Developing Countries*, WT/DS246/AB/R, adopted 20 April 2004.

21 The preferred countries were: Bolivia, Colombia, Costa Rica, Ecuador, El Salvador, Guatemala, Honduras, Nicaragua, Pakistan, Panama, Peru and Venezuela.

22 The arrangements were officially known as the 'Special arrangements to combat drug production and trafficking'. Council Regulation (EC) No 2501/2001 of 10 December 2011 applying a scheme of generalised tariff preferences for the period from 1 January 2002 to 31 December 2004 [2001] OJ L346/8, art 1.2.

23 The 'Enabling Clause' is officially known as the 'Differential and More Favourable Treatment Reciprocity and Fuller Participation of Developing Countries'. It permits developed countries to make preferential arrangements with

found that the tariff preferences were inconsistent with GATT 1994, and the measures were not justified under the Enabling Clause.

This case is a significant example of coordination between the government and the affected export promotion council, the Cotton Textiles Export Promotion Council of India (TEXPROCIL). The existing literature claims that the case was principally initiated by the Ministry of Textiles and the Ministry of Commerce and that the private stakeholders were largely absent during most of the consultations and initial investigation phase of the dispute.[24] It further observes that TEXPROCIL filed a report (requesting the government to protect its trade interests) with the Ministry of Commerce only *after* the government had invoked WTO DSU provisions in this matter.[25] By contrast, a TEXPROCIL representative who participated throughout the proceedings confirms that the measure was identified by TEXPROCIL and that he himself was a part of the national delegation during all stages of dispute settlement, including the stage of formal consultation and Panel proceedings.[26] It can therefore be seen that findings from the existing literature and the empirical research contradict each other and are difficult to reconcile.

The literature and empirical findings confirm that TEXPROCIL provided the government with the required information relating to India's performance before and after the EU's implementation of Drug Arrangements. It supplied data on the declining exports of Indian textiles and cotton to the EU, and other related information required at the litigation stage.[27] A TEXPROCIL representative notes the following:

> TEXPROCIL provided data on the lost market access, the impact it is having on textile exporters and industry, what kind of amount we are losing, and what we could have gained in the absence of the preferential regime. The entire datasheet was provided by us, along with the commercial arguments.[28]

---

developing countries in goods trade. It is the WTO's legal basis for the Generalised System of Preferences. (Decision of 28 November 1979 (L/4903) para 2).

[24] Biswajit Dhar & Abhik Majumdar, 'Learning from the India-EC GSP Dispute: The Issues and the Process' in Gregory C Shaffer & Ricardo Melendez-Ortiz (eds), *Dispute Settlement at the WTO: The Developing Country Experience* (Cambridge University Press 2010) 182–185.

[25] Ibid.

[26] Interview with an official, TEXPROCIL, Mumbai, India, 27 June 2013.

[27] Dhar & Majumdar (n 24) 183; interview with an official, TEXPROCIL (n 26).

[28] Interview with an official, TEXPROCIL (n 26).

A TPD official confirms this claim as he states that 'TEXPROCIL had very close association with the government and it provided all the required evidence and information during the dispute.'[29] TEXPROCIL in this case supplied vital resources to the government and their lawyers with the aim of regaining the lost market access in the EU. At the same time, the government had to ensure that the interests of the textiles industry were not injured at the cost of beneficial treatment extended by the EU to India's immediate neighbouring competitors (including Pakistan). Both sectors had overlapping interests in exchanging their resources and litigating the case together. The resources were exchanged between them on the basis of mutual benefit and reciprocity.

In this case, the government relied heavily on the subsidised legal services provided by the ACWL. The ACWL's legal team was further assisted by a trade lawyer based in India, Mr Krishnan Venugopal. However, as the ACWL was the main legal service provider in this case, Mr Venugopal's participation was limited. Nevertheless, attaching an in-house lawyer (Mr Venugopal) to the ACWL legal team indicates the government's commitment to enhance its own legal expertise in WTO laws through engaging with private sector legal experts in such matters.

The Ministry of Commerce has claimed, in an explicit manner, that all WTO disputes are financed entirely by the government, and that 'no financial assistance is taken from the industry'.[30] However, a private sector representative claims with certainty that, in this specific case, a part of the ACWL's legal fees was paid by TEXPROCIL.[31] This claim is supported by a trade adviser to the government in the following statement: 'Because TEXPROCIL had its commercial interest in the dispute, and was backed by the concerned exporters, it also incurred some of the legal costs for hiring lawyers to prepare and litigate this case at the WTO'.[32] The government's overall inhibition in acknowledging the acceptance of financial contributions from the affected private sector could be explained in light of its political and social settings. Its highly democratic set-up on one hand and previous records of rent-seeking allegations including corruption and lobbying against various public sector authorities in India on the other hand can explain this inhibition. In other words, this cautious behaviour could be attributed to the government's willingness to avoid the allegations of favouritism towards a specific economic sector or company.

---

29 Interview with an official, Ministry of Commerce (n 10).
30 Written response to RTI Application (n 10).
31 Interview with an official, TEXPROCIL (n 26).
32 Interview with an official, Centre for WTO Studies IIFT, Delhi, India, 5 June 2013.

Another striking feature of this dispute settlement partnership was that an official from TEXPROCIL was part of the national delegation during consultations and Panel proceedings. Direct participation of a private sector representative at the official meetings was a unique feature of this partnership as the government has usually preferred to keep private sector representatives out of the official meeting rooms. A private sector representative further explains this aspect of PPP in the following statement:

> . . .This is how we felt like a part of the system and the feeling motivated us to invest our resources and time in the process. I was an equal participant and a partner with the government in the process throughout. When you are kept outside the room, you become an indirect contributor. But when you participate directly to this extent, the problems and the issues can be raised in consultation with the private sector and be answered there and then, and the momentum of the proceedings is therefore not lost.[33]

In other words, it is suggested that the momentum of the arguments during consultations and adjudicatory proceedings can be maintained with the help of regular and close cooperation between the industry and the government, more so through direct participation of industry representatives. A private sector representative claims that this approach has its merits, as it enables an industry to fully contribute to the settlement of a dispute, and it allows the government to gain full confidence and support from an industry. However, there could be possible drawbacks to the approach as it might enable an industry to directly dominate the intergovernmental process at WTO. As seen in the previous chapter, it might provide an industry with an opportunity to protect its own special economic interests at the cost of wider national interests. However, that risk could be counterbalanced to some extent in the present case as the participating industry representative (TEXPROCIL) is a body established and sponsored by the government.

2.1.2 EC – Bed Linen

In the case of *EC – Bed Linen*,[34] India requested consultations with the EU in respect of anti-dumping proceedings initiated by the EU against the imports of cotton-type bed-linen products from India. India alleged

---

33 Interview with an official, TEXPROCIL (n 26).

34 Appellate Body Report, *European Communities – Anti-Dumping Duties on Imports of Cotton-Type Bed Linen from India*, WT/DS141/AB/R, adopted 12 March 2001.

that the anti-dumping duties imposed by the EU violated the provisions of the Anti-Dumping Agreement and GATT 1994. It contended that the EU had not taken into account the developing country status of India and had erred in making determinations, establishing the facts and evaluating them. The Panel and the Appellate Body partially upheld the claims made by India and recommended that the EU should bring its measures in conformity with its obligations under the Anti-Dumping Agreement.

This case is an instance where an export promotion council coordinated with the government from the initial stage of identification to the final stages of implementation. A private sector representative claims that the barrier was identified by TEXPROCIL, which subsequently approached the Ministry of Textiles and the Ministry of Commerce with the representation that the duties imposed by the EU were infringing the interests of the textiles industry. The Ministry of Commerce, in coordination with the Textiles Ministry and PMI, preliminarily examined the issue and decided to investigate the matter further. Following detailed investigation, the government was convinced that the duties were inconsistent with WTO rules and that they were causing a significant loss of market share to its textiles exporters.

A trade policy adviser to the Ministry of Commerce confirms that 'TEXPROCIL was actively involved at each stage of the dispute in the *EC-Bed Linen* case' and that 'TEXPROCIL participated in the investigations, consultations, in meetings with the Panel, and in preparation of the legal documents for the litigation. It provided all the required information'.[35] It also played a proactive role at the enforcement stage of the dispute. After receiving a favourable ruling from the Panel and the Appellate Body, TEXPROCIL continued to monitor the EU's progress in implementing the award. On finding that the award was not being implemented, TEXPROCIL again approached the Ministry of Commerce with the evidence of non-implementation and convinced the government to initiate compliance proceedings against the EU. Subsequently, the government requested the launch of compliance proceedings on the basis of facts provided by TEXPROCIL. This case therefore shows that an industry can play an instrumental role, not only in the investigation, preparation and litigation of the case, but also during the compliance proceedings.

TEXPROCIL hired a Brussels-based law firm to prepare and present

---

[35] Interview with an official, Centre for WTO Studies (n 32).

the case at WTO and paid a substantial amount of the firm's legal fees.[36] A part of that expenditure was later reimbursed to TEXPROCIL by the government, and the other part of the expenditure was met by TEXPROCIL through industry contributions.[37] This payment arrangement worked well for both entities. TEXPROCIL initially incurred the entire expenditure from the funds gathered through industry contributions, and a part of those expenses were later reimbursed by the government. Similar financing arrangements, based on mutual understanding and trust, can foster such partnerships between the government and industry by creating a relationship of confidence between them.

One of the most effective features of this partnership arrangement was the openness in the channels of communication between the government and the industry. A TEXPROCIL representative confirms the importance of 'open channels of communication' in the following statement:

> The *EC-Bed Linen* is a classic case of PPP in India as the lines of communication between the Government and TEXPROCIL were very open. The entire set of information was disseminated and discussed in an open manner between the two. We never got the feeling that we were outsiders. We were very much a part of the proceedings and were updated on a regular basis by the Government.[38]

The government was alert throughout the proceedings, and it reacted promptly to the updates provided and requests raised by the industry. A representative from TEXPROCIL was provided with a forum in which to express opinions and respond to commercial enquiries raised during official consultations. TEXPROCIL's representative was seen as a commercial expert in the matter, and the inputs provided by TEXPROCIL were given serious consideration at every stage of the proceedings. The free flow of information and resources between the industry and the government was largely down to the efforts of the export promotion council involved in the matter; that is, TEXPROCIL.

The industry and the government in this case cooperated 'like never before'.[39] One of the key reasons behind the formation of this distinct PPP arrangement could be that the government, by this stage, had started

---

[36] Vermulst Verhaeghe & Graafsma, although the firm is now known as VVGB law firm. The lawyers engaged in the matter were Edwin Vermulst and Folkert Graafsma.

[37] The claims were made by an official representative from TEXPROCIL (interview with an official, TEXPROCIL (n 26)).

[38] Interview with an official, TEXPROCIL (n 26).

[39] Ibid.

to confide in TEXPROCIL. This EPC, as a repeat participant in dispute settlement processes, had established relevant contacts in the ministries. Through recurring participation, TEXPROCIL generated a relationship of confidence between the Ministry of Commerce and the textiles industry because it served as a reliable, trustworthy interface between the two. This could be seen as a possible reason for the smooth interaction between them throughout the pre-litigation, litigation and post-litigation phases of this dispute. The discussion to some extent indicates that political influence and pre-established contacts, especially in the absence of a legal right to petition, can help industries seeking to protect and expand their foreign market access.

2.1.3 US – Carbon Steel (India)

In the case of *US – Carbon Steel (India)*,[40] India challenged the imposition of countervailing duties by the United States on imports of certain hot rolled carbon steel flat products from India. India alleged that the duties violated the provisions of GATT 1994 and the SCM Agreement. Regarding the claims that were within the scope of the DSU proceedings, the Panel concluded that the US had acted in contravention of the SCM Agreement. Hence, one of the main allegations raised by India was upheld by the Panel. However, the Panel rejected numerous claims made by India against the US trade remedy laws and determinations made by the US Department of Commerce with regard to the imports of certain steel products from India. The Appellate Body reversed the Panel's recommendations with respect to the US Department of Commerce (USDOC) findings that were found to be inconsistent with Articles 1, 14, 12 and 15 of the SCM Agreement and Article 11 of the DSU. Hence, the Appellate Body ruling was a favourable decision for India as it ruled that the challenged countervailing duties were inconsistent with the SCM Agreement and that the US should bring its measures in conformity with its WTO obligations.

The government, in the present instance, was approached directly by the affected companies. It was unlike the previous disputes where companies approached the government departments through trade associations and export promotion councils. Essar Steel, along with Tata Steel and Jindal Steel, filed an application with the Ministry of Commerce. In their application, they alleged that the countervailing duties imposed by the US on the

---

40 Appellate Body Report, *United States – Countervailing Measures on Certain Hot-Rolled Carbon Steel Flat Products from India*, WT/DS436/AB/R, adopted 19 December 2014.

imports of certain hot rolled carbon steel flat products were detrimental to their exporting interests and were inconsistent with WTO provisions. This application was a bulky file with an extensive collection of informational facts, evidential data and commercial arguments.[41] The matter was subsequently investigated by TPD. Following that, the file was referred to PMI for further investigation and preparation of a request for consultation.[42]

Essar Steel was the chief private sector participant as its business was the most affected when compared to the other two companies. Most of the information provided to the government therefore came from Essar Steel. The government held consultations with all three affected companies. The national delegation during formal consultations, Panel and Appellate hearings comprised lawyers (Lakshmikumaran & Sridharan Attorneys), officials from the Ministry of Commerce, officials from PMI and advisers from the Centre for WTO Studies. The affected companies or their representatives were not directly involved in the formal proceedings held at Geneva, but their physical absence during meetings or formal hearings should not suggest that they were not an essential and active part of the process. 'They were indeed extensively consulted while making preparations for the consultation meetings and while preparing the consultative briefs. Their physical presence in the meeting was just not required in this case.'[43]

The case confirms that the private sector (which in this case comprised the giant steel companies of India) would generally be more forthcoming and active in assisting the government during the settlement of disputes if it has high stakes in the matter and is anticipating substantial gains from the removal of a trade barrier. Therefore, as initially discussed, one of the vital stages of the dispute settlement process is the stage where the private sector examines the benefits to be gained from the removal of a barrier as against its expected cost of removal. The industries' decision to approach and assist its government largely depends upon the cost-benefit analysis conducted at this stage.[44]

---

41 The author gained access to the written memorandum filed by Essar Steel. It was addressed to the Ministry of Commerce, Government of India (details confidential).

42 Interview with an official, Permanent Mission of India, WTO, Geneva, Switzerland, 12 April 2012.

43 'Having an industrial representative in the national delegation during consultation meetings is need based.' (Interview with an official, Ministry of Commerce (n 10)).

44 For further details on anticipated costs and benefits, see Jan Bohanes & Fernanda Garza, 'Going Beyond Stereotypes: Participation of Developing

Finally, the case adds a new perspective to the ways in which the Government of India has coordinated with industries in the past. In this case, the government accepted and acknowledged an application filed by private businesses and proceeded to the stage of investigation, consultation and litigation on the basis of the evidence provided by these companies. There is no noticeable mention of any trade association, trade union, export promotion council or chamber of commerce assisting the government and the private companies to coordinate and exchange resources in the case. This finding provides a testimony to the fact that resourceful and influential companies such as Essar Steel can directly (and with comparative ease) approach their government if they have a trade matter to be resolved. They may not require the intervention of an industry representative as they often themselves possess the capacity to supply required resources to the government. On the other hand, the previous two cases (EC – *Tariff Preferences* and *EC – Bed Linen*) have established the significance of institutionalising and strengthening the private sector representative organisations as it may not be possible for the smaller and less resourceful companies (such as MSMEs) in India to directly access their government individually for the resolution of foreign trade conflicts. In this manner, the PPP approach can possibly discriminate in favour of resourceful business entities by providing them comparatively straightforward access to international adjudicatory provisions at WTO DSU. Hence, the PPP approach should not be considered without caution and the country aspiring to evaluate this approach should do so in light of its potential limitations and impediments, some of which are discussed in the following section.

3.1 CHALLENGES AND 'LESSONS LEARNT': A CRITICAL LOOK

The informal and ad hoc PPP arrangements have clearly strengthened India's dispute settlement capacity. However, it is important to note that there are multiple domestic conditions in India that may impede the formation of effective partnership arrangements – an arrangement which in itself is not free from certain weaknesses. Hence, before reaching any conclusions on the effectiveness of the PPP strategies employed in India, it is important to analyse the challenges and limitations that confront this

---

Countries in WTO Dispute Settlement' (2012) 4(1) *Trade Law and Development* 45, 66–67.

approach. These challenges and limitations, along with certain suggestions to overcome them, are discussed in the following subsections.

3.1.1 Unorganised Private Sector in India

One of the biggest constraints that India faces in effectively utilising the PPP approach is its largely 'unorganised' private sector.[45] The economic sector in India is heavily fragmented, with multinational businesses leading a handful of industries including steel, automobile and information technology on one hand, and a large number of economic sectors being run by MSMEs on the other hand. Together, the MSMEs contribute significantly to foreign trade, but their individual volumes of exports and profit margins may constrain their capacity to form and finance representative organisations, gather information, and approach the government with a well-researched trade issue.

An interviewee provides an example to illustrate the problem of India's insufficiently organised private sector. The fisheries industry in India, a significant exporting sector, comprises micro and small producers and exporters. They are partially represented by trade associations (such as SEAI) and an export promotion council (MPEDA), but the main problem lies in the fact that the industry is not 'sufficiently institutionalised' as trade associations and councils have failed to coordinate and represent the interests of unorganised and unaware exporters and producers of seafood – the fishermen in India. The interviewee explains this in the following words:

> By and large, there is poor awareness among the fishermen about the exports market, efficient and environment friendly ways of fishing, the technological developments for minimising wastage, and the opportunities offered to them by the increasingly liberalising world trade. Some of the WTO agreements actually protect the interest of the poor fishermen who are the actual producers, but the

---

[45] An unorganised sector in India is defined as a sector that consists 'of all unincorporated private enterprises owned by individuals or households engaged in the sale or production of goods and services operated on a proprietary or partnership basis and with less than ten total workers.' Over 90% of the country's working population is employed in the unorganised sector. (National Commission for Enterprises in the Unorganised Sector, Government of India, *Report on Conditions of Work and Promotion of Livelihoods in the Unorganised Sector* (Academic Foundation 2008) 1774).

fishermen think that the international agreements and rules are not for them but are only intended to serve the interests of the exporters.[46]

The above statement illustrates an important point; that is, poor awareness amongst the economic sectors may be an obstacle to the formation of PPP arrangements as it can lead to a situation of psychological disconnect between the two. Effective interaction between an industry and a government is possible only when the private sector is well-organised, aware, interconnected and strongly institutionalised. This may not be the case with many industries, especially in developing and least developed countries. Investment should therefore be made in developing the institutional and resource capacity of the private sector by creating interconnected and well-funded trade cooperatives, trade associations, chambers of commerce and export promotion councils.

Matthew, a representative from the Indian Fisheries industry, suggests that trade cooperatives can discharge multiple functions. The cooperatives can coordinate with the government departments and make attempts to strike bargains for beneficial domestic and international conditions in the interest of producers and exporters.[47] They can assist producers in producing and marketing goods to their optimum capacity by imparting the right training in production and marketing techniques. They can also assist exporters in finding the right markets for their products and to divert their exports to new markets in case of trade disagreements or barriers arising in existing markets.

Many of India's present-day export promotion councils and trade associations are a product of the 'export promotion import substitution' economic policy introduced in the 1950s. So they date back to the pre-liberalisation period when the markets were closed and protected; hence, the councils and associations continue to employ an inward-looking approach. In today's global economy, however, businesses are expected to identify their markets across national borders and to negotiate their interests nationally and internationally. Hence, in the wake of different trade rules and international trade conditions, an institutional reform of representative organisations is a much-needed step towards building an organised private sector in India. An organised industry comprising pow-

---

46 Interview with an official, Fisheries & Fishing Communities in India (audio conferencing) 17 June 2013.

47 For example, the trade cooperatives in Europe have in the past bargained successfully for subsidised fuel for consumption by fishing vessels in the country. This has decreased the costs of operation and increased the profit margins of the fisheries industry.

erful trade associations with expert officials that can coordinate with the government on a regular basis can facilitate the process of government-industry coordination. On the other hand, an industry with 'less sophisticated' associations, and a 'fragmented industry' with 'small companies' and 'disintegrated representatives' may diminish the attractiveness of the capacity-building partnership approach.[48]

3.1.2 Lack of Coordination

Another obstacle that not only hampers government-industry coordination but also impedes India's participation at WTO DSU is the problem of coordination between various divisions of the government and between the government and industries. The problem can be illustrated with the help of an example. In the case of *China – Electronic Payment Services*,[49] certain restrictions and requirements with respect to the electronic payment services for payment card transactions maintained by China were challenged by the US. An official from China's Permanent Mission to WTO approached his counterpart at PMI to apprise him of the matter, which, according to Chinese officials, also affected the financial interests of India. On being informed of the matter, the PMI officials made relevant enquiries with the Reserve Bank of India and the Ministry of Finance. The Mission officials found out that the financial sector of India could also be impacted by the resolution of this matter because of the restrictions and requirements on e-payments and card transactions that existed at that time in India. However, due to delay in identifying this possible threat to its payment procedures, India was on the verge of missing the opportunity to join this case as a third party participant.

Lack of communication and coordination between the financial sector and the government, and between the Ministry of Finance and the Ministry of Commerce in India becomes evident here. Such instances reflect that coordination between the government departments should be strengthened by devising cost-effective focal points and practical procedures of inter-ministerial coordination. In addition, coordination between the government and industries should also be improved by devising effective and open

---

[48] Bohanes & Garza (n 44) ('It would make little sense for one individual company to lobby the government to initiate action at the WTO against a trade barrier. Rather, a more rational course of action for that one company would be to adjust to the trade barrier and/or seek other export markets, especially when the company cannot tolerate revenue fluctuations').

[49] Panel Report, *China – Certain Measures Affecting Electronic Payment Services*, WT/DS413/R, adopted 31 August 2012.

channels of communication between the two. This could facilitate regular exchanges between the affected public and private stakeholders in India, which may in turn provide the government with adequate amount of time to coordinate and receive information from the concerned industry.

3.1.3 Lack of Confidence

Lack of confidence between the government and industries is another reason why the formation of effective networks between the two can be impeded. The problem is described by an Indian seafood association official:

> We have at times faced scepticism from the government when we approached them for certain trade concerns our exporters had. We were asked to establish that the affected exporters had not done anything wrong, and that the financial loss they were facing was due to a foreign measure and not due to other internal reasons. The burden of proof was entirely on us to prove the legitimacy of our complaint. . . .The industry, which was asked to supply detailed evidence, felt that the government is trying to discourage them from raising their complaints. This and similar other experiences have caused a major trust deficit between us.[50]

The statement shows that the first 'battle' that the private sector must win in its attempt to overcome foreign trade barriers is an internal one; that is, the battle of convincing its own government to investigate the problem and to launch an action at WTO. This signifies distrust between the government officials and the private sector entities as 'they both believe that they have different interests and their interests cannot coincide'.[51] It is therefore important that the mindset of the government and business entities should change. The government should view industry interests as forming part of a broad spectrum of economic needs affecting the entire nation, and should recognise that the protection of legitimate trade interests will foster international trade and economic growth in India. At the same time, industries must have faith that their government will strive to protect their legitimate business interests.

---

50 Confirmed by an official representative, Seafood Exporters Association of India, in an interview (audio conferencing) of 9 September 2013.

51 Interview with an official, TEXPROCIL (n 26).

3.1.4 Possible Discrimination between Resourceful and Resource-constrained Industries

Irrespective of the above-mentioned impediments and limitations, the public and the private sector entities in India have demonstrated an emerging 'pattern of coordination' through a series of jointly managed disputes. However, it may be recalled that only a few industries have partnered the government with the leading repeat participant being the textiles industry. The partnership between the government and TEXPROCIL should be seen as more of an 'exception' than a 'rule' in India, as it may not be possible for other industries to approach the government in similar ways. A comparable level of private participation is not evident in cases affecting the interests of other major exporting industries, such as pottery[52] and seafood.[53]

Economies of scale and the involvement of substantial stakes are arguably the main reasons for India's textiles and steel industries' active participation at WTO DSU. On the other hand, the lack of established procedures facilitating the interaction between the two sectors, weak representation, the prospective nature of WTO remedies, low trading stakes, and poor economies of scale may account for the nonparticipation of India's other significant exporting industries in cases filed at WTO DSU. These observations further confirm that the formation of dispute settlement partnerships may lead to a situation of discrimination between the 'haves' and the 'have nots' in a country with widespread corruption and poor observance of the rule of law. Regulatory concerns described in Chapters 2 and 5 may also be the plausible limitation of this approach for a developing country with similar domestic conditions.

4.1 CONCLUDING REMARKS

Past practice dictates that the government departments and industries in India have contacted each other through pre-established contacts, political influence, semi-governmental export promotion councils and other informal ways including phone calls, emails and unscheduled meetings. Public and private entities have collaborated with the help of flexible and

---

52 Appellate Body Report, *India – Measures Concerning the Importation of Certain Agricultural Products from the United States*, WT/DS430/AB/R, adopted 19 June 2015.

53 Appellate Body Report, *United States – Import Prohibition of Certain Shrimp and Shrimp Products*, WT/DS58/AB/R, adopted 6 November 1998.

undefined procedures chosen on an ad hoc basis during the pre-litigation, litigation and post-litigation stages. The government remains overtly reluctant towards formalising such procedures of coordination because of its democratic set-up amidst the widespread level of corruption. The lawmakers in India, being in theory directly accountable to their voters, would generally refrain from codifying or explicitly establishing a procedure of private-funding for the settlement of intergovernmental trade conflicts as some of these conflicts could pertain to the protection of social, environmental, consumer and other national interests.

The government, which acts as the lead partner, has received several practical benefits from private sector engagement, including better litigation strategies, wider access to information and commercial evidence, enhanced financial capacity, comprehensive legal and commercial analysis, better monitoring and identification of barriers, and increased capacity to seek compliance. On the other hand, wealthy and well-represented business entities (such as those operating in the textiles and steel industries) have gained a voice in the purely intergovernmental DSU proceedings that are in reality conducted for the protection of their business interests. This shows that, as with the formal and semi-formal partnership arrangements, an informal partnership arrangement also enjoys the benefit of capacity building. All three mechanisms have certain limitations, and they can face multiple impediments during their formation and functioning; however, they clearly demonstrate the potential to bridge the dispute settlement capacity-gap between the developed and developing Members States of WTO.

India's experience also confirms that pre-established contacts and interfacing private institutions (such as TEXPROCIL) can create a relationship of confidence, leading to open channels of communication and close interaction between and among the multiple stakeholders of the process. Repeat participation of a specific trade association or export promotion council can also contribute to the building and furtherance of this relationship. Finally, India's experience confirms that the key partners in a partnership arrangement, whether it is formal, semi-formal, informal or ad hoc in nature, are the concerned government authorities and affected business entities. However, they are closely supported by their respective subject-specific government departments, permanent missions, trade lawyers, economists and civil society representatives. The complex nature of foreign trade conflicts and WTO dispute settlement proceedings demands such multidisciplinary approach.

7. Devising dispute settlement partnerships: 'lessons learnt'

The previous chapters have underlined a number of capacity-building strategies. Some of them have proved advantageous in creating a more enabling dispute settlement environment, while others have remained largely ineffective. However, as initially argued in Chapter 2, and subsequently confirmed in the following chapters, it is not possible to generalise the effectiveness (or ineffectiveness) of these strategies as they may not produce similar results in all developing countries, especially because of the different economic and political conditions of WTO members. Hence, in place of arguing in favour of a standard PPP mechanism, this chapter presents guidelines that will analyse and build upon the dispute settlement experiences discussed in the previous chapters. The proposed guidelines are discussed under the following five categories:

1. A system of rights and obligations;
2. Provisions enhancing transparency and regulation;
3. Creation of strong industry representatives;
4. Financing dispute settlement procedures; and
5. Small claims provisions for non-litigable matters.

Developing Member States with levels of development, dependency on foreign trade and political economies similar to Brazil, India and China (BIC) can particularly benefit from the experiences of BIC. Moreover, advanced MICs with considerable DSU experience and the desire to achieve a more enabling dispute settlement environment can consider the guidelines proposed in this chapter. However, it is important to note that the proposed strategies are limited in their application as they may not be suitable for developing Member States that are classified under the World Bank's list of 'low income countries' and 'heavily indebted poor countries', along with the ones listed as 'least developed countries' by the UN. These countries do not fit within the parameters of this work due to their almost non-existent DSU participation experience, small market size, low aggregate trading stakes and other domestic conditions that may impede them from participating at WTO DSU. However, findings distilled in this chapter can certainly apprise them of the challenges, benefits and prerequisites for engaging the affected private sector should they seek to invoke the provisions of WTO DSU in the future.

As observed in the previous chapters, China, Brazil and India have different domestic circumstances. Multiple domestic conditions prevailing in these countries, including the nature of governance, structure of economy, political conditions, policies and social values, and bureaucratic frameworks have shaped the PPP approach employed by these countries. Accordingly, each country considering the following guidelines should assess the suitability of the proposed strategies in light of their particular domestic circumstances. During this assessment, the countries may be guided by the examination of multiple domestic factors and potential challenges to the PPP approach discussed in Chapters 2, 3, 4, 5 and 6. With this understanding, this chapter draws for consideration some of the 'lessons learnt' from the dispute settlement and partnership experiences presented throughout this book.

1.1 A SYSTEM OF RIGHTS AND OBLIGATIONS

A legal framework generally aims to achieve equilibrium of rights and obligations between the concerned parties. The guidelines presented in this section will propose certain rights and obligations to achieve this equilibrium between a government and an industry. The proposed rights and obligations are rooted in and built upon the existing legal provisions in the US, the EU and China. However, these proposals should be read with a caveat: the proposed rights and obligations are not essential for the formation or functioning of dispute settlement partnerships because, as seen in Chapters 5 and 6, such arrangements can be formed in the absence of any established rights and obligations. Governments and industries can coordinate in a very informal and ad hoc manner without any legal, institutional or procedural interface. Hence, the rights and obligations proposed in this section should rather be treated as alternative or complementary capacity-building strategies that may work for some Member States but may not work for others. To assist policymakers assess the country-wise suitability of these proposals, each proposal is presented along with its possible strengths and shortcomings.

1.1.1 Individual's Right to Petition

The Section 301 mechanism in the US, the TBR mechanism in the EU, and the Rules on the Investigation of Foreign Trade Barriers in China are legal gateways that are established to facilitate PPP during the settlement of foreign trade disputes. Most importantly, they provide individuals with a right to file a petition at the concerned government unit (hereinafter referred to as 'the unit') if and when their trade interests are infringed by foreign measures.[1] The right can provide individuals with the confidence that their legitimate trade interests will be protected by the government and that they will have the right to access their government if and when their trade interests need protection. The right can also assist small and medium level enterprises and their representative organisations, which may not otherwise be financially or politically strong enough to approach and influence their government. Hence, as mentioned initially in Chapter 2 and explained subsequently in Chapters 3 and 4, a similar legal provision can 'empower' industries.

At the same time, it is possible to argue that granting the right to petition may not be an effective way to enhance a country's dispute settlement capacity as similar rights in the US, the EU and China have not been utilised frequently by the industries and the governments. Formal dispute settlement mechanisms impose a high evidential burden of proof on the petitioner, which is one of the key reasons that have dissuaded the private sector from invoking such provisions.

Many industries in developing countries, for example the infant private industries in China and MSMEs in India, may not have the capacity to provide the supporting evidentiary inputs that their governments may require them to file with a formal petition. Hence, the provision may not grant an effective right to petition to those business entities that cannot afford to satisfy the resource obligation that comes with the right to peti-

---

[1] See, for example, Council Regulation (EC) No 3286/94 of 22 December 1994, art 3, which gives a right to a natural or legal person, an association, enterprise or industry to file a written complaint when it considers that it has 'suffered injury as a result of obstacles to trade that have an effect on the market of the community'. (Hereinafter referred to as 'Council Regulation'). Investigation Rules of Foreign Trade Barrier (2005), art 5 states that 'Domestic enterprises and industries or natural persons, legal persons on behalf of domestic enterprises and industries or other organisations (hereinafter referred to as "the applicants") may make an application for trade barrier investigation to the Ministry of Commerce'. (Hereinafter, referred to as the 'TBI Rules'). The US Trade Act 1974, s 302(a)(1) states that 'Any interested person may file a petition with the Trade Representative requesting that action be taken under Section 301 and setting forth the allegations in support of the request.' 'Interested person' under the Act refers to, but is not limited to, 'domestic firms and workers, representatives of consumer interests, United States product exporters, and any industrial user of any goods or services that may be affected by actions taken under s 301 (a) or (b)'. (Hereinafter referred to as 'Trade Act 1974').

tion. It therefore becomes important that a right to petition is accompanied by a right to seek exemption from the obligation of satisfying evidential requirements.[2] This enabling right will encourage resource-constrained industries to approach the unit with their trade concerns. An exemption application filed under this provision should contain the petitioner's precise reasons and constraints for seeking an exemption. The exemption may be granted by the unit after preliminary inspection of the filed petition and exemption application.

The right to petition could also be accompanied by a right to seek the unit's assistance in drafting a petition. The unit can extend advisory services to the potential petitioners upon request. It can also provide potential petitioners with an initial guide on drafting petitions and gathering evidence, possibly in the form of a simple, well-designed brochure. This obligation is vital because petitioners may initially struggle to draft their complaints without such guidance. The level of resources required for drafting and information-gathering depends upon the nature of each case. If a case is very complicated, then the preparation of documents may require the expert (and costly) services of lawyers and consultants. These requirements can make the legal provision of petitioning an unaffordable option for under-resourced and small private stakeholders, particularly those in developing countries. If the unit were to provide a reasonable level of assistance at this early stage of the dispute settlement process, the utilisation of the 'right to petition' would be considerably enhanced.

1.1.2 Government's Obligation to Administer and Examine Petitions

Corresponding to an individual's right to petition, the receiving unit should have an obligation to administer and scrutinise any petitions or applications received from the private sector.[3] The unit should ensure that the petition satisfies the evidential requirements, unless an exemption application is filed by the petitioner. If an exemption application has

---

[2] TBI Rules, art 8 contains details about the evidence required with a petition. But at the same time, it relaxes this requirement with a qualification: 'Any applicant who could not submit above materials should explain the reason by writing'.

[3] A similar obligation is imposed on MOFCOM under TBI Rules, art 10 which states that 'Ministry of Commerce should examine the application materials and make the decision on starting an investigation or not within 60 days at the receipt of the application letter and relevant evident materials'. However, it appears that art 4 confers a discretionary right on MOFCOM to administer complaints, as against an obligation, as it states that 'Ministry of Commerce *may* place the case on file for trade barriers investigation on its free will as it deems necessary' (emphasis added).

explained the reasons for seeking exemption from the evidential requirements, the unit should examine that application along with the petition. The unit should have the right to make the final decision on the exemption application. On the filing requirements being met, or on the exemption application being approved, the unit should come under an obligation to accept the petition and refer the same to its team of trade professionals to initiate preliminary investigation into the legitimacy of the complaint.

To determine the issue of launching further investigation, the unit may, during initial examination, consider additional documents and evidence. It may also consult the affected private sector and subject matter experts to evaluate the economic, legal and political implications of an alleged barrier and of launching an investigation in the matter.[4] Such analysis should be conducted within a fixed period of time. On its completion, the unit should decide on the issue of commencement or non-commencement of detailed investigation within a stipulated time limit.[5] If the initial examination finds that a given complaint does not raise a trade issue that is incompatible with WTO rights, or if it does not significantly harm the interests of the nation, or if it is economically or politically unviable to launch investigations on a measure, or if it deems the continuance of investigations inappropriate for any other reason, the unit should have a right to dismiss the petition at this stage. The petitioner should be notified of the outcome of the examination process within a stipulated time limit. The notification at this stage should state the unit's key findings on the legitimacy of a complaint, along with a statement of reasons, especially if the petition is rejected.[6]

Suitability of this provision should be considered by individual countries in accordance with their available resources, administrative capacity, political climate, trade and litigation policies and their relationship dynam-

---

[4] The European Commission is at this stage obliged to consult an Advisory Committee constituted under art 7, which comprises representatives from each Member State and a representative from the Commission. The decision on investigations which are referred to as 'Community Examination Procedure' in the Council Regulation is taken on the basis of such consultations.

[5] See, for example, TBI Rules, art 10, which obliges MOFCOM to make a decision on initiation or non-initiation of investigation within 60 days of the date of receipt of the application. Under s 301(2) of the Trade Act 1974, USTR has 45 days in which to make a similar decision. Council Regulation, art 5(4) also prescribes a time limit of 45 days from the date of lodging the complaint.

[6] TBI Rules, arts 14 and 17 oblige MOFCOM to inform applicants of the decision relating to investigations. Art 17 further obliges MOFCOM to 'inform the applicant by writing and make clear the reason why it does not start an investigation'.

ics with the industries. A possible limitation of the proposed government obligation could be the curtailment of flexibility offered by informal exchanges between the participants. An element of flexibility is important for such procedures, especially when they are devised for developing countries. However, a flexible dispute management process may to some extent reduce the benefits of 'industry empowerment' and 'certainty'. This proposed obligation can therefore be considered by countries that weigh the benefits of certainty and industry empowerment on a scale higher than the benefits accruing from flexible government-industry coordination.

1.1.3 Individual's Right to Provide Information

A petitioner or an interested person could discover new facts or find additional evidential documents at any stage of dispute settlement proceedings. Such information may be valuable for the government to strengthen its case at WTO, or to negotiate a settlement. The petitioners should therefore have a right to provide the unit with supplementary information and evidence at any stage of dispute settlement.

The unit should have a corresponding duty to accept and examine any relevant additional information provided by a petitioner or an interested person at any stage. However, the unit should have the discretion to decide whether additional inputs are relevant to the stage at which the dispute is, or whether these could be used at any subsequent stage of dispute settlement. The right to provide documents may also be extended to interested persons,[7] such as individuals, business entities, NGOs or consumer organisations. This will, to some extent, ensure that the investigation and dispute settlement procedure is widely informed in relation to different concerns and developments. Upon a legitimate request made by an interested person or a petitioner, the unit should be obliged to hold 'public hearings' for the presentation of opinions and submission of additional information.[8] The right to determine the legitimacy of a request for a 'public hearing' should vest in the unit.

On the other hand, the unit should have the right to seek additional

---

[7] These are the persons who are not petitioners but are otherwise interested in the case.

[8] Trade Act 1974, s 305 (b)(1)(A) states that USTR shall provide an opportunity for presentation of views to the interested persons and shall hold a public hearing if the same is requested by any interested person, before making determinations required under s 305 (a)(1). The same request can be rejected if USTR thinks that an expeditious action is required. Trade Act 1974, s 306 (c) imposes an obligation on USTR to consult the petitioner and other representatives of the

information from the petitioning parties and other participating individuals, as and when required during the conduct of a dispute.[9] This right should also include the right to issue a call for public comments and public hearings.[10] Correspondingly, the petitioning individual should have the responsibility to cooperate with the government and to provide such information as it can viably gather.[11] However, a negative inference should not be drawn if the petitioning individuals are unable to provide the solicited information or comments due to financial difficulties or other justifiable constraints. Therefore, the unit's right to seek further information should be limited to the consent and capacity of the petitioner providing or expected to provide the same.[12]

1.1.4 Individual's Right to Withdraw Petition

It may happen that, during the course of investigation or consultation, the commercial obstacle which a petitioning industry was seeking to remove is no longer there because that obstacle has been removed or the matter has been settled between the industries and the governments. Alternatively, the petitioning entities, at a later stage, may realise that the cost of litigating a concern would be higher than its potential benefits. It may also find that the business prospects in the offending nation have diminished and are no longer lucrative for various political, social or economic reasons. For instance, an exporter of luxury bags from Country A, whose biggest importer is Country B, may find that its profit margins have declined due to a prohibited subsidy granted to domestically produced luxury bags

---

concerned industry, and provide an opportunity to interested persons for the wider presentation of views, during consultations.

9 Council Regulation, art 8(2)(a) confers a similar right to seek information on the Commission, and art 11 of the TBI Rules confers a similar right on MOFCOM during the examination stage.

10 The US seeks public opinion on their proposed regulations and related documents via an online portal <www.regulations.gov> accessed 29 October 2012.

11 See, for example, TBI Rules, art 8, which imposes an obligation on the petitioner to provide sufficient evidence to prove the existence of an impugned measure and the causal injury to its interests. TBI Rules, art 16(2) further confers a right on MOFCOM to not start an investigation in cases where the applicant does not provide additionally sought materials within the time limit fixed by MOFCOM.

12 Council Regulation, art 8(2)(a) states that: 'If necessary the Commission shall seek all the information it deems necessary and attempt to check this information with the importers, traders, agents, producers, trade associations and organizations, *provided* that the undertakings or organizations concerned give their consent' (emphasis added).

by Country B's government. The luxury bag exporter from Country A therefore files a petition with its government to investigate the matter and to seek the removal of this measure. Meanwhile, the market of Country B no longer remains lucrative for the exporter as the demand for luxury bags in that country significantly diminishes due to the onset of recession in Country B. In that case, the exporter from Country A would prefer to divert its exports to a more lucrative market and will no longer be interested in restoring its market access and hence pursuing this conflict further. Therefore, there should be a provision allowing the petitioner to withdraw its petition if the anticipated benefit of pursuing a complaint, due to changed circumstances, has significantly reduced or changed for any legitimate reason.[13]

In these circumstances, the unit should be under an obligation to consider the request for withdrawal and grant the request if it deems it appropriate and not harmful to the interests of the nation. Conversely, the unit should have the right to reject the request for withdrawal if the dismissal of an investigation or discontinuance of a settlement procedure is not in the best interests of the nation or the wider commercial community.

1.1.5 Government's Right to Determine a Suitable Course of Action

Once the unit is convinced that a trade measure should be pursued bilaterally and/or multilaterally and that the government should make efforts for the removal of a foreign trade barrier, the unit can make recommendations to the relevant government department to commence bilateral/multilateral consultations with the offending Member State(s). The unit should have an obligation to complete the investigation process and make a determination on the pursuance or non-pursuance of an issue within a stipulated time limit.[14] If the unit decides not to pursue the matter, it should notify the petitioning and other interested parties of its decision. Such notifications can also simultaneously be published online. The government should have complete discretion on deciding the issues of pursuance or non-pursuance of a complaint or determining an appropriate course of action. The government should have the right to decide

[13] TBI Rules, art 9 allows petitioners to recall their petitions before a decision on investigation is made by MOFCOM.

[14] TBI Rules, art 31 r/w art 32 provides that MOFCOM should make a decision on a trade barrier and complete the investigation within six months from the date of its launch.

whether to initiate bilateral consultations or multilateral consultations or to pursue the matter using a different approach.[15]

An international economic law scholar observes that 'the hands of the government should not be tied while deciding such matters so that the social welfare interests of the nation are not overridden by special private interests'.[16] The government at this stage should therefore have complete discretion for making informed determinations on pursuing a matter and deciding on an appropriate course of action. Additionally, the unit should have the right to terminate further proceedings of dispute settlement if, during or after consultations, it becomes clear to the unit that a trade barrier no longer injures the market access interests of the nation.[17] The unit could also terminate the proceedings if the barrier has been withdrawn by the offending nation, or if a lack of information, evidential material or other resources warrants discontinuation of the settlement process. The settlement process may also be discontinued if the concerned industries and government departments reach a settlement, or if discontinuation of the process would be in the best interests of the nation.

1.1.6 Individual's Right to Appeal Government Decisions

The unit should have an obligation to justify its determinations. If the government says 'no' to a petition filed by the private sector, the government should have an obligation to explain that 'no'.[18] If the private sector is not satisfied with the explanation, it should have the right to file an appeal

---

[15] TBI Rules, art 33 grants a discretionary right to MOFCOM to decide which action to take if it finds that a barrier exists. It may hold bilateral consultations, initiate multilateral proceedings, or take other appropriate action.

[16] Interview with an international trade law scholar (audio conferencing) 10 June 2013.

[17] See, for example, Council Regulation, art 11, which confers a right on the Commission to terminate the proceedings if, after having consultations with an offending Member State, or after conducting the examination of a complaint, it feels that it is in the interest of the 'community industry', or in the wider national interest, to suspend or terminate the dispute. Council Regulation, art 14 prescribes the procedure for such suspension and termination. A similar provision is found in TBI Rules, art 16, wherein MOFCOM has the right to refuse further investigation and pursuance of a complaint under certain circumstances specified in the provision. Further, TBI Rules, arts 26, 28 and 30 stipulate the conditions under which MOFCOM has the right to terminate investigation proceedings in a case.

[18] For example, TBI Rules, arts 13, 14 and 17, and Council Regulation, arts 8 and 12 implicitly confer such a right on the individual to seek a statement of reasons for decisions made by the government and the Commission.

against these determinations in the national courts or a quasi-judicial authority established for such purpose.

It is important that the right to appeal is used with caution as it may delay the settlement of trade disputes. This delay may cause further trade injuries to an affected industry which might already be dealing with a continuing trade barrier. Furthermore, the provision may also increase the amount of resources expended on the entire process, as it will increase the workload of the adjudicators and lawyers. Hence, the right to appeal could further increase the government's workload and make the process more time-consuming and resource-demanding, consequently making this provision unaffordable for some developing countries.

The developing (and particularly the least developed) countries may not have the resources to introduce such a provision as it will eventually add to the cost, time and risks involved. Therefore, an alternative option could be to confer the 'right to seek review' of determinations in place of the proposed 'right to appeal' determinations. The provision can include judicial and/or administrative reviews. Reviews involve less time and procedural commitment and are comparatively less resource-demanding. They can be carried out by the unit or by an expert committee appointed for this purpose. The right may yield a result similar to the appeals process, but with some diminished effects.

1.1.7 Confidentiality and Anonymity Requirements

The individuals, representatives of industry or interested person(s) who provide information should have the right to request non-disclosure of documents, evidence and information provided by them in the interest of their business.[19] In the absence of such a right, the private sector may be hesitant to supply any information to the unit. The unit should therefore be obliged to consider the request for confidentiality made by parties supplying information and documents. The request may be accepted if the unit deems it appropriate and in the legitimate commercial interests of the requesting party.[20] If the request for confidentiality is granted, the documents supplied can only be used in furtherance of the trade dispute

---

[19] Trade Act 1974, s 308(c)(1)(A) provides that USTR shall not disclose any information received for the purpose of investigation to any person if the person providing the information certifies that the information is business confidential, not generally available or the 'disclosure of such information would endanger trade secrets or profitability'. USTR holds the right to determine whether such certification is well founded (s 308(c)(1)(C)).

[20] See, for example, TBI Rules, art 24, which obliges MOFCOM to 'treat the

under consideration. The documents cannot be used for any other purpose or for the furtherance of a different trade dispute without the specific consent of the providers of the confidential information.

The anonymity requirement is equally important to business entities making use of the dispute resolution procedure. Companies may be discouraged from approaching the government if the provisions do not grant a right to complainants to remain anonymous. It may be recalled that EU enterprises seldom use the European Commission's TBR mechanism partly because it does not contain any anonymity provisions. The absence of such a provision can generate a fear of adverse trade ramifications. Hence, to enable industries to overcome such fears, a country's dispute settlement framework should contain a provision that could make the domestic handling of disputes and procedures of coordination completely anonymous.

1.1.8 A Specialised Dispute Settlement Unit

Government should establish a specialised dispute settlement unit under a designated ministry or department. This unit can be known as the WTO dispute settlement unit.[21] It is essential that the officers recruited to this unit have basic training in, and experience of, international dispute settlement, WTO rules, and the foreign trade policies and procedures of the national government. They should remain updated on recent WTO disputes, other international trade law developments, and market access concerns. This unit can serve as the key contact point between the government and the private sector working towards the enforcement of WTO rights. Shaffer describes the institutionalisation of PPP as the establishment of a central contact point that is easily accessible by the private sector, and a dedicated international trade law unit that enables the private sector to contribute to the intergovernmental dispute settlement process.[22] The proposed unit can therefore be the primary institution responsible for discharging the obligations and giving effect to the rights mentioned under this section.

---

materials provided by the interested parties as classified' if it thinks that the request for confidentiality is proper.

21 Virachai Plasai, 'Coordinating Trade Litigation' (April 2013) ICTSD Issue Paper No 14, 4, accessed 24 September 2016 at <http://www.ictsd.org/sites/default/files/research/2013/04/coordinating-trade-litigation1.pdf>.

22 Gregory C Shaffer & Ricardo Melendez-Ortiz (eds), *Dispute Settlement at the WTO: The Developing Country Experience* (Cambridge University Press 2010) 26–27.

The primary functions which can be performed by the proposed unit are as follows:

1. *Administer, scrutinise and investigate the trade concerns of the private sector*: The unit can work closely and in partnership with private stakeholders in order to manage the dispute settlement process. The unit can be given certain quasi-judicial powers to investigate and determine the legitimacy of complaints filed by private entities or barriers identified by other sources or on a *suo moto* basis.
2. *Prepare and present cases at WTO*: Once a government has decided to initiate an action against a foreign measure, the unit can prepare a legal case with the help of lawyers, economists and subject-specific experts, private sector participants, research centres and concerned government departments. The unit can also engage in informal and formal consultations with the offending Member State. Unit officials can draft documents and gather relevant evidence that is required to be filed with the briefs. It can also present briefs and arguments at the Panel hearings with the assistance of the permanent WTO mission and the public sector and private sector lawyers. Moreover, a government may vest decision-making powers in the proposed unit and can subject the same to judicial review or appeal. Alternatively, the proposed unit can submit an investigation report and recommendations to the department of commerce or external affairs for final decision-making.
3. *Conduct training workshops and seminars*: The unit can use workshops and seminars to educate industries about the national provisions available to them for approaching the government, changes and developments in foreign trade policies, and developments in international trade law and jurisprudence. The mere existence of rights and obligations will not be useful unless the private sector is given the opportunity to know about these and their benefits. Confidence-building events can also be organised to nurture the relationship between the representatives of government and industries. The unit may therefore perform these awareness- and trust-building functions by organising joint workshops and consortiums, holding periodic meetings with different trade associations and confederations, and issuing regular newsletters on relevant subjects.
4. *Publish relevant material*: The unit can further bridge the communication gap between industries and governments in developing countries by regularly publishing: (i) foreign trade policies and amendments; (ii) a summary of trade disputes and their potential impact on various industries; (iii) determinations and status updates on various disputes under investigation or litigation; (iv) information about ongoing

negotiations, trade agreements and other international developments; (v) potential threats to and opportunities for trade; and (vi) other related issues.[23] Publishing requirements are also discussed under the guidelines on regulatory practices (discussed later in this chapter).

5. *Interministerial management of disputes*: To handle trade disputes effectively, the proposed unit would require close coordination with various government departments. For example, the unit may need expert opinion, information and evidence from the department of textiles if an issue pertains to textiles. The participation of the concerned government departments is vital for litigating such disputes in a cost-effective and timely manner. Therefore, it is important for the Member States to consider devising an interministerial process of dispute management to facilitate effective coordination between various government departments.

   For example, Thailand's International Committee on Economic Policy is an interministerial forum that provides required inputs and expert analysis gathered from different subject-specific departments.[24] Brazil is also known for its interministerial approach to managing trade disputes. It has created an interministerial body known as the 'Chamber of Foreign Trade' (or 'CAMEX'), 'to formulate, adopt, coordinate and implement foreign trade policy'.[25]

   These experiences can be a useful guide for those Member States that are considering consolidating their approach towards the management of disputes with optimum utilisation of available resources. A specialised body or a small unit or a committee can be established to enhance the coordination between the ministries, but its

---

23 The US and the EU, for example, have been publishing similar reports regularly. See, for example, Ambassador Ronald Kirk, '2011 National Trade Estimate Report on Foreign Trade Barriers' (Office of the United States Trade Representative, March 2011) <http://www.ustr.gov/webfm_send/2751>; '2010 Trade and Investment Barriers Report' (European Commission, March 2011) <http://trade.ec.europa.eu/doclib/docs/2011/march/tradoc_147629.pdf>, both accessed 24 July 2016. The Ministry of Commerce, Government of India regularly publishes a WTO newsletter containing information about and analysis of WTO cases and ongoing WTO discussions. See Ministry of Commerce, Government of India <http://commerce.nic.in/publications/india_wto_newsletter.asp> accessed 20 June 2016.

24 Pornchai Danvivathana, 'Thailand's Experience in the WTO Dispute Settlement System: Challenging the EC Sugar Regime' in Shaffer & Melendez-Ortiz (eds), *Dispute Settlement at the WTO* (n 22) 212–213.

25 Gregory C Shaffer, Michelle Raton Sanchez Badin & Barbara Rosenberg, 'The Trials of Winning at the WTO: What Lies Behind Brazil's Success' (2008) 41(2) *Cornell International Law Journal* 383, 427.

establishment would largely depend upon the bureaucratic structure of, and the resources available to, the government considering the matter. Besides consolidating the resources and expertise of various government departments, the proposed body can also provide an interface between the government and the country's Permanent Mission to WTO.

2.1 PROVISIONS ENHANCING TRANSPARENCY AND REGULATION

Good regulation is the key to an effective PPP arrangement. The EC Guidelines on PPPs acknowledge the importance of the regulatory aspect in the following statement:

> Successful PPPs depend on the effectiveness of national and municipal legislative and regulatory structures. Legal due diligence is required to define the constraints to PPP implementation and to define project scope.[26]

To achieve the right balance between public and private interests, the Guidelines affirm the importance of developing 'effective regulatory and watchdog mechanisms'. The Guidelines also affirm the importance of devising effective regulatory procedures to 'manage and monitor the PPPs'.[27] It is crucial that a PPP mechanism should have regulatory provisions to ensure that the operation of such arrangements remains immune from any form of regulatory threat. An effective regulation should also aim to ensure that the resources contributed by the public and private sectors are optimally utilised in line with the public and private interests at stake.

Robert Wolfe observes that a regulation is effective only when the 'regulatees' (i) 'know the existing rules'; (ii) 'have the ability to shape new rules' through 'effective consultation' procedures with the government; and (iii) 'have the confidence that the rules will be implemented fairly'.[28] An effective regulatory framework in developing countries can be established on

---

26 European Commission, 'Guidelines for Successful Public-Private Partnerships' (March 2003) 39, accessed 29 July 2016 at <http://ec.europa.eu/regional_policy/sources/docgener/guides/ppp_en.pdf>.

27 Ibid.

28 Robert Wolfe, 'How Transparency Brings Standards to Life' Standard-Setting in International Trade, Academy of Global Governance Executive Training Seminar Series, European Research Institute, Florence, 18-20 February 2013.

the basis of these or similar transparency- and accountability-enhancing principles.

The guidelines on best regulatory practices outlined in the following subsections are in line with the principles and values Wolfe describes. Due to the diverse requirements and social, economic, cultural and political conditions of different developing countries, these guidelines may or may not work and may not produce similarly positive results for all. Hence, the potential constraints and obstacles which some developing countries might face in adopting or adapting to these suggestions are also outlined alongside the proposals.

2.1.1 Publishing Requirements

It is important that participants in a dispute settlement process follow certain transparency-enhancing practices. Regular publication of relevant material, such as the determinations made during the conduct of trade disputes, proposed regulations and negotiation plans, information on the proposed trade policies and agreements, developments in international trade law and practice, including developments in the settlement of trade disputes, and details of briefs filed at WTO, can potentially be the first step towards enhancing transparency in the handling of disputes. Recent trends necessitate that the government's obligation to publish should also include the obligation to publish online. Online availability of information has now become a crucial requirement for dissemination of information.[29]

An interviewee notes that 'the online and offline publication should include information on various issues including what a trade dispute is, what impact it is having on the national wellbeing, and what can be the benefits from the removal of a foreign trade barrier, what policies and regulations are being proposed, what agreements and treaties are under negotiation'.[30] Online publication of such information can to some extent ensure that private stakeholders and other interested persons are kept informed and are better engaged with the government during the process

---

[29] For example, WTO has launched the Integrated Trade Intelligence Portal (I-TIP) for improving the transparency of trade policy measures. I-TIP 'provides a single entry point for information compiled by the WTO' on both tariff and non-tariff measures. For details, see World Trade Organization, Statistics, Integrated Trade Intelligence Portal <http://www.wto.org/english/res_e/statis_e/itip_e.htm>, accessed 20 September 2016.

[30] Confirmed in interview with an official, ICTSD, Geneva, Switzerland, 11 April 2012.

of dispute settlement. However, the requirements of confidentiality should be adhered to when publishing online and in public registers.

Some developing countries may find it difficult to manage and update online publication systems due to underdeveloped information and communications technology (ICT). Governments may also consider that too expensive and not in the best interests of the administration to make international trade related information freely available on the internet. A trade lawyer explains this obstacle in the following words.

> If a developing country has a proactive bunch of environmental activist groups and consumer organisations, the government might prefer to disclose selective information owing to the fears of increased resistance against growth and development of international trade. Wide publication of such material might also generate resistance from international NGOs.[31]

Hence, a government might prefer selective disclosure of information as unfiltered disclosure may give rise to some unwarranted resistance. Full disclosure obligations may also increase the government's workload and the amount of resources required to be spent on administration, consultations and reviews. However, one should not underestimate the importance of open dissemination and exchange of information between and among multiple stakeholders during the overall management of trade disputes.

2.1.2 Expert Consultative Committees

Expert consultative committees can be established to assist the government with the management of foreign trade disputes. These committees can ensure that the determinations made by the unit are well-informed and extensively consulted. An example of a consultative committee system is one established under the US Trade Act 1974. For example, Section 302(b)(1)(B) of the Act provides that the Office of the United States Trade Representative (USTR) shall consult the Committee established under Section 135 of the Act before making any determinations on the initiation of trade barrier investigations. Additionally, Section 305(b)(1)(A) states that USTR 'shall establish an advisory panel to recommend measures which will promote the competitiveness of the domestic industry affected by the export targeting'. USTR shall submit a report to the US Congress on the actions taken to restore or improve the international competitiveness of the domestic industry within 30 days of receiving recommendations

---

[31] Interview with a Brussels-based trade lawyer, Brussels, Belgium, 25 June 2013.

from the advisory panel (Section 305(b)(1)(c)). Section 305(b)(2)(A) further provides that the advisory panel shall consist of individuals who are employed in the affected private sector.

It may not be viable to import and apply the above-mentioned provisions of developed countries in developing countries. Nevertheless, governments in developing countries can consider these provisions and devise their own committee systems. In doing so, they can also consider the following suggested functions that expert committees could perform:

1. The committees can analyse the findings of the unit through the spectrum of law, economics, diplomacy and public good. If the committee members are experts in the subject matter of the trade dispute, legal policy, economics and trade law, they can provide a specialised and comprehensive opinion on the suitability of determinations and actions.
2. The unit may not necessarily be obliged to adhere to the advice of the proposed committee; however, the committee's advice should have a considerable influence on decision-making and functioning of PPP arrangements.
3. Maintaining a permanent advisory body might be a resource-demanding option; furthermore, the advisory body might remain underutilised in periods of peace. Hence, these consultative committees can be created on an ad hoc basis depending upon the subject matter of the dispute at hand.
4. The committee can comprise academics, researchers, scientists, industry representatives, consultants and lawyers, some of whom may be willing to work on a pro bono basis to gain experience and practical insights on various aspects of trade dispute settlement, in which case the process is likely to be more cost-effective. The appointment of members to the committee should depend upon the subject matter and nature of the dispute under review.

An ICTSD official observes the following:

> It would be ideal to have a consultative process which can be organised and altered in accordance with the nature of the dispute at hand. The process should be open to all interested persons and stakeholders and not just confined to commercial stakeholders, at a domestic level.[32]

The benefits of devising an ad hoc and tailor-made system of expert consultation are clear. However, the proposal may not be suitable for

---

[32] Interview with an official, ICTSD (n 30).

some developing countries, especially those with small trading stakes and poor economies of scale due to the additional resources the process may call for. Least developed countries will for the same reason be even less likely to pursue this option.

The proposal may also be criticised for its potential to delay the decision-making process and the launching of formal dispute settlement proceedings. But it has its own merits, and these merits have been realised by several developed and developing countries that have constituted similar committee systems. For example, China has introduced provisions that allow MOFCOM to constitute and consult an expert consultation committee during the investigation, consultation and litigation process.[33] This approach enables the government to analyse trade measures through a wide spectrum of expertise and thereby make informed determinations. The committee can also act as a kind of filter and a monitoring mechanism to ensure that the procedure of dispute management upholds and harmonises national interests with special private interests.

2.1.3 Judicial Review

The provision of judicial review can also enhance regulation as it enables the national courts or quasi-judicial authorities to review the decisions made by the unit on important trade issues.[34] The right to request judicial review should be a limited right, and it should have certain control mechanisms. *First*, the provision should only cover determinations made in respect of strategic disputes of significant national importance. *Second*, judicial review applications should only be approved against determinations made in connection with the initiation or non-initiation of action for the removal of an alleged trade barrier. (However, the provision could be extended to cover the ways in which determinations are arrived at.) *Third*, judicial review should not be granted against other ancillary determinations (for example, determinations pertaining to the initiation or suspension of investigations), since that might cause undue delay in the process. The control mechanisms should impose limitations concerning

---

[33] TBI Rules, art 20 provides that the 'Ministry of Commerce may establish an expert consultation group constituted by relevant departments of State Council, experts and scholars when it deems necessary. The expert consultation group is responsible for providing comments on technical and lawful issues relating to the investigation.'

[34] The proposal was made in Asif H Qureshi, 'Participation of Developing Countries in the WTO Dispute Settlement System' (2003) 47 *Journal of African Law* 174, 197.

(a) the stage at which review applications can be filed; (b) limitation periods; (c) applicable court fees; (d) categories of matters admissible in judicial review; (e) the parties who can apply for judicial review; and (f) the national courts or quasi-judicial bodies having jurisdiction in these matters.

The authority to decide whether a trade issue is of strategic importance should vest in the courts or quasi-judicial bodies where an application for judicial review is filed. The right to file such applications may be granted to the petitioning parties and other interested participating parties as may be defined and determined by the national provisions. The right to review determinations can also be exercised by the proposed expert consultative committee.

China has devised a similar provision of judicial review. China's Accession Protocol provides that 'all administrative actions relating to the implementation of international trade laws and regulations shall be subject to judicial review'.[35] Accordingly, Chinese laws provide complainants and other interested persons with the right to file applications for judicial review if they disagree with MOFCOM's decisions taken under the TBI Rules.[36] Additionally, right to file for administrative review is also provided within China's regulatory framework as an alternative simpler remedy for TBI complainants and interested persons.[37] Hence, the provision of administrative review could be considered by other developing countries that find the provision of judicial review unaffordable or unviable.

Judicial review is not explicitly provided for under the EU's TBR. However, the European Court of First Instance in *FICF v Commission of the European Communities*[38] found that the 'procedural safeguards in the TBR show that "a complainant under Article 4 (of the TBR) has the right to submit for review by the court any decision of the Commission terminating an examination procedure initiated as a result of his complaint".[39,40]

---

[35] Protocol of Accession of the People's Republic of China (23 November 2001) WT/L/432, s 2.D.

[36] Zhong Hua Ren Min Gong He Guo Xing Zheng Su Song Fa [Administrative Procedural Law] (Promulgated by the National People's Congress, 4 April 1989, effective 1 October 1990), art. 2, LAWINFOCHINA (P.R.C.) (as cited in Junrong Song, 'A Comparative Study on the Trade Barriers Regulation and Foreign Trade Barrier Investigation Rules' (2007) 41(4) *Journal of World Trade* 799, 821).

[37] Ibid.

[38] *FICF v Commission of the European Communities* Case T-317/02, 41 (as cited in Song (n 36) 813, 821).

[39] Ibid.

[40] Song (n 36) 821.

Although the court rejected the complainant's allegation relating to violations of Articles 2.1, 8.5, 10.5 and 11.1 of the TBR, it nevertheless settled the question of whether the Commission's decision under TBR provisions could be subjected to judicial review. The court laid down that the right originates from Article 263 of the Treaty on the Functioning of the European Union, which provides a right to the Court of Justice to review the acts of the Commission. The treaty also confers a right on any natural or legal person to file review applications against Commission decisions.[41]

A possible shortcoming of the provision could be that an application for judicial review would delay the launch of dispute settlement proceedings. The provision could be misused by unscrupulous foreign or domestic commercial entities as they could file fraudulent applications for judicial review to cause deliberate delays in the dispute settlement procedure. Business entities, operating in offending Member States or elsewhere, could use this provision to 'buy extra time', which might cause additional injury to the innocent industry's already infringed interests.[42] In addition, it might not be possible to implement the provision of judicial review in resource-constrained countries (that is, low income developing countries and least developed countries); the incorporation of the provision would further increase the workload of an already overburdened judiciary and administration. Hence, if the proposed provision is considered by Member States for better regulation and access to justice, it is equally important to devise in-built control mechanisms that can filter out meritless and frivolous applications, leaving only the genuine ones to be considered.

2.1.4 Public Interest Litigation (PIL)

The right to file a PIL can be conferred on individuals, NGOs and institutions. A PIL can be filed in the national courts against determinations made by the unit. Applications based on individual or special private interests should not be admissible as a PIL as the provision should

---

41 Treaty on the Functioning of the European Union [26/10/2012] OJ C326/49, art 263 [ex Treaty Establishing the European Community [26/10/1997] OJ C430 3, art 133]. Council Decision 93/350 of 8 June, 1993 grants the Court of First Instance the right to exercise the jurisdiction conferred on the Court of Justice at the first instance. (Council Decision 93/350/ECSC, EEC, Euratom of 8 June 1993 amending Council Decision 88/591/ECSC, EEC, Euratom establishing a Court of First Instance of the European Communities [1993] OJ L144/21, art 1.1).

42 Concerns have been expressed in 'Ministers line up curbs on "frivolous" judicial reviews' *BBC News: Politics* London, 23 April 2013, accessed 12 July 2016 at <http://www.bbc.co.uk/news/uk-politics-22260063>.

specifically protect public interests. The authority to define 'public interest' should lie with the national courts. Many democratic governments grant the right to file a PIL to their citizens for the protection of public interests.[43] However, although such provisions may already be in existence in many national jurisdictions, it is additionally important to make individuals aware that the provision may also be invoked in respect of important international trade matters. Expansion in the scope of the PIL provision may add to the workload of national courts and introduce complexities to the adjudication and administration process. It may also increase the cost of administration required for the management of trade disputes. However, it deserves to be considered as it can bring about the desired regulatory implications with comparatively fewer costs, procedures and complexities.

2.1.5 Institutionalisation

The regulatory practices can be institutionalised through the creation of a regulatory agency or a committee, which should be independent of the government departments. The committee can take the form of a permanent institution, its members appointed on an ad hoc basis depending upon the nature and subject matter of the trade issues at hand. The primary functions that the proposed regulatory agency can perform are numerous. Mainly, it can be made responsible for performing the following tasks:

1. To monitor the performance of legal rights and obligations of the unit and the private sector during the process of dispute settlement.
2. To ensure that a proper balance is maintained between the interests of the partners and to minimise the occasions of one interest overriding the other. These interests can generally be classified as: special private interest and national interest.
3. To ensure that the partnership process remains immune from regulatory threats emerging from different forms of rent-seeking activities. This can be achieved through various watchdog procedures devised by the government in consultation with the regulatory committee from time to time.
4. To recommend judicial review of any determination made by the unit on a complaint filed by a private individual or on *suo moto* basis.

---

[43] For example, art 32 of the Indian Constitution provides Indian citizens with a right to file litigation in the courts of law for the protection of public interest.

5. Compulsory information disclosure processes may also be enforced by the regulator on the unit if the regulator believes that there are adequate reasons for such enforcement.
6. To ensure public participation and the regular publication of relevant material (as discussed above). The regulatory body may further enhance public participation through public hearings, seminars, symposiums, online releases and notifications.

Regulatory institutionalisation may not be viable for some developing countries (particularly LDCs) as their governments may find it difficult to invest the financial and human resources required for establishing the proposed agency. Moreover, the proposed regulatory committee may itself face the risk of being lobbied, bribed or captured by a private stakeholder, by the unit or the concerned departments of the government. But the appointment of members on an ad hoc basis and wider representation from industry, consumer organisations, trade unions, academics, chambers of commerce and government departments may ensure that these threats are kept at bay, at least to some extent.

Member States can refer to the guidelines proposed and discussed above when devising a regulatory framework for monitoring the formation and functioning of PPP arrangements. These 'regulatory provisions' should be known as 'best practices' or 'good practices' so that their enforcement does not convey a negative connotation to the regulated subjects. The regulatees should not be made to feel that they are being regulated as that might hamper the process of optimum exchange of resources between the two.

3.1 CREATION OF 'STRONG' INDUSTRY REPRESENTATIVES

The examples of TEXPROCIL, Jiangsu Laver Association, Brazilian Soluble Coffee Industry Association, and Global Sugar Alliance discussed in the previous chapters show that dispute settlement partnerships can work smoothly if the private sector is well-represented. It may also be recalled that one of the reasons cited for the underutilisation of TBI rules in China is 'the lack of industry associations truly representing the interests of private firms in China'.[44] On the other hand, one of the most touted reasons for Brazil's success at WTO DSM is its organised

[44] Henry Gao, 'Taking Justice into Your Own Hand: The TBI Mechanism in China' (2010) 44(3) *Journal of World Trade* 663, 650.

private sector. These dispute settlement experiences make a strong case for the organisation and integration of the private sector community in developing countries. The guidelines proposed in the following subsections are intended to facilitate the development of an organised business community in a developing country.

3.1.1 Creation of Export Promotion Councils

The government should establish regional export promotion councils in various regions of the country. The key aim of these councils should be the development and promotion of exports in their respective jurisdictional region. The export promotion councils can act as a focal point for exporters operating in that region and the concerned government departments. These councils can bridge the intra- and inter-industry gap by providing a common forum where exporters can interact and coordinate. The proposed council can perform a number of key functions, including the following:

1. Councils can assist the affected private stakeholders in investigating trade concerns.
2. On being challenged by a Member State, the government will require information and evidence to prepare a defence case. The proposed council (through their established contacts with individual firms and associations) can seek information from the private sector on behalf of the government. The council can gather information from various exporters, importers, producers and manufacturers in its region.
3. It can provide a forum to establish a dialogue between the business fraternity, various government departments, trade associations and consumer organisations.
4. It can organise outreach programmes to raise awareness in the business community of pertinent trade-related issues, such as the government's trade policies, procedures and regulations (and changes thereto), international trade law and its ramifications, the status and impact of various trade disputes affecting business interests in the region, and so on.
5. It can also conduct training programmes for business entities on matters such as export skills development, product development and adaptation, marketing and product information, and adopting a proactive approach to deal with trade issues.
6. It can also facilitate the formation of trade associations in its area and prompt individual entities to join these representative associations. Workshops and symposia can be organised by the council (i) to

explain the benefits and incentives of organisation, and (ii) to provide a common forum of interaction between private companies and their representatives.

These councils can be supervised by a central export promotion council. Additionally, it is important to keep the regional and central councils active and incentivised with the help of regular consultative meetings, training programmes and awareness workshops. These councils can either be sector-specific or region-specific, or both, depending upon the structure and dynamics of commerce in the individual Member State.[45]

3.1.2 Formation of Trade Cooperatives

India's dispute settlement experience shows that trade cooperatives can play an instrumental role in an industry's institutional development. Trade cooperatives can inform governments of what needs to be done to protect, promote and advance the business interests of the private sector entities in various sectors of the economy. They can coordinate with the providers of goods and services, the national and international markets, exporters, trade associations and the government in order to strike the best bargains for producers and exporters. For example, trade cooperatives in Europe have in the past bargained successfully for subsidised fuel for consumption by fishing vessels in the region. This has decreased the costs of operation and increased the profit margins of the EU fisheries industry.

The cooperatives can also run training programmes to educate farmers and fishermen in developing countries to enable them to maximise their productivity, as well as to channel and sell their produce in the most optimum manner. They can also potentially identify the right markets for the producers and exporters and can assist them in exporting their produce to that foreign market in a cost-effective manner. For example, if the demand for prawns in the market of Country A diminishes or disappears, the cooperatives can identify an alternative market in Country B where this perishable produce can be exported with maximum gain and minimum wastage. These trade cooperatives can be sector-specific or region-specific, or both.

It may be argued that similar functions could also be performed by

---

[45] For example, the export promotion councils in India are established on a sector-wise and regional basis. Whereas, the export promotion councils in various countries of Africa are not sector-specific, but are established on a central or a regional basis.

export promotion councils. It is an acceptable argument, but the reason behind the present suggestion is to put forward various alternative options for the integration and organisation of the private sector. Trade cooperatives will not only be expected to coordinate with the exporters, but also with the producers of goods and services, with the purpose of enhancing the overall economic and social welfare of the nation. Their members will be stakeholders at different levels – working closely, sharing knowledge and exchanging opportunities in an optimum manner. Further guidance on the potential functions of the proposed cooperatives can be obtained from studying the successful models of trade cooperatives in developed countries such as those in Europe.[46]

3.1.3 Creation of Chambers of Commerce

The formation of chambers of commerce or confederations of industry is a way of organising business communities from different industries under a single umbrella. Chambers of commerce can represent a wide range of business interests, irrespective of their size, nature and sector. These chambers can encourage the sharing of opportunities, knowledge and expertise between and among various industries in the nation. They can provide companies, 'with practical support, useful connections and valuable access to new ideas and innovations'.[47] Historically, chambers of commerce have played an important role in the handling of disputes in many developed and developing Member States. They have commonly rendered various important services, including the following:

1. They have organised workshops and conferences at the national and international levels for different sectors and stakeholders.
2. They have provided members with access to international conferences and workshops at a discounted rate.
3. They have prepared guidelines for industries to help them conduct national and international trade effectively.
4. They have conducted investigations, risk assessments and cost-benefit analyses on behalf of trade associations and enterprises when the need has arisen.

---

46 Cooperatives Europe claims to be the voice of enterprises in Europe, with 91 member organisations from 35 European countries across all business sectors.

47 British Chambers established in UK <http://www.britishchambers.org.uk> accessed 21 July 2013.

5. They have advised members on national and international trade policies and regulations, and their potential impact on different sectors.
6. They have published newsletters and reports on topical issues for the benefit of their members.
7. They have assisted the private sector in accessing the government and in convincing it to protect business interests.
8. They have provided logistical and practical support to small and resource-constrained members. For example, they have offered translation, drafting and editing services, which are often required in foreign trade matters.

Determining the role and functions of a chamber of commerce should be left to the discretion of each Member State, as it will depend upon the commercial expectations and concerns of the business community and the national government in question.

3.1.4 Compulsory Taxation: the Brazilian Approach

As seen in Chapter 5, Brazilian trade associations are well established and properly resourced. One reason often cited for this development is the legislative provision of compulsory taxation levied on business entities in the country. Under this legislation, the government collects taxes from domestic businesses and distributes the revenue received among trade associations. This provision enhances the financial capacity of Brazil's trade associations, and hence, it may be of interest to other developing country governments that wish to do the same. As with the other guidelines discussed here, the suitability of this proposal will depend upon a country's level of economic development.

4.1 FINANCING THE DISPUTE SETTLEMENT PROCEDURES

WTO litigations have become costly and complicated. Most developing countries therefore find it challenging to finance the dispute settlement procedures. Additionally, some countries may struggle, not because they have insufficient resources, but simply because the funds needed to litigate the dispute are not immediately available, usually because the funds allocated for this purpose fall outside the financial year in which the trade dispute arises. The following comment describes this situation:

> ACWL won a dispute for a developing Member State which was litigated with a delay of six months. The litigation was delayed for this period because there were no funds available for litigation with the concerned department at that time of the financial year. It was a winning case, and it would have been commercially more viable to have won the case sooner than that, but the Member State had to wait until the start of the next financial year for the allocation of required funds to the issue.[48]

The strategy of financing the management of trade disputes should therefore have a dual function: *one* that enables developing countries to generate funds and *another* that helps them to channel these funds. However, it is not possible to propose specific provisions for financing WTO disputes in developing countries, as this depends on several country-specific factors (such as a country's share of global trade, its economic size, the stakes involved in foreign trade and the volume of foreign trade, the level of engagement and organisation of the private sector, and existing political, economic and social conditions). Nevertheless, it is possible to propose several general guidelines for financing dispute settlement procedures litigated at WTO.

4.1.1 Creation of a Standing Budget with Government

The prospect of establishing a standing budget with the concerned government department can be explored by developing countries.[49] The provision of a standing budget allows the government to access the funds required to litigate a trade dispute as and when a dispute arises. An annual amount can be allocated to the concerned department for this purpose, and can be calculated on the basis of the following variables: (i) annual share of foreign trade (as a percentage of the country's GDP); (ii) pending and potential trade disputes; (iii) vulnerability of important economic sectors; and (iv) availability of funds.

The provision of a standing budget may not work for some developing countries, especially for low income and least developed countries with very limited financial resources. It may be the case that a government has insufficient funds in a particular year or a decade due to recession or a natural calamity. Also, governments might prefer to utilise their limited funds to provide for basic needs such as education, food and shelter. Moreover, the provision might not work owing to a country's small share of global trade, low GDP, poor economies of scale and small trading stakes, or to

48 Interview with a trade lawyer, ACWL, Geneva, Switzerland, 11 April 2013.

49 Ibid.

its inability (through lack of capacity) to litigate or defend cases at WTO. Thus, the suitability, form and scope of this provision should be explored in light of the conditions and needs of the Member State considering the prospect of creating a standing budget.

4.1.2 Creation of a Standing Budget with Chambers of Commerce or Trade Associations

If a country's foreign trade amounts to an insignificant share of its annual GDP, or if a Member State has only been involved in a small number of trade issues, or if it does not anticipate trade frictions arising in the future, then it may not be feasible to create a standing budget with the concerned government department. In these circumstances, the creation of a standing budget with the most prominent chambers of commerce in the country would be a better alternative. The chambers could set up a contingency fund with the help of annual contributions paid by its business members towards the contingency expenses and its membership fee. Prominent chambers with large memberships may be able to raise sufficient funds to finance the entire, or a considerable part of, the dispute settlement process. Contributions to the contingency fund can also be sought from government departments and trade associations.

The provision would be most beneficial for financially weak, poorly organised industries. It will enable such industries to protect and restore their market access as the cost of doing so will be uniformly spread across the entire commercial sector of the country. However, it could be argued that it is not fair to distribute the burden of financing a dispute (affecting the interests of one industry) over various other industries by way of an increased annual contribution charged by the chambers. The counterargument to this would be that spreading the cost of financing trade disputes as widely as possible will lead to better protection of trade interests, and this may eventually result in increased foreign trade and overall economic growth in the country. There is no right or wrong perspective or a single answer to this dilemma, as it is largely an ideological issue for Member States to reflect on.

Alternatively, the contingency fund may be created with trade associations representing the interests of a particular industry. This may seem to be a fairer proposition as the contributions will be made by business entities that are actively seeking the removal of a trade barrier. Contributions could be in the form of an enhanced annual membership fee, where part of the fee is set aside for the purpose of conducting trade disputes at WTO. The cost of hiring lawyers and consultants, or of gathering information and evidential documents could be paid for out of the fund created.

Member States considering this proposal need to consider one obstacle. It may be that a specific industry in the country is insufficiently organised or inadequately represented, which means that trade associations (assuming they exist) may struggle to raise the funds needed to set up a contingency. Without a healthy membership base, the creation of a contingency fund becomes less of a possibility. It may also be the case that the business entities in an affected industry do not have adequate resources or are unwilling to pay an annual fee or make regular contributions to the contingency fund. The effectiveness of this proposal therefore largely depends on how organised the private sector is, and how well established the trade associations and chambers of commerce are in a given country.

4.1.3 Creation of Think Tanks

Think tanks can provide legal and economic analysis of trade matters to a government or an industry in a cost-effective manner. They can also assist a government with the collection of information in the absence of a participating private sector. They can help in evaluating the genuineness of claims made by an industry. An industry can only provide information from its individual perspective and therefore it is essential that a government should be able to obtain further information to gain a wider, more comprehensive understanding of the matter at hand. In addition, think tanks can assist governments in conducting the cost-benefit analysis of litigating a measure at WTO.

The think tanks in Brazil, for example, are created by entrepreneurs to advise, inform and assist the government and industry on various trade issues. There are both profit-based and non-profit-based think tanks. Several think tanks in Brazil are also associated with and run by universities. In this respect, India has followed in Brazil's footsteps. The Centre for WTO Studies in India, for example, has performed the following functions: (i) it has engaged in robust research in the field of WTO law; (ii) it has created a specialised e-repository of important WTO documents, especially those relating to India; (iii) it has provided analytical inputs to the Government of India concerning various trade negotiations and WTO disputes; and (iv) it has interacted with industry and government through its various outreach and capacity-building programmes.

Developing countries can create think tanks and research centres with the help of academics, trade and policy experts, retired foreign trade officers and government administrators. These institutions can be funded partly by the government and partly by the chambers of commerce or trade associations. Alternatively, these institutions can self-finance their operation through the provision of international trade law courses and programmes to students, lawyers, industry officials and policy experts. The emergence of think tanks reduces the need to hire policy experts and consultants to evaluate contentious trade measures, or specialised agencies to gather information and documents in support of a case brought before WTO, and this in turn lowers the cost to government of launching and pursuing a trade dispute at WTO DSU. Finally, these institutions can bridge the communication gap between industry, academia and government through organising outreach programmes such as workshops, joint meetings and field trips.

4.1.4 NGOs for Monitoring

NGOs have played an instrumental role in assisting governments during the process of dispute settlement and in various other international trade related matters. They have engaged in fact-finding and gathering required information.[50] They have also analysed trade frictions, negotiations and agreements.[51] Additionally, they have engaged in public relation activities for the generation of support during the enforcement stages of WTO awards.[52] Moreover, they have contributed by actively monitoring the foreign market access of various developing countries. Encouraging NGOs to support the government and the private sector in matters relating to international trade disputes is therefore of crucial importance.

Developing countries often have weak monitoring mechanisms. NGOs can address this problem as they can provide cost-effective monitoring services to the governments and business entities. These NGOs can be intergovernmental, international, national or regional in nature, and they can be funded by the private sector, law firms or government. The NGOs can maintain a database of market access practices and commitments, and

---

50 In the *US – Upland Cotton* dispute, Oxfam International, ICTSD and IDEAS Centre provided information to the Brazilian government and also mobilised support from the cotton farmers in other countries (Chad P Bown, *Self-Enforcing Trade: Developing Countries and WTO Dispute Settlement* (Brookings Institution Press 2009) 188).

51 Technically sophisticated NGOs have offered to conduct legal and economic analysis of trade matters for the governments and private sectors in developing countries. Examples of such NGOs are: the Center for International Environmental Law and the Earth Island Institute (Bown, *Self-Enforcing Trade* (n 50)175–207).

52 For example, in the *US – Upland Cotton* case, Oxfam worked on behalf of West African cotton-producing countries and it engaged the US media through a campaign aimed at generating political and public support (Bown, *Self-Enforcing Trade* (n 50) 195).

update this on a regular basis. They can also monitor databases to identify any violations in trade commitments and emerging trade barriers affecting the interests of industries in developing countries. The WTO's Trade Policy Review Mechanism (TPRM) performs this function to some extent, as it reviews the trade policies of all WTO members with different time frames set for each member. However, TPRM is insufficient to meet the monitoring needs of developing (and especially least developed) countries because its frequency of reviews is based on the country's share of world trade. Under this mechanism, some members are reviewed once every two years, others once every four years, and certain least developed countries even less frequently than that. It is therefore crucial for developing countries to have additional monitoring mechanisms to enable them to monitor their market access on a more regular basis.

Some developing countries may not be able to utilise their national or regional NGOs for the monitoring purpose. It may be the case that the NGOs in developing countries are also developing as organisations and are therefore not sufficiently resourced. They may not have the expertise required to conduct monitoring exercises. Bown has argued that NGOs can assist developing countries to overcome the problems of monitoring, at least to some extent, and an enhanced monitoring capacity can lead to the achievement of national development goals through expanded foreign trade.[53] However, Bown recognises that an NGO may have its own limitations in doing the same. Bown therefore proposes to establish the 'Institute for Assessing WTO Commitments'. The proposed Institute can monitor compliance on behalf of developing countries and generate requisite information for the private sector and the government.[54] Hence, there are several ways through which developing countries can monitor their trade interests in a cost-effective manner.

4.1.5 Creation of Domestic Legal Expertise

The creation of in-house legal expertise has the potential to significantly reduce the cost of dispute settlement. The creation of a standing legal team (trained in WTO laws) within certain government departments, business confederations or industry associations is one way to upgrade a country's domestic legal expertise. However, this would make no financial sense for developing countries with a low WTO caseload as they would experience poor economies of scale from maintaining a standing legal unit. An

---

[53] Bown, *Self-Enforcing Trade* (n 50) 176.
[54] Ibid 208.

alternative approach would be to make use of the ACWL's subsidised legal services. Another way forward for developing countries could be to encourage private domestic law firms to develop expertise and experience in WTO laws. Evidence shows that many developing countries have followed one or more of these routes.

India and China are important examples of developing countries that have recently increased their trade law expertise at the domestic level. The Government of India has encouraged domestic law firms to develop their international trade law expertise. A trade lawyer working for an Indian law firm observes the following:

> India has started to build its domestic legal capacity by following a unique approach. The government has hired various local law firms which had some trade law expertise and it has thrown them into a deep end, as if the government was telling them to 'learn to swim or sink'. We were, and we are being encouraged by the government to gain knowledge and expertise over international trade laws.[55]

The Ministry of Commerce in India has started to hire India-based trade lawyers to manage foreign trade disputes on behalf of the government. Until the year 2000, India mainly hired Geneva- or Brussels-based lawyers for litigating WTO cases,[56] and until the year 2001, a single Indian lawyer was repeatedly hired for preparing defences.[57] However, the government has started engaging a higher number of domestic trade lawyers[58] (most noticeably from 2006 onwards).

China has also significantly expanded its domestic legal capacity during the past decade. It has consistently required international law firms to work with the domestic law firms while preparing and presenting WTO cases.

---

[55] Interview with a trade lawyer, Luthra & Luthra, Delhi, India, 21 June 2013. (The interviewee further observes the following: 'With more number of cases being litigated by and against India mainly from the year 2001, the government decided to expand its legal expertise. It was not feasible anymore to hire expensive Geneva-based lawyers, especially in the cases where India was challenged. It was also not wise to exclusively rely on a sole trade lawyer in India [Mr Krishnan Venugopal]. The government therefore started to hire other Indian lawyers from different law firms based in India.').

[56] The foreign lawyers hired by India in the years before 2000 were: Dr Frieder Roessler, Edwin Vermulst and Folkert Graafsma.

[57] Krishnan Venugopal was the sole lawyer hired by the Government of India for disputes challenging Indian trade measures from the year 1996 to 2000.

[58] The new generation of trade lawyers hired by the government after 2005–2006 were: ACWL lawyers, Krishnan Venugopal, Lakshmi Kumaran and Sridharan, Economic Law Practices, Luthra & Luthra, and Cloras Law Firm.

With this approach, China has gradually trained its domestic lawyers to handle future WTO cases. Moreover, it has further enhanced its legal expertise and experience through third party participation. This 'learning by observation' approach has greatly improved the WTO DSU experience of government officials and local law firms. These two approaches (lawyer-pairing and third party participation) are cost-effective strategies that can help developing country governments '...face lower start-up costs for subsequent participation'.[59] High start-up costs can initially make WTO DSM an unaffordable option for most developing countries, but the DSU-related experience gained through third party participation can substantially decrease this cost in the long run.[60]

4.1.6 'In-house Ambulance Chasing' by Law Firms

International law firms, on their own initiative, have started the practice of monitoring foreign policies and their implications on market access. Without receiving an instruction from a corporate client or a government, these international law firms identify and examine potential barriers, gather information and approach the affected business and governmental entities with their findings and analysis. The firms carry out this exercise with the hope that they will be able to generate new clients. In this arrangement, they normally propose to share the information concerning market access and violations in exchange for an agreement with the receiving client that the supplying law firm will be hired for further monitoring, investigation or litigation of the potential dispute.[61]

This practice could be a useful tool for developing countries that cannot afford to have their own specialised monitoring institutions. At present, the law firms engaging in 'ambulance chasing' are mostly Geneva-, Brussels- or Washington-based international law firms, and hiring their services in exchange for their ambulance-chasing practices could be an unaffordable option for many developing countries. Hence, it is proposed that in developing countries, domestic law firms should perform the 'ambulance chasing' practices traditionally undertaken by overseas law firms. The practice of 'in-house ambulance chasing', as it could be termed, would enhance domestic legal expertise, provide additional monitoring services, and reduce the overall cost of dispute settlement,

---

59 Christina L Davis & Sarah Blodgett Bermeo, 'Who Files? Developing Country Participation in GATT/WTO Adjudication' (2009) 71(3) *The Journal of Politics* 1033, 1034.

60 Ibid 1047.

61 Bown, *Self-Enforcing Trade* (n 50) 124.

all of which would benefit the government and industry of the country concerned.

The proposed 'in-house ambulance chasing' strategy may enable the government and affected business entities to gain information on WTO violations as this may be required to investigate the WTO-incompatibility of a particular measure. The services provided by domestic law firms are likely to be more affordable than those of internationally based law firms.

A similar practice has recently shown an emerging trend in India. Luthra & Luthra, an Indian law firm, was hired by the Government of India in the *India –Agricultural Products*[62] case after the law firm had provided the initial information and legal analysis concerning the measure to the Ministry of Commerce. A trade advisor to the Ministry of Commerce confirms that Luthra & Luthra provided the initial analysis and informational support and that its initial assistance was the main reason for its subsequent engagement in this case.[63]

With such practices in place, the private sector and the government have enhanced access to monitoring services and legally marshalled information and evidence at a comparatively affordable rate. On the other hand, domestic law firms in developing countries with minimal trade law expertise (mainly due to shortage of business and/or lack of professional or internship opportunities) will be able to generate more business and expand their expertise and experience. This trend can also increase demand for courses in international economic law at universities, leading to an overall enhanced trade law expertise and awareness in the country.

4.1.7 Creation of a Multidisciplinary Dispute Management Team

The BIC experiences demonstrate that multiple public and private sector entities have been engaged in the handling of WTO disputes. The extent of their participation has been different from case to case, but the composition of the different dispute management teams reflects a common pattern. It may be recalled that in the *Japan – Quotas on Laver* case, China's key participants were: officials from the Ministry of Commerce, subject-specific experts from the Bureau of Fisheries of the Ministry of

---

62 Appellate Body Report, *India – Measures Concerning the Importation of Certain Agricultural Products from the United States,* WT/DS430/AB/R, adopted 19 June 2015.

63 Interview with an official, Ministry of Commerce, Government of India, Delhi, India, 12 June 2013.

Agriculture, economic consultants from the China Chamber of Commerce of Import and Export of Foodstuffs, privately hired trade lawyers, the Jiangsu Laver Association, and laver exporters from China. In the *EC – Sugar* case, Brazil's key participants were: officials from the Ministry of Foreign Affairs and other concerned government departments, a team of lawyers from Sidley Austin, Datagro's team of economic consultants, NGO officials from Oxfam and the Netherlands Economic Institute, sugar cane trade association officials, and sugar exporters from Brazil. And in the *EC – Bed Linen* case, India's key participants were: officials from the Ministry of Commerce and the Ministry of Textiles, trade advisers from the Centre for WTO Studies, officials from an export promotion council, and a team of lawyers from a Brussels-based law firm. These, along with other disputes, point towards the multidisciplinary composition of their dispute management teams.

The BIC experiences also illustrate the interdependent nature of the dispute management team. They demonstrate that a trade concern identified by an exporter will go unaddressed without the engagement of government officials. Government officials may find it difficult to investigate a barrier or litigate it at WTO without resource inputs from the affected industry. An exporter will find it difficult to convince its government to pursue a WTO-incompatible foreign trade measure (or even to approach the government in the first place) without seeking support from its trade association or chamber of commerce. Trade lawyers may not be able to interpret economic formulas or evidential data without assistance from economists, data analysts and subject-specific experts. Trade lawyers are needed to assess the WTO-compatibility of a trade measure, and if needed, to prepare and present a case at WTO. Trade policy experts and diplomats are required to assess the political ramifications of adjudicating a measure.

In light of these observations, it is suggested that each dispute should be handled by a multidisciplinary team comprising government officials, trade policy advisors, diplomats, industry representatives, private companies, civil society organisations, trade lawyers, economic consultants, data analysts, subject-specific experts and academics. However, as argued earlier in Chapter 2, the government should remain the lead participant in the team. It should have complete discretion for making *informed* determinations on handling foreign trade disputes and deciding on an appropriate course of action.

5.1 SMALL CLAIMS PROCEDURES FOR NON-LITIGABLE MATTERS

The management of trade conflicts should follow a procedural hierarchy that allows a trade concern to gradually scale up to the level of formal WTO dispute settlement proceedings. Figure 7.1 indicates the phases in the proposed life cycle of a trade conflict. A 'full-blown' dispute may survive up to the phase of litigation or post-litigation, but some frictions will fall away as they make their way up the trajectory, usually as a result of the parties reaching agreement on the matter or the offending Member State removing the alleged trade barrier.

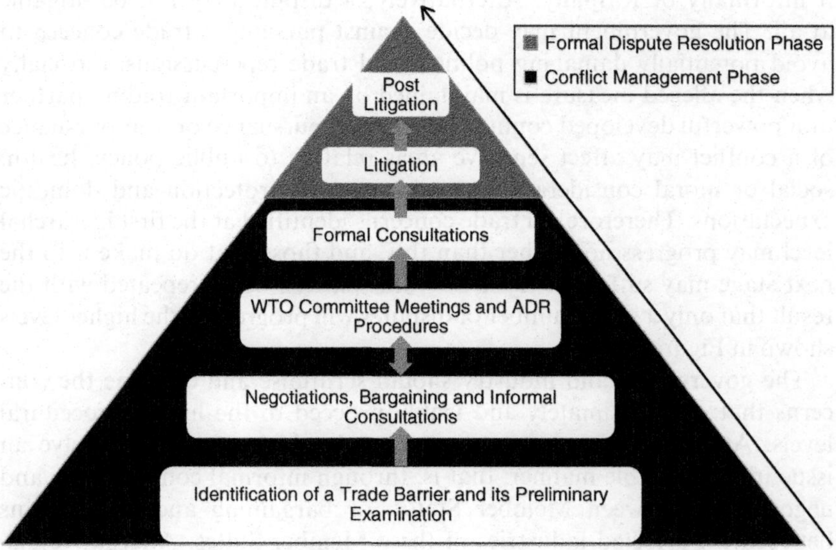

Figure 7.1 International trade conflicts: proposed life cycle

Figure 7.1 illustrates the desired multi-tiered procedural hierarchy that a trade concern should go through, following an upward trend. Up until the stage of formal consultations, governments and industries should try to diffuse or settle trade conflicts as amicably as possible through discussions, negotiations and consultations. These stages are broadly viewed as the stages of 'conflict management'.[64] If a trade friction has not been

[64] Robert Echandi, 'How to Successfully Manage Conflicts and Prevent Dispute Adjudication in International Trade' (2013) ICTSD Issue Paper No 11,

diffused or resolved by the time it reaches the stage of formal consultations, it enters the terrain of 'formal dispute settlement' as the affected Member State can now invoke formal provisions of international adjudication. It is important to note that the process of 'conflict management' is not a substitute for the process of 'formal dispute settlement'; the former is a phase that precedes the latter in the life cycle of a 'full-blown' dispute.

Not all trade concerns identified by industry or government will be pursued. There are several reasons why a particular industry might decide not to pursue the matter. The industry may fear retaliation by the offending trade partner(s), or it may think that the stakes involved are smaller than the resources required for investigating the measure and pursuing it informally or formally. Alternatively, a dispute may not be litigable at all. The government may decide against pursuing a trade concern to avoid potentially damaging political and trade repercussions, especially when the alleged measure is maintained by an important trading partner or a powerful developed country. Moreover, pursuance or non-pursuance of a conflict may affect sensitive areas relating to public policy, health, social or moral considerations, environmental protection and domestic expectations. Therefore, all trade concerns identified at the first hierarchal level may progress no further than this, and those that do make it to the next stage may suffer the same fate; this pattern being repeated with the result that only a small number of disputes will progress to the higher levels shown in Figure 7.1.

The government and industry should scrutinise and examine the concerns that can legitimately and viably proceed to the higher procedural levels. At the first instance, an attempt should be made to resolve an issue in an amicable manner; that is, through informal consultations and negotiations between Member States, or bargaining and negotiations between the affected industries of these Member States. Alternative dispute resolution (ADR) procedures may also be considered and invoked to discuss the matter and find a mutually acceptable solution.[65] The issue can also be raised at the relevant WTO Committee as the WTO Committee

4–6, accessed 22 September 2016 at <http://www.ictsd.org/downloads/2013/04/how-to-successfully-manage-conflicts-and-prevent-dispute-adjudication-in-international-trade.pdf>.

[65] The DSU offers various informal alternatives to litigation, including good offices, and conciliation and mediation (DSU, art 5, contained in Annex 2). It also offers arbitration, which is a more 'expeditious' process than the typical Panel process (DSU, art 25, contained in Annex 2). These provisions are not used frequently as they require the consent of both parties and their processes are not pre-determined, but rather decided on an ad hoc basis.

System (particularly for Technical Barriers to Trade (TBT) and Sanitary and Phytosanitary Measures (SPS) related concerns) has efficiently led to the settlement of multiple trade concerns. This approach may be especially well suited to developing countries as they have actively participated in WTO committee discussions, as compared to their relative rate of participation at WTO DSM. This is evidenced with the help of the indicative data shown in Figures 7.2 and 7.3. These figures provide data on the number of times a given country has raised concerns at the SPS and TBT Committees vis-à-vis the number of times it has launched WTO litigations concerning SPS and TBT issues.

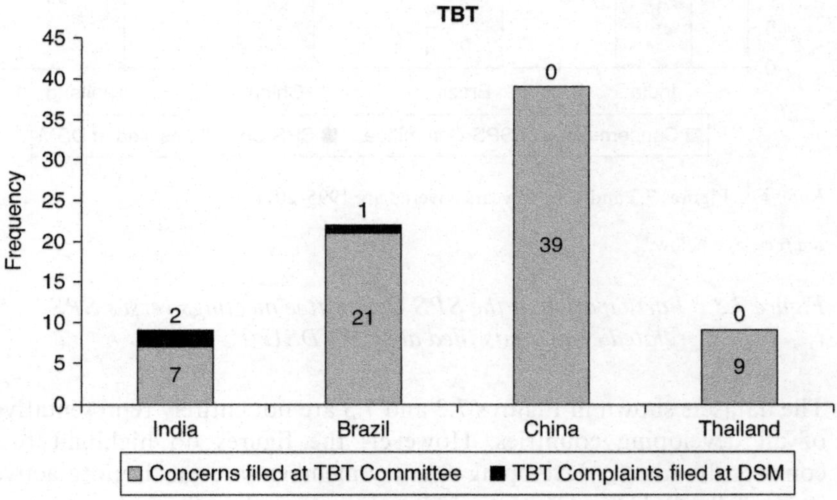

Figure 7.2 Participation at the TBT Committee meetings versus TBT-related complaints filed at WTO DSU

Figure 7.2 shows that, from the years 1995 to 2011, India, Thailand, Brazil and China raised 7, 9, 21 and 39 TBT concerns respectively at the TBT Committee meetings. In comparison, these developing countries merely raised one or two or zero TBT-related complaints at WTO DSU over the same period.

Figure 7.3 depicts a similar (or an even wider) disparity between the usage of the WTO committee system and WTO DSU by these developing countries with respect to SPS concerns. From 1995 to 2011, India, Thailand and China each raised only one dispute concerning SPS at WTO DSU, while Brazil raised none. Contrastingly, India, Thailand, Brazil and China raised 15, 14, 38 and 44 trade concerns respectively at the SPS Committee meetings.

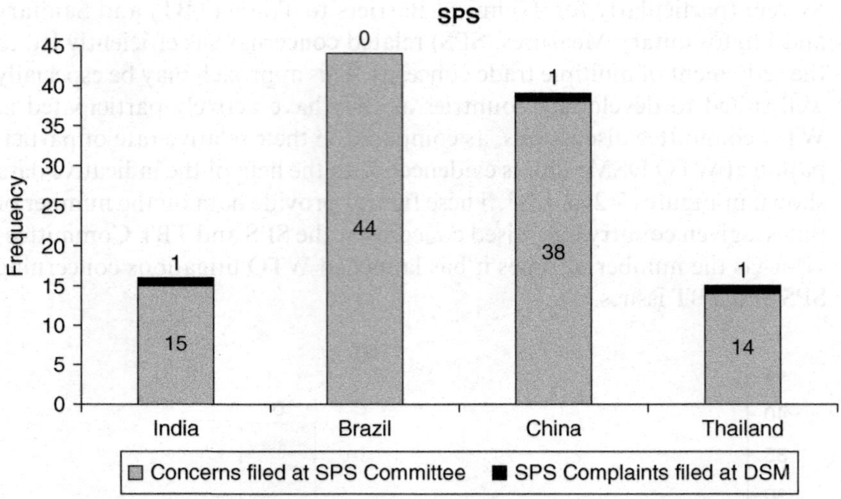

Note: For Figures 7.2 and 7.3, the years covered are 1995–2011.[66]

Sources: See below.[67]

Figure 7.3 Participation at the SPS Committee meetings versus SPS-related complaints filed at WTO DSU

The datasets shown in Figures 7.2 and 7.3 are not entirely representative of all developing countries. However, the figures do highlight two common trends: (i) developing country members are much more active users of the WTO committee system as compared to their participation

[66] Some qualifications should be noted here: (a) The dataset indicates members raising and supporting the concerns, and not maintaining the concerns. (b) Only specific trade concerns raised for the first time in these years are included in the calculations. Their frequency of notifications and re-notifications in the same year and subsequent years are not included in the dataset. Hence, each specific trade concern raised in that year for the first time is counted as one. (c) These numbers may not be fully accurate (as there are slight variations in the numbers provided in the Meeting Reports and those in the new dataset prepared by the Committees), but these figures are very close to the actual number of TBT and SPS concerns filed and supported by these members.

[67] The data on TBT and SPS complaints filed at WTO DSM was compiled from information held on the WTO database and accessed on 24 September 2014. The year of dispute indicates the year in which consultations were requested by the complainant(s). The data on concerns filed at the TBT Committee Meetings was compiled from the TBT Committee Paper entitled 'Specific Trade Concern Raised in the TBT Committee: Note by the Secretariat' [G/TBT/GEN/74/Rev9] 17

at WTO adjudicatory mechanism. (b) The figures dismiss the view that developing countries participate at WTO DSU less frequently than the developed countries mainly because the developing countries have fewer or no trade concerns. (c) The data suggests that developing countries have trade concerns and frictions too.[68] But the wide discrepancy between the number of TBT- and SPS-related concerns filed at the Committees and those launched at WTO DSU goes to show that these developing countries have preferred to raise their concerns at the Committee meetings, and that a very minute percentage of trade concerns give rise to formal WTO disputes.

On the contrary, some may argue that if most of the specific trade concerns raised at the TBT and SPS Committees in these years were (supposedly) resolved, there would be no reason for these countries to further invoke the DSU provisions. However, this argument can be dismissed, especially with regard to the SPS-related concerns, as data suggests that out of 312 SPS-related trade concerns raised between 1995 and 2010, only '. . . ninety five (30 per cent) were reported as resolved by WTO members to the SPS Committee. Eighteen (6 per cent) were reported as partially resolved'.[69] The remaining 215 SPS-related trade concerns (64 per cent) raised at the Committees were either 'not addressed', or reported as 'unresolved', or 'not reported'.[70] Hence, although a significant number of

---

October 2011, which was accessed on 4 June 2016 at <docsonline.wto.org/imrd/directdoc.asp?DDFDocuments/t/G/TBT/...doc>; the New Dataset on Specific TBT Trade Concerns was taken from the WTO webpage <http://www.wto.org/english/res_e/publications_e/wtr12_dataset_e.htm>, which was accessed on 4 June 2016. The data on concerns filed at the SPS Committee Meetings was compiled from the SPS Committee Paper entitled 'Specific Trade Concerns: Note by the Secretariat' [G/SPS/GEN/204/Rev13], which was accessed on 26 February 2013. <https://docs.wto.org/dol2fe/Pages/FE_Search/FE_S_S006.aspx?Query=(@Symbol=%20g/sps/gen/204/rev.13*)&Language=ENGLISH&Context=FomerScriptedSearch&languageUIChanged=true#> accessed 4 June 2016; the New Dataset on Specific SPS Trade Concerns was taken from the WTO webpage <http://www.wto.org/english/res_e/publications_e/wtr12_dataset_e.htm>, which was accessed on 4 June 2016.

68 Henrick Horn, Petros C Mavroidis & Erik Wijkstrom, 'In the Shadow of the DSU: Addressing Specific Trade Concerns in the WTO SPS and TBT Committees' (2013) 47(4) *Journal of World Trade* 729, 730. ('By raising STCs, Members often are not only requesting information or clarification; but they also send a strong signal that they already have reasons to believe that obligations under the agreements have not been met.')

69 WTO, 'An Inventory of Non-Tariff Measures and Services Measures' (2012) World Trade Report 106, accessed 25 July 2024 at <http://www.wto.org/english/res_e/booksp_e/anrep_e/wtr12-2c_e.pdf>.

70 Horn, Mavroidis & Wijkstrom (n 68) 751–752.

trade conflicts have been raised and discussed at the WTO Committees, relatively few of these have been fully resolved.

These arguments and counterarguments, when read together, strengthen the assertion that developing countries have preferred to utilise softer mechanisms of dispute resolution, including the WTO committee system. The committee system is not, strictly speaking, a forum for the resolution of trade conflicts and disagreements. However, in practice, it has notably contributed to 'diffusing trade tensions' in its respective trade disciplines.[71] The committee system has shown itself to be a less-demanding, non-political, pragmatic, and expert-driven forum for discussing and resolving trade conflicts.

Trade concerns that cannot be resolved amicably will require further analysis. The government at this stage must determine whether it is appropriate to launch formal consultations with the offending Member State, closely followed by litigation if consultations fail. If the government decides to proceed with the matter, it translates its disagreement into well-defined, substantiated and documented claims based on WTO legal texts. It is at this stage that a trade concern can properly be termed a 'trade dispute', as it leaves the terrain of 'conflict management' and enters the process of 'formal dispute settlement'.[72] The formal process of dispute settlement may not only involve Panel hearings, but it may also extend to the equally time-consuming and resource-demanding stages of appeal and compliance. Hence, it is desirable that trade concerns should gradually pass through these informal and formal stages and that the government's preference should be to resolve or diffuse conflicts before they enter the cumbersome and expensive phase of formal dispute settlement.

The issues that go through WTO DSM are those arising from continuing trade obstacles that can survive the time-consuming process of dispute settlement. However, there will be some trade frictions between industries or traders that are non-litigable and non-continuing in nature and such issues may not viably go through the hierarchy of stages indicated in Figure 7.1. It is advisable that the government should resolve such non-litigable issues and trade frictions through informal procedures, or at WTO Committees, or with the help of ADR procedures provided in the DSU Agreement. But how will an industry approach its government if a non-litigable trade concern is jeopardising its exports or imports? What procedure should an industry follow if it wants the government to promptly raise an issue at

71 Ibid 754.
72 Echandi (n 64) 6.

the TBT or SPS Committee? How should an industry and a government coordinate when trade issues are to be resolved more informally, through negotiations or other ADR procedures? There should be a simpler and more expeditious procedure for private stakeholders to approach their government if and when such trade concerns arise.[73] A 'small claims procedure' of coordination should be devised at the domestic level and be treated as a part of the proposed PPP framework.

Small claim provisions as an alternative to litigation have worked efficiently in many national jurisdictions. For example, the US courts provide small claims proceedings as an alternative to litigation in claim areas such as minor civil claims, public law claims, and tax claims.[74] England and Wales have established small claims procedures as a cost-effective means of settling claims,[75] and the state of California has a Small Claims Legal Advisor Program.[76] Another interesting example is the European Small Claims Procedure, which addresses cross-border claims up to the value of €5,000 for several categories of claims.[77] These procedures are not relevant to public private coordination and to disputes concerning international trade, but they nevertheless recognise the importance of small claims procedures as an effective alternative to costly and time-consuming procedures leading to litigation.

Certain features of the proposed small claims procedure are suggested below:

1. A specific government unit should remain the single point of contact for the private sector in respect of all trade concerns.

---

[73] The proposal was discussed during an interview with a trade lawyer, ACWL, on 11 April 2013. Prof Gregory C Shaffer has proposed the establishment of a 'Small Claims Procedure' at the international level; that is, at the WTO, to deal with certain trade claims with the help of fewer resources and less time. (Hakan Nordstrom & Gregory Shaffer, 'Access to Justice in the World Trade Organization: The Case for a Small Claims Procedure?' (2008) 7(4) *World Trade Review* 587).

[74] See William C Whitford, 'The Small-Case Procedure of the United States Tax Court: A Small Claims Court that Works' (1984) 9(4) *American Bar Foundation Research Journal* 797.

[75] Pablo Cortes, 'Does the Proposed European Procedure Enhance the Resolution of Small Claims?' (2008) 27(1) *Civil Justice Quarterly* 83.

[76] James C Turner & Joyce A McGee, 'Small Claims Reform: A Means of Expanding Access to the American Civil Justice System' (2000) 5(1) *University of the District of Columbia Law Review* 177.

[77] Regulation (EC) 861/2007 of the European Parliament and of the Council of 11 July 2007 establishing a European Small Claims Procedure [2007] OJ L199/1.

2. The private sector should be able to invoke its right to petition the government through a specially devised small claims procedure which should exempt a small claims petition from regular evidential requirements.
3. Online and offline application forms should be available from chambers of commerce and relevant government departments. These forms should be formatted in such a way that they are easy to understand and complete, and should include precise instructions regarding the information to be supplied by the petitioner.
4. The requirement to provide accompanying evidential documents and information should be kept to a minimum so that private sector entities are not discouraged from promptly reporting their concerns to the government.
5. Once a small claims form is administered, the unit should examine the issue and determine an appropriate measure to deal with it. The unit should have the right to make an initial determination on pursuing the measure through a viable approach, which may include negotiations, bilateral consultations, WTO Committee discussions or ADR procedures.
6. The right to seek updates on the progress of the matter, request consultations at any stage, and seek confidentiality and anonymity in the matter should be conferred on petitioners making use of the small claims procedure.
7. The government should have the right to call for additional information and evidence, and for public comments, to hold consultations and public hearings, and to appoint advisory committees.
8. The unit should have discretion to define explanatory provisions. This may require the unit to answer questions such as: What is a small claim? Who can make use of the small claims mechanism? Is the small claims procedure available to NGOs and consumer groups? Are appeals or reviews permitted in this procedure?

These domestic features are by no means exhaustive. Developing country members will need to develop their own specific government-industry coordination approach for the handling of small claims in an expeditious and cost-effective manner. However, Member States can consider these suggestions while they are devising a PPP framework for the management of day-to-day disagreements concerning international trade. Finally, it is important to note that these provisions cannot replace the previously proposed procedures of PPP. They are only suggested as an alternative strategy for the handling of claims that are small, perishable and non-continuing, and therefore non-litigable in nature.

6.1 CONCLUDING REMARKS

This chapter, along with the previous ones, explores the possibilities of engaging the private sector in the intergovernmental process of dispute management, the elements required for government-industry coordination, the possible methods of coordination, and the reforms needed to ensure the predictability of the rules and procedures governing the reciprocal exchange of resources. It examines the important issues and elements that should be considered by a country that is aspiring to enhance its dispute settlement capacity through the PPP approach.

Brazil, India and China have provided an indicative roadmap of what is required and what can be done at the domestic level to take advantage of opportunities (created by WTO DSU) at the international level. Other developing countries can 'learn lessons' from peer reviewing the experiences of BIC and then considering the strategies presented in this chapter. They can learn how their peers have overcome the problems, at least to some extent, which they face today at WTO DSU.

It is important for future research and scholarship to investigate the suitability of these proposals in light of the economic, political and social circumstances of individual countries. The proposed strategies can be adopted or adapted by individual Member States on a trial basis and their performance can be reviewed after a fixed period of time. Depending upon the individual domestic circumstances of each Member State, these features and strategies can be modified or additional features can be introduced for the purpose of devising an effective mechanism of dispute management.

Conclusion

1.1 LESSONS LEARNT: IN A NUTSHELL

Two key observations inform and pervade through the guidelines proposed in the previous chapter. *First*, the dispute settlement experiences examined in this work reinstate the claim that the participation problems that developing countries face at WTO DSU are embedded in their domestic conditions and, hence, the participation challenges should be addressed at the domestic level. In other words, findings exhibit that effective dispute settlement procedures employed at the domestic level can strengthen the WTO Member States' capacity to litigate and defend trade disputes at WTO DSM. *Second*, the engagement of affected industries during the management of trade disputes is a crucial enabling element for the protection and enforcement of WTO rights, and therefore the developing country governments should handle WTO disputes in close coordination with the affected industries.

The abovementioned observations are confirmed by investigating three central issues: (i) how governments can manage disputes by engaging the affected private stakeholders; (ii) how governments can engage the affected private stakeholders for capacity building; (iii) how governments can overcome the impediments they may face during the formation and functioning of dispute settlement partnerships. An investigation of these issues provided a detailed account of how China, Brazil and India have strengthened their DSU participation with the help of dispute settlement partnerships.

Dispute settlement partnerships have enabled the governments to identify and investigate barriers, consult and negotiate settlements, and litigate and defend cases at WTO. On the other hand, PPP arrangements have enabled private sector entities, and the representatives acting on their behalf, to protect and restore their foreign market access through governmental processes. Hence, these arrangements have provided industry with indirect access to international adjudicatory procedures. In light of these benefits, dispute settlement partnerships represent a 'win-win' strategy for the governments and industries of developed and developing countries.

The PPP mechanism has several capacity-building advantages. However, there are also several reasons why developing countries may find it difficult to design, implement and regulate such dispute settlement partnerships. The private sector in a developing country may not be sufficiently organised or resourceful to form such complex partnerships with the government. Additionally, the government may not possess the expertise and resources required for the management of disputes through the engagement of the private sector. For example, a government may not have the legal expertise to oversee the work of privately hired lawyers, or it may not have the resources to establish a specialised division for coordinating with the private sector. The interaction and exchange of resources between the public and private sector entities can also give rise to regulatory concerns arising from rent-seeking activities such as bribery and lobbying. A developing country government may not have the capacity to monitor and regulate the functioning of PPPs in order to keep the real threat of regulatory capture at bay. Because these reasons add to the complexity of the PPP mechanism, it was important to derive practical insights from the experiences of those developing countries that have engaged the private sector during various stages of dispute settlement. This has been done in Chapters 4, 5, 6 and 7.

Chapters 3 and 4 have shown that the governments in certain developed and developing countries have devised formal laws and regulations for exchange of resources with the private sector during the management of trade disputes. For example, the private sectors in the US, the EU and China have the right to petition and request their respective governments to protect or restore their infringed trade interests. The governments, on the other hand, can ask the petitioners to provide information and commercial evidence that may be required during the investigation, consultation and litigation stages of a dispute. In practice, however, these formal PPP arrangements are frequently accompanied and shadowed by informal procedures. The most preferred and commonly invoked PPP method is not the formal mechanism of Section 301 in the US or the TBR in the EU or the TBIM in China. Mostly, interaction and resource exchange in these countries has taken place by means of informal strategies or through a combination of formal and informal procedures.

A distinct approach to the management of WTO disputes has been observed in Chapter 5. Dedicated and specialised institutions in Brazil facilitate the formation and functioning of PPP arrangements. An organised business community, a specialised group of government professionals, and an interministerial management of trade disputes in Brazil have supported the functioning of institutionalised partnerships. The Brazilian PPP has been described as a quasi-formal partnership, having elements of both a formal mechanism (as its institutionally supported PPP resembles the US, the EU and China's PPP in some respects) and an informal system of coordination (as it operates without a legal framework).

Chapter 6 has enunciated the nature and features of two forms of partnership systems: a patterned system of coordination, and an informal, ad hoc system of coordination. Having some overlap with the Brazilian institutionalised partnership mechanism, these two coordination mechanisms introduce a different category of arrangement to those discussed in the chapters before. Chapter 6 clearly demonstrates how the government and industries in India have worked in tandem to achieve successful outcomes in landmark WTO litigations through informally formed partnership arrangements. The chapter also demonstrates how repeat industry participants with prior understanding of the process, familiarity of law, experience, and pre-established contacts with concerned government officials can strengthen a country's dispute settlement capacity. This 'patterned system of coordination', which creates a relationship of confidence, trust and understanding between public sector and private sector participants, allows both sides to reap the benefits of international trade.

Together, the book's chapters have presented the nature of formal, informal and ad hoc dispute resolution partnerships. Irrespective of whether a government has formed a partnership with the private sector in a formal, semi-formal or informal manner, the end result has been the enhancement of the country's dispute settlement and overall WTO participation capacity. The government, as the lead partner, has received several benefits from the private sector engagement, including better litigation strategies, wider access to information and commercial evidence, increased financial capacity, comprehensive legal and commercial analysis, better monitoring and identification of barriers, and increased capacity to seek compliance. However, these valuable resources have not come for free. The private sector, in exchange for these resources, has actively sought to protect, restore or enhance its foreign market access and benefits from international trade.

The dispute settlement experiences of the US, the EU and China present several distinguishing features of the partnerships formed and facilitated with the help of formal laws and regulations. These features include: (i) legal provisions conferring rights and obligations on individuals and governments; (ii) institutional processes for administering, scrutinising, investigating and litigating legitimate trade concerns; and (iii) regulatory provisions for monitoring interactions. These features outline the nature of formal processes of coordination. However, in practice, their operation draws a thin and a blurred line of distinction between formal and informal partnership procedures.

The blurred line of distinction between formal and informal partnership systems has become evident in Chapters 5 and 6 as the operational nature of different PPP arrangements has overlapped, and the ways in which different partnership procedures have been conducted have revealed several similarities. For instance, the existence of a specialised institution for receiving private sector petitions has demonstrated a similarity between Brazil's institutionalised PPP and the EU's formal mechanism. The complete financial support, political lobbying and use of informal contacts by the affected business entities to persuade the Government of India to pursue the matter at WTO in the *EC – Tariff Preferences* case reveal several commonalities between India's PPP experience and the US's approach to dispute resolution. Hence, the typology of 'formal PPPs' and 'informal PPPs' is imprecise as it is not possible to define these types of arrangements in a clear-cut manner. However, it has not been the focus of this work to distinguish between and define the different forms of public private coordination. Rather, the focus has been to illustrate and examine certain dispute settlement strategies that developing countries can use to devise an effective PPP mechanism (not necessarily a formal one) for the management of international trade disputes. In other words, the existence of a 'formal' or an 'informal' system of coordination will only be relevant in so far as this procedure makes the partnership more effective in a specific developing country.

2.1 WHAT HAPPENS NEXT?

The dispute settlement experiences of selected developed and developing countries have outlined a number of elements which have been effective and those which have not worked well. The elements of PPPs that have introduced complexities into the handling of disputes are the following: (i) evidential requirements accompanying an individual's right to petition; (ii) increased complexity and procedural burden imposed on government authorities by formal mechanisms; (iii) government's expectations of, and extensive resource dependence on, the private sector; (iv) possible conflict between national interest and special private interest; (v) the likelihood of government authorities being captured by private interests, and consequentially, a possible protection of private business interests that might in certain situations go against national interests; and (vi) the consequent discriminatory protection of business interests dictated by wealth and influence.

The elements of PPP arrangements that have worked well and have therefore informed the proposed guidelines are the following: (i) a strongly represented private sector community; (ii) an institutional interface between the public and private sectors; (iii) open channels of communication and resource exchange; (iv) the building of trust and confidence between the partners; (v) interministerial and multidisciplinary management of trade disputes; (vi) building of domestic legal expertise through the 'bidding' process for the selection of lawyers, the lawyer-pairing approach, and third party participation; (vii) pre-defined procedures for financing the dispute settlement process; and (viii) the establishment of regulatory provisions to ensure a balance between national interests and business interests.

The effective elements identified above, if incorporated into a PPP strategy, will not produce similarly positive results in all developing countries. The institutionalised PPP in Brazil may not be as effective in India as it is in Brazil.[1] The formalised procedures of the EU or the US may introduce further resource and procedural complexities if employed as such by India. One size cannot fit all in this case, especially because of the heterogeneous nature of developing countries and their varied social, economic and political climates. Hence, the guidelines proposed in Chapter 7 should be examined by Member States in accordance with their individual circumstances.

It is essential for developing countries to formulate a clear plan or a 'roadmap' of how they will engage with the private sector, and the individual business entities in it, as the nature and quality of the relationship with the private sector directly affects the government's ability to enhance its dispute settlement capacity. It is important that governments enhance their capacity in order to navigate the complex system of WTO DSU. It is one thing to be a part of WTO agreements and know the WTO rules, but quite another to know how to use and take advantage of those agreements and rules in practice. The strategies which have ensued from the dispute settlement experiences of Brazil, India and China have provided an illustration of how other developing countries can utilise WTO DSU by engaging the affected private stakeholders.

It is outside the scope of this work to provide a complete methodology for implementing the strategies proposed in Chapter 7. Nor would it be useful as any standardisation of methodology would defeat the desired flexibility which the countries with very different domestic circumstances may require for adopting or adapting these proposals. Hence, these

---

1 The institutionalised PPP process of Brazil may not be as effective in India because there are stark differences in the structural development and composition of various industries in Brazil and India.

proposals should be viewed as practical suggestions aimed at the identification, examination and development of certain features which can be considered for establishing dispute settlement partnership mechanisms. The country-specific implementation plans and their methodologies should, in future, be individually devised by policymakers, economists and lawyers. A degree of flexibility should be maintained throughout the planning and implementation of the suggested reforms because, generally, 'PPPs are inherently flexible and situation-dependent' in nature.[2] Notions of flexibility should also be inherent in the interpretation of the provisions and procedures so that the circumstances and needs of the participating parties are taken into account during the management of trade disputes.

At the same time, it is important that the provisions and procedures devised for the handling of disputes and formation of partnerships are robustly defined to enhance the transparency and predictability of rules. They can be devised either in the form of laws and regulations, or PPP arrangements can be facilitated by an institutional framework devised at the domestic level. The Member States could also manage disputes and engage the private sector without a legal, regulatory or an institutional framework, as long as the procedures of partnership and dispute management are effectively and clearly defined.

To derive optimum advantage from the partnership arrangements, the public and private sector participants should have a clear understanding of the methods and procedures that they can utilise to form and structure their coordination. This can be achieved through organising outreach programmes and joint consultative meetings between the participants. Think tanks can also play an important role, as they can provide training facilities to apprise government officials and private sector representatives about the available methods of coordination. It is also important to devise effective channels of information-sharing and communication between the partners so that the information concerning the government's laws, regulations and procedures can reach the private sector and the information on trade barriers and their impact on commercial interests can promptly be communicated to the government. One way of doing this could be to create a web portal that can be accessed and updated by the authorised government and industry representatives. Government updates regarding new or amended laws and regulations could be accompanied by simple guides explaining how the new or amended legal provisions affect the

---

[2] Major Christopher E Martin, 'Sovereignty, Meet Globalization: Using Public-Private Partnerships to Promote the Rule of Law in a Complex World' (2009) 202 *Military Law Review* 91, 140.

private sector generally, and / or how they affect different industries within the private sector community. The portal could also allow for the registration of requests and complaints by private sector entities, and provide details of existing and proposed procedures concerning the private sector's engagement with the government on trade issues.

3.1 KEY CHALLENGES AND TASKS AHEAD

The proposed partnership approach, especially the proposed system of 'rights and obligations', can face stern criticism from Neorealist scholars of international law. Their disapproval can be based on the following arguments: *First*, placing a formal right to petition in the hands of private individuals can vitiate the principles of public international law and further diminish the already blurred line of distinction between public international law and private international law. *Second*, a mandatory obligation imposed on public sector entities to launch investigations and other dispute settlement procedures on the 'mandate' of private stakeholders can obscure the principle of state sovereignty. *Third*, it can also obscure the role of the state as the sole guardian of national interests. This *de facto* delegation of public (that is, government) authority to profit-motivated industries can allow special private interests to trump national interests in crucial areas such as public health, public policy, public morality, the environment, and sustainable economic development. *Fourth*, undue interference by industries in intergovernmental dispute settlement affairs can put at risk future trade, political and diplomatic relationships between different states. This can give rise to adverse repercussions not only for international trade alliances but also for the alliances working towards cumulative social development, and international peace and security.

These points of criticism can be dismissed with the help of three suggestions already discussed in the previous chapters. *First*, the concerns raised in the previous paragraph can be kept at bay if the proposed coordination arrangements are regulated effectively. As the guidelines contained in Chapter 7 demonstrate, effective monitoring and transparency-enhancing procedures can ensure that the government remains the sole caretaker of national interests in this public-private exchange and retains overall authority to decide whether a matter merits investigation, consultation, litigation or retaliation. *Second*, the guidelines also highlight a number of capacity-building strategies that can be employed without or outside of the formal framework of 'rights and obligations'. If a state feels that the proposed regulatory provisions do not satisfactorily address the first and second points of criticism mentioned above, the concerned Member State can consider the informal procedures of interaction and exchange where no explicit right is conferred on the private stakeholders. *Finally*, developing countries with concerns regarding state sovereignty and supremacy can consider the arguments provided against the Mandatory Action Requirements imposed by the US Trade Act 1974 in Chapter 3 and the role that the author has proposed for the governments in Chapter 7.

Once these concerns are addressed, readers should turn their attention to the possible limitations of this proposed capacity-building approach. One significant challenge for this approach is how to engage the private sector in defence cases at WTO DSU. The BIC experiences have consistently shown that the concerned industries have mostly been willing to participate and invest resources in cases where their government has acted as a complainant. This is why the PPP approach has mainly been examined through a spectrum of WTO cases from the complainants' point of view. As seen in the previous chapters, complaints at WTO are generally filed after receiving a request from the concerned private sector. In such cases, the affected industry is usually willing to support the government and has the financial resources required to bear the cost of litigation. By contrast, industries generally do not engage in cases where an existing trade policy is challenged by a foreign government, unless they have a substantial stake in maintaining the challenged home measure. Due to this imbalance, the suggested PPP approach may not be able to directly benefit a defending country at WTO DSU. However, the use of partnership strategies would enhance the overall legal expertise and experience of a country, and that would also gradually have a positive externality impact on its defence capacity.

Another limitation of this approach is its inability to fully engage the poorly organised, small and resource-constrained commercial sectors. With their poor economies of scale, low per capita stakes and insufficient resource clout, they will find it difficult or rather unaffordable to protect their business interests through governmental actions. One way of mitigating this problem would be to relax the resource burden that a private sector entity would normally be expected to discharge through use of a waiver. However, it is beyond the scope of this book to suggest strategies for engaging private entities which cannot afford or otherwise discharge the partnership obligations. Nevertheless, the aspect of wider and fuller engagement of private sector is a topical issue and should be the subject of further research.

Similarly, additional research on the subject of non-governmental and non-commercial bodies participating in the dispute settlement process would be welcome. Chapters 4, 5 and 6 have briefly outlined the potential of coordination and resource exchange between the government and private entities other than businesses, including voluntary organisations, think tanks, research centres, academia, and intergovernmental and international organisations. The observations made in these chapters can offer an initial food for thought to individuals and organisations working in the field of international trade dispute resolution and should, hopefully, stimulate further investigation into the role that can be played by these institutions.

The concept of PPP can have wider application in the field of international trade law, that is, beyond the framework of WTO DSM. The strategies of partnership can be employed during the settlement of trade disputes under various bilateral and regional agreements, such as Preferential Trade Agreements (PTAs) and Free Trade Agreements (FTAs). Moreover, the proposed partnership strategies can also be utilised by governments to develop the capacity required for implementing commitments agreed under the WTO Trade Facilitation Agreement (TFA). The facilitation of trade by the simplification of customs rules and a reduction in red tape at the borders has a direct bearing on the private sector's trade interests, as this will expand the exporting market for available products and will also reduce the cost and time involved in the cross-border movement of goods. Hence, the private sector can work with the border authorities in devising effective and fast track procedures for clearance, inspections, compliance, licensing and approvals. Coordination arrangements between private company officials and government officials can therefore be envisaged in this respect. Broader application of the PPP mechanism and its suitability in the context of this capacity-building aspect offer interesting avenues for future investigation projects.

Bibliography

BOOKS

Baldwin RR, *Doha and Beyond: The Future of the Multilateral Trading System* (Cambridge University Press 2004)

Bhagwati J, *India in Transition: Freeing the Economy* (Clarendon Press 1993)

Blink J and Dorton I, *Economics* (Oxford University Press 2007)

Bown CP, *Self-Enforcing Trade: Developing Countries and WTO Dispute Settlement* (Brookings Institution Press 2009)

Bryman A, *Social Research Methods* (Oxford University Press 2012)

Frankfurt FR, *India's Political Economy 1947–2004: The Gradual Revolution* (Oxford University Press 2005)

Goh BC, *Law Without Lawyers, Justice Without Courts* (Ashgate, Dartmouth 2002)

Grossman GM and Helpman E, *Special Interest Politics* (The MIT Press 2001)

Hertel TW and Winters A (eds), *Poverty and the WTO: Impacts of the Doha Development Agenda* (co-publication of the World Bank and Palgrave Macmillan UK 2006)

Honkonen T, *The Common But Differentiated Responsibility Principle in Multilateral Environmental Agreements* (Wolters Kluwer 2009)

Johnson D and Turner C, *European Business: Policy Challenges for the New Commercial Environment* (Taylor & Francis 1998)

Kirton JJ, *G20 Governance for a Globalised World* (Ashgate 2013)

Komesar N, *Imperfect Alternatives: Choosing Institutions in Law, Economics and Public Policy* (University of Chicago Press 1994)

Maclean RM, *EU Trade Barrier Regulation: Tackling Unfair Foreign Trade Practices* (London: Thomson, Sweet & Maxwell 2006)

Mastel G, *American Trade Laws After the Uruguay Round* (M.E. Sharpe 1996)

Michalopoulos C, *Developing Countries in the WTO* (Palgrave 2001)

Petersmann EU, *Constitutional Functions and Constitutional Problems of International Economic Law: International and Domestic Foreign Trade Law and Foreign Trade Policy in the United States, the European Community and Switzerland* (University Press 1991)

Pollack MA and Shaffer GC (eds), *Transatlantic Governance in the Global Economy* (Lanham MD: Rowman & Littlefield 2001)
Pollack MA and Shaffer GC, *When Cooperation Fails: The International Law and Politics of Genetically Modified Foods* (Oxford University Press 2009)
Robles AC, *The Asia-Europe Meeting: The Theory and Practice of Interregionalism* (London: Routledge 2008)
Shaffer GC, *Defending Interests: Public-Private Partnerships in WTO Litigation* (Brookings Institution Press 2003)
Shaffer GC and Melendez-Ortiz R (eds), *Dispute Settlement at the WTO: The Developing Country Experience* (Cambridge University Press 2010)
Sinha A, *The Regional Roots of Developmental Politics in India: A Divided Leviathan* (Bloomington: Indiana University Press 2005)
Watkins D and Burton M, *Research Methods in Law* (Routledge 2013)

ARTICLES

Alesina A, Londregan J and Rosenthal H, 'A Model of the Political Economy of the United States' (1993) 87(1) *The American Political Science Review* 12
Bohanes J and Garza F, 'Going Beyond Stereotypes: Participation of Developing Countries in WTO Dispute Settlement' (2012) 4(1) *Trade Law & Development* 45
Bown CP, 'Participation in WTO Dispute Settlement: Complainants, Interested Parties and Free Riders' (2005) 19(2) *World Bank Economic Review* 287
Bown CP and Hoekman BM, 'WTO Dispute Settlement and the Missing Developing Country Cases: Engaging the Private Sector' (2005) 8(4) *Journal of International Economic Law* 861
Caliskan O, 'An Analysis of the Airbus-Boeing Dispute From the Perspective of the WTO Process' (2010) 10(4) *Ege Academic Review* 1129
Charnovitz S, 'Opening the WTO to Non-Governmental Interests' (2000) 24(1) *Fordham International Law Journal* 173
Cortes P, 'Does the Proposed European Procedure Enhance the Resolution of Small Claims?' (2008) 27(1) *Civil Justice Quarterly* 83
Davis CL and Bermeo SB, 'Who Files? Developing Country Participation in GATT/WTO Adjudication' (2009) 71(3) *The Journal of Politics* 1033
Delimatsis P, 'Transparency in the WTO's Decision-Making' (2014) 27(3) *Leiden Journal of International Law* 701
Deshman AC, 'Horizontal Review between International Organizations:

Why, How, and Who Cares about Corporate Regulatory Capture' (2011) 22(4) *European Journal of International Law* 1089

Ewing-Chow M, 'Are Asian WTO Members Using the WTO DSU "Effectively"?' (2013) 16(3) *Journal of International Economic Law* 669

Galanter M, 'Contract in Court; or Almost Everything You May or May not Want to Know about Contract Litigation' (2001) 3 *Wisconsin Law Review* 577

Gao H, 'China's Participation in the WTO: A Lawyer's Perspective' (2007) 11 *Singapore Year Book of International Law* 72

Gao H, 'Taking Justice into Your Own Hand: The TBI Mechanism in China' (2010) 44 *Journal of World Trade* 633

Gao H, 'Public-Private Partnership: The Chinese Dilemma' (2014) 48(5) *Journal of World Trade* 983

Grossman G and Helpman E, 'Protection for Sale' (1994) 84(4) *The American Economic Review* 833

Guzman AT and Simmons BA, 'Power Plays and Capacity Constraints: The Selection of Defendants in WTO Disputes' (2005) 34 *Journal of Legal Studies* 557

Horn H, Johanneson L and Mavroidis PC, 'The WTO Dispute Settlement System 1995–2010: Some Descriptive Statistics' (2011) 45(6) *Journal of World Trade* 1107

Horn H, Mavroidis PC and Wijkstrom E, 'In the Shadow of the DSU: Addressing Specific Trade Concerns in the WTO SPS and TBT Committees' (2013) 47(4) *Journal of World Trade* 729

Hsieh PL, 'China's Development of International Economic Law and WTO Legal Capacity Building' (2010) 13(4) *Journal of International Economic Law* 997

Jayaram R and Lanjaw PF, 'Small Scale Industry, Environmental Regulation and Poverty: The Case of Brazil' (2004) 18(3) *The World Bank Economic Review* 443, 447

Jiang X and Tan S, 'Non-Litigation Tradition in China' 2008 4 *Legal System and Society* 239

Lau LJ, 'Gain Without Pain: Why Economic Reforms in China Worked' 1998 *China's Political Economy* 43

Leibowitz LE, Polino TM and Frank MA, 'WTO Negotiations on Trade Facilitation: Prospects for Cutting Red Tape at the Borders and Opening Doors for Developing Countries' (2007) 1 *International Trade Law Review* 4

Li X, 'Understanding China's Behavioral Change in the WTO Dispute Settlement System: Power, Capacity, and Normative Constraints in Trade Adjudication' (2012) 52(6) *Asian Survey: University of California Press* 1111

Lu C, 'Legal Services in China: Facing the WTO' (2003) 20 *UCLA Pacific Basin Law Journal* 278

Makkai T and Braithwaite J, 'In and Out of the Revolving Door: Making Sense of Regulatory Capture' (1992) 12(1) *Journal of Public Policy* 61

Martin CE, 'Sovereignty, Meet Globalization: Using Public-Private Partnerships to Promote the Rule of Law in a Complex World' (2009) 202 *Military Law Review* 91

Mitchell AD, 'A Legal Principle of Special and Differential Treatment for WTO Disputes' (2006) 5(3) *World Trade Review* 445

Nishijima M and Saes MS, 'Tariff Discrimination on Brazil's Soluble Coffee: An Economic Analysis' (2010) 30(2) *Brazilian Journal of Political Economy* 293

Nordstrom H and Shaffer GC, 'Access to Justice in the World Trade Organization: The Case for a Small Claims Procedure?' (2008) 7(4) *World Trade Review* 587

Prost O, 'Can European Businesses Trust the WTO?' (2004) *European Lawyer* 22

Qian H, 'Trade Associations and Private Antitrust Litigation in China' (16 April 2013) 4(1) *CPI Antitrust Chronicle* 2

Qureshi AH, 'Participation of Developing Countries in the WTO Dispute Settlement System' (2003) 47(2) *Journal of African Law* 174

Rhodes RAW, 'The New Governance: Governing without Government' (1996) 44 *Political Studies* 652

Shaffer GC, 'The Challenges of WTO Law: Strategies for Developing Country Adaptation' (2006) 5(2) *World Trade Review* 177

Shaffer GC, Badin MRS and Rosenberg B, 'The Trials of Winning at the WTO: What Lies Behind Brazil's Success' (2008) 41(2) *Cornell International Law Journal* 383

Shaffer GC, Busch M and Reinhardt E, 'Does Legal Capacity Matter? A Survey of WTO Members' (2009) 8 *World Trade Review* 559

Sharma SD, 'From Central Planning to Market Reforms: India's Political Economy in Comparative Perspective' (1997) 23(1/2) *Humboldt Journal of Social Relations* 175

Snyder F, 'We Need a Global Food Safety Agency: Reflections on the Hidden Jurisprudence of the WTO' (2013) 1(2) *Peking University School of Transnational Law* 162

Song J, 'A Comparative Study on the Trade Barriers Regulation and Foreign Trade Barrier Investigation Rules' (2007) 41(4) *Journal of World Trade* 799

Takeuchi H, 'Political Economy of Trade Protection: China in the 1990s' (2013) 3 *International Relations of the Asia-Pacific* 1

Tietje C and Nowrot K, 'Forming the Centre of a Transnational Economic

Legal Order? Thoughts on the Current and Future Position of Non-State Actors in WTO Law' (2004) 5(2) *European Business Organization Law Review* 321

Turner JC and McGee JA, 'Small Claims Reform: A Means of Expanding Access to the American Civil Justice System' (2000) 5(1) *University of the District of Columbia Law Review* 177

Whitford WC, 'The Small-Case Procedure of the United States Tax Court: A Small Claims Court that Works' (1984) 9(4) *American Bar Foundation Research Journal* 797

Yongnian Z, 'Will China Become More Democratic? A Realistic View of China's Democratisation' (1998) *China's Political Economy* 167

BOOK CHAPTERS

Bown CP and Ruta M, 'The Economics of Permissible WTO Retaliation' in Bown CP and Pauwelyn J (eds), *The Law, Economics, and Politics of Retaliation in WTO Dispute Settlement* (Cambridge University Press 2010)

Busch M and Reinhardt E, 'Testing International Trade Law: Empirical Studies of GATT/WTO Dispute Settlement' in Kennedy DLM and Southwick JD, *The Political Economy of International Trade Law: Essays in Honor of Robert E. Hudec* (Cambridge University Press 2002)

Busch M and Reinhardt E, 'With a Little Help from Our Friends? Developing Country Complaints and Third-Party Participation' in Thomas C and Trachtman JP (eds), *Developing Countries in the WTO Legal System* (Oxford University Press 2009)

Cao F, 'PPP in China' in Tvarno CD (ed), *Public-Private Partnerships: An International Analysis – From a Legal and Economic Perspective* (Asian Link Europe Aid Conference Office 2010)

Cunningham R, 'Trade Law and Trade Policy: The Advocate's Perspective' in Deardorff AV and Stern RM (eds), *Constituent Interests in U.S. Trade Policies* (University of Michigan Press 1998)

Danvivathana P, 'Thailand's Experience in the WTO Dispute Settlement System: Challenging the EC Sugar Regime' in Shaffer GC and Melendez-Ortiz R (eds), *Dispute Settlement at the WTO: The Developing Country Experience* (Cambridge University Press 2010)

Degregarie C, 'Assets and Access: Linking Lobbyists and Lawmakers in Congress' in Herrnson PS, Shaiko RG and Wilcox C (eds), *The Interest Group Connection: Electioneering, Lobbying, and Policymaking in Washington* (Chatham House Publishers 1998)

Dhar B and Majumdar A, 'Learning from the India-EC GSP Dispute:

The Issues and the Process' in Shaffer GC and Melendez-Ortiz R (eds), *Dispute Settlement at the WTO: The Developing Country Experience* (Cambridge University Press 2010)

Goldberg R, Lawrence R and Milligan K, 'Brazil's WTO Cotton Case: Negotiation Through Litigation' in Devereaux C, Lawrence R and Watkins M (eds), *Case Studies in US Trade Negotiation: Resolving Disputes* 235 (Volume 2, Peterson Institute Press 2006)

Hoekman BM and Mavroidis PC, 'WTO Dispute Settlement, Transparency and Surveillance' in Hoekman B and Martin W (eds), *Developing Countries and the WTO: A Proactive Agenda* (Blackwell Publishing 2001)

Hoekman BM, Horn H and Mavroidis PC, 'Winners and Losers in the Panel Stage of the WTO Dispute Settlement System' in Thomas C and Trachtman JP (eds), *Developing Countries in the WTO Legal System* (Oxford University Press 2009)

Howse R and Nicolaïdis K, 'Legitimacy and Global Governance: Why Constitutionalizing the WTO is a Step Too Far' in Porter R, Sauve P, Subramanian A and Zampetti A (eds), *Efficiency, Equity, Legitimacy: The Multilateral Trading System at the Millennium* (Brookings Institution Press 2001)

Joseph S, 'The WTO, Poverty, and Development' in Joseph S (ed), *Blame it on the WTO: A Human Rights Critique* (Oxford Scholarship Online, September 2011)

Kniivila M, 'Industrial Development and Economic Growth: Implications for Poverty Reduction and Income Inequality' in Department of Economic and Social Affairs, *Industrial Development for the 21st Century: Sustainable Development Perspectives* (United Nations 2007)

Kooiman J, 'Findings, Speculations and Recommendations' in Kooiman J (ed), *Modern Governance: New Government – Society Interactions* (Sage Publications 1993)

Liyu H and Gao H, 'China's Experience in Utilizing the WTO Dispute Settlement Mechanism' in Shaffer GC and Melendez-Ortiz R (eds), *Dispute Settlement at the WTO: The Developing Country Experience* (Cambridge University Press 2010)

Powell W, 'Neither Market nor Hierarchy: Network Forms of Organization' in Frances J, Levacic R, Mitchell J and Thompson G (eds), *Markets, Hierarchies & Networks: The Coordination of Social Life* (Sage Publications 1991)

Rechenberg HK, 'NGOs' in Bernhardt R (ed), *Encyclopaedia of Public International Law* (Vol 9, North – Holland 1986)

Roessler F, 'Special and Differential Treatment of Developing Countries Under the WTO Dispute Settlement System', in Ortino F and Petersman

EU (eds), *The WTO Dispute Settlement System 1995–2003* (Kluwer Law International 2004)

Shaffer G, 'Developing Country Use of the WTO Dispute Settlement System: Why it Matters, the Barriers Posed, and its Impact on Bargaining', in Hartigan J (ed) and Elsevier, *Trade Disputes and the Dispute Settlement Understanding of the WTO: An Interdisciplinary Assessment* (Vol 6, Emerald Group Publishing 2009) 172

Shaffer GC, Badin MRS and Rosenberg B, 'Winning at the WTO: The Development of a Trade Policy Community Within Brazil' in Shaffer GC and Melendez-Ortiz R (eds), *Dispute Settlement at the WTO: The Developing Country Experience* (Cambridge University Press 2010)

Shaffer, G, Nedumpara J, Sinha A and Bahri A, 'Equalizing Access to the WTO: How Indian Trade Lawyers Build State Capacity' in Wilkins D, Khanna V and Trubek D (eds), *The Indian Legal Profession in the Age of Globalization* (Cambridge University Press 2017)

Shaffer GC and Sutton C, 'The Rise of Middle-Income Countries in the International Trading System' in Peerenboom R and Ginsburg T (eds), *Law and Development of Middle-Income Countries: Avoiding the Middle-Income Trap* (Cambridge University Press 2014)

Taslim MA, 'How the DSU Worked for Bangladesh: The First Least Developed Country to Bring a WTO Claim' in Shaffer GC and Melendez-Ortiz R (eds), *Dispute Settlement at the WTO: The Developing Country Experience* (Cambridge University Press 2010)

Veiga PDM, 'Trade Policy-making in Brazil: Changing Patterns in State-Civil Society Relationship' in Halle M and Wolfe R (eds), *Process Matters: Sustainable Development and Domestic Trade Transparency* (Geneva, IISD 2007)

INTERVIEWS

Interview with Former Ambassador of The Permanent Mission of the People's Republic of Bangladesh to the World Trade Organization (Video conferencing) 21 August 2013

Interview with Former Ambassador/WTO Permanent Representative of India (Audio Conferencing) 9 April 2010

Interview with an India-based trade lawyer, Delhi, India, 27 August 2013

Interview with an international economic law scholar, Singapore Management University (Audio conferencing) 24 June 2013

Interview with an international trade law scholar (Audio conferencing) 9 September 2014

Interview with an international trade law scholar, Xiamen Academy

of International Economic Laws (Audio conferencing) 6 December 2013
Interview with an official representative, Advisory Centre on WTO Law (ACWL), Geneva, Switzerland, 11 April 2013
Interview with an official representative, Centre for WTO Studies, Indian Institute of Foreign Trade, New Delhi, Delhi, India, 5 June 2013
Interview with an official representative, Cotton Textiles Export Promotion Council (TEXPROCIL), Mumbai, India, 27 June 2013
Interview with an official representative, European Commission (Audio conferencing) 3 June 2013
Interview with an official representative, Fisheries & Fishing Communities in India, Mumbai, India, 17 June 2013
Interview with an official representative, Government of Thailand (Audio conferencing) 3 February 2014
Interview with an official representative, International Centre for Trade and Sustainable Development, Geneva, Switzerland, 8 March 2013
Interview with an official representative, International Centre for Trade and Sustainable Development (ICTSD), Geneva, Switzerland, 11 April 2013
Interview with an official representative, Ministry of Commerce, Government of India (Audio conferencing) 3 May 2013
Interview with an official representative, Ministry of Commerce, Government of India, Delhi, India, 12 June 2013
Interview with an official representative, Ministry of Commerce, Government of India, Delhi, India, 15 June 2013
Interview with an official representative, Ministry of Law and Justice, Government of India, Delhi, India, 3 June 2013
Interview with an official representative, The Permanent Mission of Brazil to the World Trade Organization (Audio conferencing) 16 September 2013
Interview with an official representative, The Permanent Mission of India to the World Trade Organization, Geneva, Switzerland, 12 April 2012
Interview with an official representative, The Permanent Mission of People's Republic of China to the World Trade Organization, Geneva, Switzerland, 17 September 2013
Interview with an official representative, Seafood Exporters Association of India (SEAI) (Audio conferencing) 9 September 2013
Interview with an official representative, Trade Policy Division, Ministry of Commerce, Government of India, Delhi, India, 16 June 2013
Interview with a trade lawyer, Luthra & Luthra, Delhi, India, 21 June 2013
Interview with a trade lawyer, White & Case (Geneva), London, United Kingdom, 16 May 2013

CONFERENCE PAPERS

ACWL, 'The ACWL at Ten: Looking Back, Looking Forward' WTO Conference, Geneva, Switzerland, 4 October 2011 <http://www.acwl.ch/e/documents/reports/ACWL%20AT%20TEN.pdf> accessed 20 September 2013

Dhar B and Majumdar A, 'The India-EC GSP Dispute: The Issues and the Process' ICTSD Asia Dialogue on WTO Dispute Settlement and Sustainable Development, Jakarta, Indonesia, 25 January 2006 <http://www.ictsd.org/downloads/2008/06/dhar.pdf> accessed 21 September 2014

Shaffer GC, Badin MRS and Rosenberg B, 'Brazil's Response to the Judicialized WTO Regime: Strengthening the State through Diffusing Expertise' ICTSD South America Dialogue on WTO Dispute Settlement and Sustainable Development, Sao Paolo, Brazil, 22–23 June 2006 <http://www.ictsd.org/downloads/2008/05/brazils-response-to-the-judicialized-wto-regime-strengthening-the-state-through-diffusing-expertise.pdf> accessed 10 October 2014

Wolfe R, 'How Transparency Brings Standards to Life' Standard-Setting in International Trade, Academy of Global Governance Executive Training Seminar Series, European Research Institute, Florence, Italy, 18–20 February 2013

ONLINE PAPERS AND RELEASES

'2010 Trade and Investment Barriers Report' European Commission, March 2011 <http://trade.ec.europa.eu/doclib/docs/2011/march/tradoc_147629.pdf> accessed 24 July 2016

'An Inventory of Non-Tariff Measures and Services Measures' in *World Trade Report* 2012 *Trade and public policies: A closer look at non-tariff measures in the 21st century* <http://www.wto.org/english/res_e/booksp_e/anrep_e/wtr12-2c_e.pdf> accessed 25 July 2016

Aydin M, 'WTO Dispute Settlement Mechanism and Developing Countries: Lessons for Turkey' (June 2007) Fletcher School of Law and Diplomacy <www.ekonomi.gov.tr/upload/BF09AE98-D8D3-8566.../Mesut_Aydin.pdf> accessed 15 June 2016

Centre for WTO Studies, 'India, WTO and Trade Issues' (July–August 2008) 1(1) Bi-monthly Newsletter of the Centre for WTO Studies, IIFT <http://wtocentre.iift.ac.in/NewsLetters/NewsLetter_01.pdf> accessed 20 September 2015

Charnovitz S, 'The WTO and the Rights of the Individual' (March/April

2001) Intereconomics <http://ssrn.com/abstract=282021> accessed 28 November 2015

Directorate-General I Press Conference, 'EU Launches New Market Strategy' *Eurocom Monthly Bulletin*, December 1996 <www.eurunion.org/news/eure-com/1996/ecom1296.htm> accessed 17 September 2016

'Global Sugar Alliance to Monitor EU Implementation of WTO Sugar Decision' Global Alliance for Sugar Trade Reform and Liberalisation, 6 July 2006 <http://www.globalsugaralliance.org/resources.php?action=viewResource&id=51> accessed 17 August 2016

India's Ministry of Commerce's Response to the RTI application filed by Prashant Reddy (Advocate) vide document F No 1/13/2012-TPD, Government of India, Ministry of Commerce and Industry 6 March 2012 <https://docs.google.com/file/d/0Bxi2TzVXul5ZRTF3N3pQb05RMWktbXFRbUFoMTR3QQ/edit> accessed 17 September 2016

Kirk R, '2011 National Trade Estimate Report on Foreign Trade Barriers' Office of the United States Trade Representative, March 2011 <http://www.ustr.gov/webfm_send/2751> accessed 26 September 2016

Knowledge @ Wharton: Finance 'Lessons from Brazil: Why Is It Bouncing Back While Other Markets Stumble?' Wharton School of the University of Pennsylvania, 11 November 2009 <http://knowledge.wharton.upenn.edu/article/lessons-from-brazil-why-is-it-bouncing-back-while-other-markets-stumble/> accessed 30 October 2016

Melendez-Ortiz R, Bellman C and Mendoza MR (eds), *The Future and the WTO: Confronting the Challenges* (ICTSD Programme on Global Economic Policy and Institutions 2012) <http://www.ictsd.org/downloads/2012/07/the-future-and-the-wto-confronting-the-challenges.pdf> accessed 15 September 2014

Pio C, 'Brazil: Political and Economic Lessons from Democratic Transitions' (June 2013) Civil Society, Markets and Democracy Initiative <http://i.cfr.org/content/publications/images/csmd_ebook/PathwaystoFreedom/ChapterPreviews/PathwaystoFreedomBrazilPreview.pdf> accessed 9 July 2016

Press release, 'Cabinet Committee on WTO Matters Constituted' Prime Minister of India, 9 June 2004 <http://pmindia.nic.in/press-details.php?nodeid=11> accessed 20 September 2016

'Secex opens public consultation on negotiating agreements with the EU and Canada' CAMEX, 26 September 2012 <http://www.camex.gov.br/noticias/ler/item/218> accessed 29 October 2016

Spak WJ and Bond DE, 'Steelworkers File Section 301 Petition on China's Support of its Clean Energy Sector' White & Case LLP, ClientAlert International Trade, 10 September 2010 <http://www.whitecase.com/alerts-09132010/#.UxRuTuN_uxl> accessed 3 March 2017

'U.S. must break pay to Brazil relative to cotton, says Secretary of Agriculture of the country' ABRAPA, 8 October 2012 <http://www.abrapa.com.br/noticias/Paginas/EUA-deve-romper-pagamento-ao-Brasil-relativo-a-algodao-diz-secretario-de-Agricultura-do-pais.aspx> accessed 28 October 2016

'USTR Calls for Comments on Intellectual Property Protection and Enforcement' USTR, January 2012 <http://www.ustr.gov/about-us/press-office/press-releases/2010/january/ustr-calls-comments-intellectual-property-protecti> accessed 29 October 2016

'WTO, OECD Find U.S. – China Deficit Smaller Under "Value-Added" Approach' Inside U.S. Trade: World Trade Online, 22 January 2013 <http://insidetrade.com/Inside-Trade-General/Public-Content-World-Trade-Online/wto-oecd-find-us-china-deficit-smaller-under-value-added-approach/menu-id-896.html> accessed 28 June 2016

NEWSPAPER REPORTS

'A Rotten State' *The Economist*, 10 March 2011 <http://www.economist.com/node/18332796> accessed 12 April 2016

Beetz B, 'China retaliates, finds US in violation of free-trade rules' *PV magazine*, 25 May 2012 <http://www.pv-magazine.com/news/details/beitrag/china-retaliates--finds-us-in-violation-of-free-trade-rules_100006951/#axzz2XEW8pztO> accessed 9 October 2016

Biswas S, 'India's Billionaires and the Wealth of the Nation' *BBC News: India*, 12 October 2012 <http://www.bbc.co.uk/news/world-asia-india-19921501> accessed 24 September 2016

'Brazilian Sugarcane Industry Association Calls on European Commission Not to Authorize Sugar Exports Above WTO Ceiling' *7KPLCtv.com*, Sao Paulo, 25 January 2014 <http://www.kplctv.com/story/11878241/brazilian-sugarcane-industry-association-calls-on-european-commission-not-to-authorize-sugar-exports-above-wto-ceiling> accessed 13 June 2016

'Cabinet panel on WTO to discuss revised offer on services this week' *The Hindu: Business Line*, New Delhi, 25 May 2005 <http://www.thehindubusinessline.com/todays-paper/tp-economy/article2178513.ece> accessed 10 October 2016

Chemyshova D, 'Russia Forms Body to Protect Interests at WTO' *The BRICS POST*, Moscow, 31 July 2013 <http://thebricspost.com/russia-forms-body-to-protect-interests-at-wto/#.UfuwZpJJMYD> accessed 2 August 2016

'China says US violates WTO on renewable energy' *ahramonline* AFP, 24 May 2012 <http://english.ahram.org.eg/NewsContent/3/0/42621/

Business/0/China-says-US-violates-WTO-on-renewable-energy-.aspx> accessed 9 October 2015

'Collusive corruption: Transparency International lifts lid on public-private sector partnership on graft, mining, oil and power' *Mail Online India*, 21 March 2012 <http://www.dailymail.co.uk/indiahome/indianews/article-2118406/Transparency-International-lifts-lid-public-private-sector-collusive-corruption-graft-mining-oil-power.html> accessed 12 April 2015

Duggan J, 'China sets new world record for solar installations' *The Guardian*, 30 January 2014 <http://www.theguardian.com/environment/chinas-choice/2014/jan/30/china-record-solar-energy> accessed 12 June 2016

'EU Violates WTO Rules With Out-Of-Quota Sugar Exports, says UNICA' *UNICA News*, 17 December 2011 <http://www.unica.com.br/news/7064751920334804993/eu-violates-wto-rules-with-out-of-quota-sugar-exports-por-cento2C-says-unica/> accessed 12 June 2016

Ferreira V and Ikeda A, 'U.S. suspends compensation to Brazilian producer' *Economia & Negocios*, Brasilia & Sao Paulo, 8 August 2013 <http://www.estadao.com.br/noticias/impresso,eua-suspendem-indenizacao-a-produtor-brasileiro-,1061750,0.htm> accessed 28 October 2016

Freedman JM, 'WTO to probe U.S. Anti-Subsidy Duties on Chinese Imports' *Renewable EnergyWorld.Com*, Geneva, 28 September 2012 <http://www.renewableenergyworld.com/rea/news/article/2012/09/wto-to-probe-u-s-anti-subsidy-duties-on-chinese-imports> accessed 9 October 2016

Hirschberg P, 'China Eclipses U.S. as Biggest Trading Nation' *Bloomberg News*, 10 February 2013 <http://www.bloomberg.com/news/2013-02-09/china-passes-u-s-to-become-the-world-s-biggest-trading-nation.html> accessed 17 November 2013

'India's corruption scandals' *BBC News: South Asia*, 18 April 2012 <http://www.bbc.co.uk/news/world-south-asia-12769214> accessed 24 September 2015

Inman P, 'China overtakes US in world trade' *The Guardian*, 11 February 2013 <http://www.theguardian.com/business/2013/feb/11/china-worlds-largest-trading-nation> accessed 17 November 2016

Khanna T and Palepu KG, 'How to Define Emerging Markets' *Forbes*, 27 May 2010 <http://www.forbes.com/2010/05/27/winning-in-emerging-markets-opinions-book-excerpts-khanna-palepu.html> accessed 15 May 2016

Matthews J and Tan H, 'China's Renewable Energy Revolution Has Global Implications' *Clean Technica* <http://cleantechnica.com/2014/04/08/chinas-renewable-energy-revolution-global-implications/> accessed 12 June 2016

Mello PC, 'Cotton producers are raffle to fund the WTO panel' *PC Estado De Sao Paulo*, 18 September 2003 <http://www.scielo.br/scielo.php?script=sci_

nlinks&ref=000166&pid=S0104-44782007000100006000016&lng=es> accessed 28 October 2016

'Ministers line up curbs on "frivolous" judicial reviews' *BBC News: Politics*, London, 23 April 2013 <http://www.bbc.co.uk/news/uk-politics-22260063> accessed 12 July 2015

Osava M, 'Commodities: Brazil-EU Dispute over Instant Coffee Goes to WTO' *Inter Press Service*, Rio de Janeiro, 16 February 1998 <http://www.ipsnews.net/1998/02/commodities-brazil-eu-dispute-over-instant-coffee-goes-to-wto/> accessed 2 May 2016

Osava M, 'EU lifts tariffs on Brazilian soluble coffee' *Third World Network*, Rio de Janeiro, 11 July 2001 <http://www.twnside.org.sg/title/soluble.htm> accessed 5 July 2016

Pizzigati S, 'To End Extreme Poverty, End Extreme Wealth' *Inequality.org*, 27 January 2013 <http://inequality.org/extreme-poverty-extreme-wealth/> accessed 24 September 2016

'PM disbands four Cabinet panels, to set up four key committees' *Times of India*, Delhi, 11 June 2014 <http://timesofindia.indiatimes.com/india/PM-disbands-four-Cabinet-panels-to-set-up-four-key-committees/articleshow/36369253.cms> accessed 12 June 2014

'Right to Health: Seizure of Generic Drugs in Transit to Brazil in European Ports' *CONNECTAS: Human Rights*, 14 September 2013 <http://www.conectas.org/en/actions/foreign-policy/news/right-to-health-seizure-of-generic-drugs-in-transit-to-brazil-in-european-ports> accessed 11 November 2016

Scissors D, 'The Fall and Rise of Chinese State-Owned Enterprises' in the Testimony before the U.S.–China Economic and Security Review Commission on Chinese State-Owned Enterprises and U.S.–China Economic Relations *The Heritage Foundation*, 1 April 2011 <http://www.heritage.org/research/testimony/2011/04/chinese-state-owned-enterprises-and-us-china-economic-relations> accessed 20 May 2015

Shashikant S, 'Concerns Voiced at TRIPS Council over Seizure of Drugs' *SUNS*, 11 June 2009 <http://www.twnside.org.sg/title2/health.info/2009/twnhealthinfo20090602.htm> accessed 11 November 2016

Sinha K, 'Corruption rate in India is double of global average' *The Times of India*, Delhi, 9 July 2013 <http://articles.timesofindia.indiatimes.com/2013-07-09/india/40468760_1_global-corruption-transparency-international-huguette-labelle> accessed 24 September 2016

Walker A, 'The WTO has failed Developing Nations' *The Guardian*, 14 November 2011 <http://www.theguardian.com/global-development/poverty-matters/2011/nov/14/wto-fails-developing-countries> accessed 8 June 2016

Weinraub B, 'Economic Crisis Forcing Once Self-Reliant India to Seek Aid' *New York Times*, New Delhi, 29 June 1991 <http://www.nytimes.com/1991/06/29/world/economic-crisis-forcing-once-self-reliant-india-to-seek-aid.html> accessed 12 July 2016

Wilson B, 'Rift between developing and developed countries seen as root of WTO stalemate' *The Western Producer*, 12 July 2012 <http://www.producer.com/2012/07/rift-between-developing-and-developed-countries-seen-as-root-of-wto-stalemate/> accessed 4 June 2016

'WTO, OECD Find U.S. – China Deficit Smaller Under "Value-Added" Approach' Inside U.S. Trade: World Trade Online, 22 January 2013 <http://insidetrade.com/Inside-Trade-General/Public-Content-World-Trade-Online/wto-oecd-find-us-china-deficit-smaller-under-value-added-approach/menu-id-896.html> accessed 28 June 2016

'WTO raps EU over sugar subsidies' *BBC News*, London, 4 August 2004 <http://news.bbc.co.uk/1/hi/business/3536710.stm> accessed 24 October 2015

EU REPORTS AND DOCUMENTS

European Commission DG-Trade, 'Final Report: Interim Evaluation of the European Union's Trade Barrier Regulation (TBR)' June 2005 <http://trade.ec.europa.eu/doclib/docs/2005/october/tradoc_125451.pdf> accessed 25 September 2016

European Commission: External Trade, 'Global Europe: A Stronger Partnership to Deliver Market Access for European Exporters' <http://trade.ec.europa.eu/doclib/docs/2007/april/tradoc_134591.pdf> accessed 19 March 2016

European Commission, 'General Overview of Active WTO Dispute Settlement Cases Involving the EU as Complainant or Defendant and of Active Cases under the Trade Barriers Regulation' <http://trade.ec.europa.eu/doclib/docs/2007/may/tradoc_134652.pdf> accessed 8 April 2016

European Commission, 'Guidelines for Successful Public-Private Partnerships' March 2003 <http://ec.europa.eu/regional_policy/sources/docgener/guides/ppp_en.pdf> accessed 29 July 2016

European Commission, 'How the EU Works with the WTO' <http://trade.ec.europa.eu/doclib/docs/2013/april/tradoc_150988.pdf> accessed 19 March 2016

European Commission, 'The EU and Brazil solve dispute over soluble coffee' IP/01/987 (11 July 2001) <europa.eu/rapid/press-release_IP-01-987_en.pdf>accessed 24 October 2015

European Commission, 'Trade Barrier Regulation: Opening Markets for

European Exporters' 2008 <http://trade.ec.europa.eu/doclib/docs/2005/april/tradoc_122567.pdf> accessed 3 July 2016

WORKING PAPERS

Boehm F, 'Regulatory Capture Revisited – Lessons from Economics of Corruption' (2007) Internet Centre for Corruption Research Working Paper 22 <http://www.icgg.org/downloads/Boehm%20-%20Regulatory%20Capture%20Revisited.pdf> accessed 20 December 2014

Bown CP and McCulloch R, 'Developing Countries, Dispute Settlement, and the Advisory Centre on WTO Law' (January 2010) The World Bank, Policy Research Working Paper 5168 <http://elibrary.worldbank.org/doi/pdf/10.1596/1813-9450-5168> accessed 10 October 2015

Busch ML and Reinhardt E, 'The WTO Dispute Settlement Mechanism and Developing Countries' (April 2004) Swedish International Development and Cooperation Agency, Trade Brief <http://www9.georgetown.edu/faculty/mlb66/SIDA.pdf> accessed 15 November 2016

Echandi R, 'How to Successfully Manage Conflicts and Prevent Dispute Adjudication in International Trade' (April 2013) ICTSD Issue Paper No 11 <http://www.ictsd.org/downloads/2013/04/how-to-successfully-manage-conflicts-and-prevent-dispute-adjudication-in-international-trade.pdf> accessed 22 September 2016

Francis J, Horn H and Kaunitz N, 'Trading Profiles and Developing Country Participation in the WTO Dispute Settlement System' (December 2008) ICTSD Issue Paper No 6 <http://www.peacepalacelibrary.nl/ebooks/files/ICTSD_Francois_Trading-Profiles.pdf> accessed 21 September 2016

Ghani E, Kerr WR and O'Connell SD, 'The Exceptional Persistence of India's Unorganized Sector' (May 2013) The World Bank, Policy Research Working Paper 6454 <http://elibrary.worldbank.org/doi/pdf/10.1596/1813-9450-6454> accessed 15 July 2014

'Globalisation and Emerging Economies' (March 2009) Organisation for Economic Co-operation and Development Policy Brief <http://www.oecd.org/tad/tradedev/42324460.pdf> accessed 30 October 2015

Insights from the International Institute for Sustainable Development, 'Special and Differential Treatment' (Spring 2003) IISD Trade and Development Brief <http://www.iisd.org/pdf/2003/investment_sdc_may_2003_2.pdf> accessed 4 June 2015

Jatkar A and McFarlene L, 'Brazil in the WTO Dispute Settlement Understanding: A Perspective' (2013) Briefing Paper 1, Cuts International <http:///C:/Users/Amrita/Downloads/Briefing_Paper13Brazil_in_the_

WTO_Dispute_Settlement_Understanding-A_Perspective.pdf> accessed 10 July 2015

Kasteng J, Karlsson A and Lindberg C, 'Differentiation between Developing Countries in the WTO' (June 2004) Report 2004: 14 E, Swedish Board of Agriculture, International Affairs Division <http://www2.jordbruksverket.se/webdav/files/SJV/trycksaker/Pdf_rapporter/ra04_14E.pdf> accessed 3 August 2016

Meagher N, 'Representing Developing Countries before the WTO: The Role of the Advisory Centre on WTO Law (ACWL)' (2015) European University Institute, RSCAS Policy Paper 2015/02 <http://cadmus.eui.eu/handle/1814/35747> accessed 15 May 2016

Notage H, 'Developing Countries in the WTO Dispute Settlement System' (January 2009) Global Economic Governance Programme, GEG Working Paper 2009/47 <www.globaleconomicgovernance.org/sites/geg/files/Nottage_GEG WP> accessed 6 June 2016

Page S and Kleen P, 'Special and Differential Treatment of Developing Countries in the World Trade Organization' (2005) Global Development Studies No. 2 <http://www.worldfuturecouncil.org/fileadmin/user_upload/papers/40725_Gl_Dev_Stud_2.pdf> accessed 5 June 2016

Plasai V, 'Coordinating Trade Litigation' (April 2013) ICTSD Issue Paper No 14 <http://www.ictsd.org/sites/default/files/research/2013/04/coordinating-trade-litigation1.pdf> accessed 24 September 2016

Rodrik D, 'Industrial Policy for the Twenty-First Century' (2004) CEPR Discussion Paper No 4767 <http://ssrn.com/abstract=666808> accessed 18 November 2015

Shaffer GC, 'Developing Country Use of the WTO Dispute Settlement System: Why it Matters, the Barriers Posed, and its Impact on Bargaining' (May 2005) ICTSD Research paper: Legal Capacity <http://www.ictsd.org/themes/global-economic-governance/research/developing-country-use-of-the-wto-dispute-settlement> accessed 15 September 2016

Shaffer GC, 'How to Make the WTO Dispute Settlement System Work for Developing Countries: Some Proactive Developing Country Strategies' (March 2003) ICTSD Resource Paper No 5 <http://ictsd.org/downloads/2008/06/dsu_2003.pdf> accessed 18 July 2016

Wilke M, 'Practical Considerations in Managing Trade Disputes' (December 2012) ICTSD Information Note 11 <http://ictsd.org/downloads/2013/02/practical-considerations-in-managing-trade-disputes.pdf> accessed 27 September 2015

REPORTS AND COMMUNICATIONS

Commission (EC), 'Implementing the Community Lisbon Programme – Modern SME Policy for Growth and Employment' (Communication) COM (2005) 551 final

Commission (EC) to the Council, the European Parliament, the European Economic and Social Committee and the Committee of the Regions of 18 April 2007, 'Global Europe: A Stronger Partnership to Deliver Market Access for European Exporters' (Communication) COM (2007) 183 final

Commission (EC), 'The Global Challenge of International Trade: A Market Access Strategy for the European Union' (Communication) COM (1996) 53 final

SPS Committee Paper, 'Specific Trade Concerns: Note by the Secretariat' [G/SPS/GEN/204/Rev13] 26 February 2013 <https://docs.wto.org/dol2fe/Pages/FE_Search/FE_S_S006.aspx?Query=(@Symbol=%20g/sps/gen/204/rev.13*)&Language=ENGLISH&Context=FomerScriptedSearch&languageUIChanged=true#> accessed 4 June 2016

TBT Committee Paper, 'Specific Trade Concern Raised in the TBT Committee: Note by the Secretariat' [G/TBT/GEN/74/Rev9] 17 October 2011 <docsonline.wto.org/imrd/directdoc.asp?DDFDocuments/t/G/TBT/...doc> accessed 4 June 2016

World Trade Organization, Dispute Settlement Body, Special Session, 'Contribution of Ecuador to the Improvement of the Dispute Settlement Understanding of the WTO' submitted by Ecuador [TN/DS/W/9] 8 July 2002

World Trade Organization, Dispute Settlement Body, Special Session, 'Negotiations on the Dispute Settlement Understanding' submitted by Cuba, Honduras, India, Indonesia, Malaysia, Pakistan, Sri Lanka, Tanzania and Zimbabwe [TN/DS/W/19] 9 October 2002

World Trade Organization, Dispute Settlement Body, Special Session, 'Negotiations on Improvements and Clarifications of the Dispute Settlement Understanding' submitted by Mexico [TN/DS/W/23] 4 November 2002

World Trade Organization, Dispute Settlement Body, Special Session, 'Text for LDC Proposal on Dispute Settlement Understanding Negotiations' submitted by Haiti in the name of LDC [TN/DS/W/37] 22 January 2003

World Trade Organization, Dispute Settlement Body, Special Session, 'Text for the African Group Proposals on Dispute Settlement Understanding Negotiations' submitted by Kenya in the name of African Group [TN/DS/W/42] 24 January 2003

World Trade Organization, Dispute Settlement Body, Special Session,

'Responses to Questions on the Specific Input from China' submitted by China [TN/DS/W/57] 19 May 2003

World Trade Organization, 'Eighth WTO Ministerial Conference' Report by the Director-General [WT/MIN(11)/5] 18 November 2011 <http://www.wto.org/english/thewto_e/minist_e/min11_e/min11_5_e.pdf> accessed 28 March 2017

World Trade Organization, General Council, 'Preparation for the Fourth Session of the Ministerial Conference' [WT/GC/W/442] 19 September 2001

World Trade Organization, 'Trade Policy Review: Brazil' Report of the Secretariat [WT/TPR/S/140] 1 November 2004 <http://www.wto.org/english/tratop_e/tpr_e/tp239_e.htm> accessed 6 July 2016

United Nations Economic and Social Council, 'Committee for Development Policy' Report on the sixth session [E/2004/33] 29 March – 2 April 2004 <http://www.un.org/en/development/ desa/policy/cdp/cdp_ecosoc/e_2004_33_en.pdf> accessed 15 June 2016

Index